PALGRAVE M
GREAT DEBATES ... LAW SERIES

PALGRAVE MACMILLAN
GREAT DEBATES IN LAW SERIES

Series editor: Jonathan Herring

Criminal Law *Jonathan Herring*
Employment Law *Simon Honeyball*

Other titles are in course of preparation.

If you would like to comment on this book, or on any other law text published by Palgrave Macmillan, please write to lawfeedback@palgrave.com.

PALGRAVE MACMILLAN
GREAT DEBATES IN LAW SERIES

GREAT DEBATES:
EMPLOYMENT LAW

SIMON HONEYBALL

Senior Teaching Fellow,
School of Law, University of Exeter

Series Editor: Jonathan Herring
Fellow in Law,
Exeter College, Oxford

palgrave
macmillan

First published 2011 by PALGRAVE MACMILLAN

Palgrave Macmillan in the UK is an imprint of Macmillan Publishers Limited,
registered in England, company number 785998, of Houndmills, Basingstoke,
Hampshire RG21 6XS.

Palgrave Macmillan in the US is a division of St Martin's Press LLC,
175 Fifth Avenue, New York, NY 10010.

Palgrave Macmillan is the global academic imprint of the above companies
and has companies and representatives throughout the world.

Palgrave® and Macmillan® are registered trademarks in the United States,
the United Kingdom, Europe and other countries.

ISBN: 978–0–230–27840–0 paperback

This book is printed on paper suitable for recycling and made from fully
managed and sustained forest sources. Logging, pulping and manufacturing
processes are expected to conform to the environmental regulations of the
country of origin.

A catalogue record for this book is available from the British Library.

10   9   8   7   6   5   4   3   2   1
20   19 18 17 16 15 14 13 12 11

Printed and bound in Great Britain by MPG Books Group, Bodmin
and King's Lynn.

CONTENTS

1. THE IDEA OF EMPLOYMENT   1

2. THE EMPLOYMENT CONTRACT AND THEORY   34

3. THE EMPLOYMENT CONTRACT AND PRACTICE   73

4. DISCRIMINATION AT WORK   97

5. TERMINATION OF EMPLOYMENT   123

6. COLLECTIVE ASPECTS OF EMPLOYMENT   154

7. HUMAN RIGHTS AND EMPLOYMENT   187

8. THE EMPLOYMENT LEGAL SYSTEM   200

PREFACE

Employment law can claim to be the most fascinating of subjects in the legal canon. It has something of interest for everyone. First, it concerns one of the two main areas of ordinary human life. One's job and one's family together probably constitute the central focus in most people's lives. It is also a subject of great political importance, and in many areas of it divisions are drawn along party political lines. This is not just the case with collective employment law, such as the law on trade unions and industrial action, but also with regard to individual employment law. The extent to which employees should enjoy legal protection with regard to their jobs is one reflected in the ideologies of different political parties. This is connected to the fact that there is a major role for moral theory in employment law. Much of the debate regarding discrimination law, for example, is rooted in moral philosophy, although most people would probably be very surprised to learn that much of the law on discrimination has been driven not so much by high moral principle but rather by political and economic considerations. For those interested in theory, particularly of course legal theory, employment law also has much to offer. In this book I concentrate to a great extent on the theory of contract law. There are those who argue for the abandonment of contract as the root of the employment relation, but this idea has, until now, not made a great deal of progress. But it is highly debateable how far employment can be characterized as a contractual relationship at heart.

I cover just a few of the many debates in these pages that keep employment lawyers occupied. It is important to realize that it is not a short textbook. I do not attempt to cover the whole field of employment law. There is little here on many of the rights that arise during the course of employment, such as the law on working time, the minimum wage, pensions, health and safety, maternity rights and so on. For that reason alone this is not an introductory book either in the sense that it attempts to give a potted version or overview of employment law to provide a primer for the reader intending to move on to a more meaty textbook. Rather, what I have attempted to do here is to concentrate on areas of employment law which have provided controversy, and about which there can be debate. Some of these debates are theoretical, as with the topic I mentioned above with regard to the differing views that exist on the contractual basis of employment. Sometimes, these debates are practical, such as differing views on the effectiveness of legislation in a particular area.

A further reason why this book is not intended to be a potted introduction to the subject is that I hope it will be considered to be of most interest to those readers who already have some knowledge of employment law. I have often made this assumption during the course of this work. These readers might be undergraduates who are looking for a background to the ideas behind the subject of employment law, or perhaps also academics and practitioners working in the field. I would also hope that the book will be of interest to lawyers versed in other areas of the law perhaps seeking parallels, or at least comparisons, with the bases of their own specialist areas. It might even be of interest to the general reader.

This book is about debates in employment law. I have taken a particular view on what this means. I could have concentrated on controversies that have arisen in the field between identified protagonists. I suppose that is what really constitutes a recognizable debate. However, I take the view (and it is one I take into the field of legal philosophy or jurisprudence where this is much more acute) that the people involved in legal arguments are much less important than what it is that they are arguing about. So, most of the Debates identified in this work do not square up the gladiators on each side of the arguments against each other. Instead, I have pitted the various possible viewpoints in opposition, and let the ideas themselves fight it out. However, for much of the time I do not nail my colours firmly to the fence, but take a side, and leave it to the readers to decide for themselves if they prefer the alternative viewpoints that I lay out.

The book begins by looking at the meanings of 'employment' in law. In order to do that, I examine some issues to do with the process of ascribing meaning to legal terms, such as the difficulties in defining concepts as opposed to physical objects. So I begin with a deeply philosophical issue of much practical import. Then I consider two more controversial issues related to the meaning of employment, namely the extent to which the law should be driven by definitions or instead by policy considerations. So, should employees have rights because they are employees as recognized in law or instead because moral or other principles demand that they should? And should these questions be matters of fact or questions of law, not least because, if they are questions of fact, the law does not allow them to be appealed to the higher tribunal and courts. This may lead to unacceptable inconsistency between like cases, one of the harbingers of injustice. Linked to this idea, but by no means identical with it, is the debate as to whether employment can be considered to be a unified concept. In other words, do differing definitions of 'employment' in law indicate that one word is being used to identify different ideas, or is it that these definitions differ merely because they reflect a differing viewpoint of a single idea? So, is it more like differing things being called a table, or the same person being a father, son and brother? To complete the first chapter I then examine the idea that the concept of employment should be abandoned altogether and replaced by something else.

In Chapter 2 I stay with theory, but this time the theory of contract law and its relevance to employment. The first Debate considers how far employment is considered to be, on best analysis, a contractual relationship. This has been a matter of a great deal of controversy over many years. It is a theoretical debate, but it is one of great practical importance, and cannot be reduced simply to a matter of mere labelling. I then go on to examine if contract theory does not provide the best possible analysis of the employment relationship, what other candidates there are for this position. Is it, for example, best seen as a status relationship whereby rights and duties of the parties are not so much determined by the content of the agreement they have made but by the law placing non-negotiable rights and duties on them in virtue of the fact that they are in an employment relationship. The final Debate of the chapter then considers the extent to which contract law has been seen to provide the basis of the employment relationship simply because the judiciary here finds itself in familiar common law territory.

In Chapter 3 I move further into more practical areas of employment law, but I continue to explore, for the time being, the law of contract. So, I examine whether the contract of employment can provide a satisfactory basis for modern working relationships, or whether it is inevitable that the extent and reach of legislative intervention will continue to increase. I also examine the debate as to whether employers have too much power in determining the basis of the employment relationship and whether this is because the law inevitably allows this to be the case. I also question whether this, and other considerations, means that the law of contract, if it is, should be abandoned as the basis of employment.

I then leave behind contract and move on in the next chapter to the highly topical and interesting area of discrimination in employment. There are so many areas of controversy here that it is difficult to alight on just a few of them for discussion. However, in the first Debate I consider whether it is possible to see discrimination law as a unified whole. Until recently there has been a system, if it can be called that, of fragmented law on discrimination, with different provisions taking different approaches to different contexts of discrimination. But we now have the Equality Act 2010 which seeks to provide some sort of consolidation, but more than that, conceptual coherence to the law in this area. It is debateable, however, whether it has succeeded in that aim, or indeed whether it could. Then I go on to examine the role of equality in discrimination law and in particular whether it is the idea discrimination law should be seeking to secure. There is arguably a great deal of discrimination under recognized heads that takes place because the law does not recognize that the failure to treat people differently and unequally can itself be discriminatory. Then I spend a good deal of time examining the question of whether discrimination rights should be personal in the sense that it might be justified to have legal claims for discrimination in the context of characteristics one does not oneself have. I then move on to the rather technical, but nonetheless crucial issue, as to the correct test of causation in discrimination law. How can one recognize that an act has occurred because of a discriminatory reason? I follow that with another technical 'housekeeping' issue, and question whether the fundamental distinction between direct and indirect discrimination is as coherent as it might appear.

This takes me to debates concerning the termination of employment. In Chapter 5 I question whether it can be justified for legal remedies to be dependent upon the employee having acquired a period of continuous employment with an employer. I then explore doubts as to whether the concept of dismissal, fundamental to termination remedies, is coherent. This is followed by an assessment of the adequacy of termination remedies from the point of view of the employee, and I question the extent to which the law on unfair dismissal is really concerned with fairness in any ethical sense.

In Chapter 6 I address just two, but two very important, issues. First, I examine whether the law provides adequate protection, particularly to employees but also to employers, during industrial action. I then go on to examine the theoretical justification that could be said to exist for the law's intervention in trade union affairs. The law makes a major point of the fact that trade unions are private bodies, having the legal status of unincorporated association much like a club, but then goes on to interfere in the affairs of trade unions perhaps to an extent that is not justified with regard to a private institution.

The following chapter considers the issue of human rights in the employment sphere. Human rights law, and human rights in general, is a vast subject, and I make no attempt to consider it in any detail. However, I begin by examining the idea of human rights from the point of view of someone who has little knowledge of such detail. Is it an intelligible concept, or is it necessary to identify human rights merely from the legal contexts in which certain rights have been identified as human rights? I then examine the question whether employment rights can really be said to amount to human rights. There are several contexts in employment in which human rights have been identified, although I question whether this should really be so.

Finally, in another short chapter, I examine the system of legal adjudication in employment matters. Individual employment law is unusual in that, at least at the lower levels, it has what looks very much like a court system, and increasingly so, but which purports not to be. Two debates concern me here. The first is the question whether the system of employment tribunals is in need of reform. Then I examine whether the appeals process in employment cases could be improved.

* * *

I have been fortunate to have had help and assistance from several sources during the highly enjoyable process of writing this book. I would like to express my gratitude to Professor Andrew Tettenborn of the University of Swansea whose wisdom and deep knowledge of matters contractual and commercial have been made available to me. Dr Kevin Costello of University College Dublin also provided me with invaluable advice and information. My colleague Dr Michael Addo has also been most helpful. My Employment Law undergraduates at the University of Exeter have been a constant provider of ideas, both intentionally and otherwise, over many years. Finally, but certainly by no means least, I must thank my wife Helen and daughter Rachel for their innumerable contributions in many ways to the writing of this book. It is dedicated to them both. I have stated the law as it appeared to me at the end of 2010.

TABLE OF CASES

Adams v Lancashire CC and BET
    Catering Services Ltd [1997] IRLR
    436; [1997] ICR 834   50
Addison v London Philharmonic
    Orchestra Ltd [1981] ICR 261   7
AGCO v Massey Ferguson Ltd [2004]
    ICR 13   141
Ahmad v United Kingdom [1997]
    EHRLR 670   198–98
Airey v Ireland (1979) 2 EHRR 305   195
Airfix Footwear Ltd v Cope [1978]
    ICR 1210; [1978] ITR 513   23
Airlie v City of Edinburgh District
    Council [1996] IRLR 516   88
Allen v Flood [1898] AC 1   99, 160
Allen v National Australia Group
    Europe [2004] IRLR 847   53
Alexander v Standard Telephones and
    Cables plc [1990] ICR 291   80
Amalgamated Society of Railway Servants
    v Osborne [1910] AC 10   202
American Cyanamid Co. Ltd v Ethicon
    Ltd [1975] AC 396; [1975] 2 WLR
    316   175
Aparau v Iceland Frozen Foods plc
    [1996] IRLR 119   87
Arrowsmith v Jenkins [1963] 2 QB
    561   171
Asamoah-Boakye v Walter Rodney
    Housing Association Ltd (2000)
    EAT/44/00 (unreported)   142
ASLEF v United Kingdom [2007]
    IRLR 361   185, 193

Associated Newspapers Group v Wade
    [1979] IRLR 279; [1979] ICR
    664; [1979] 1 WLR 697   165
Attorney-General v Blake [2001] 1
    AC 268   46

B v United Kingdom (1990) 46 DR
    278   197
Bank voor Handel en Scheepvaart NV
    v Slatford [1953] 1 QB 248; [1954]
    2 WLR 867   21
Bartonshill Coal Co. v McGuire (1858)
    3 Macq. 300   25
Beaverbrook Newspapers Ltd v Keys
    [1978] IRLR 34; [1978] ICR
    582   165, 175
Belling & Lee v Burford [1982] ICR
    454   202
Belmar v Denny [1958] 1 Lloyd's
    Rep 112   45
Benveniste v University of Southampton
    [1989] IRLR 122   104
Berg and Busschers v Besselsen [1989]
    IRLR 447; [1990] ICR 396   50
Betts v Brintel Helicopters Ltd and KLM
    ERA Helicopters (UK) Ltd [1997]
    IRLR 361; [1997] ICR 792   49
Birch and Humber v University of
    Liverpool [1985] IRLR 165; [1985]
    ICR 470   141, 143
Blackpool & Fylde Aero Club v
    Blackpool Borough Council [1990]
    1 WLR 1195   41

Blue Chip Trading Ltd v Helbawi
[2009] IRLR 128   60
Bodha v Hampshire Area Health
Authority [1982] ICR 200   202
Bonsor v Musicians' Union [1956] AC
104   177
Booth v United States of America
[1999] IRLR 16   128
Bowater Containers Ltd v Blake EAT
522/81 (unreported)   156
Boyle v Equal Opportunities Commission
[1998] IRLR 717   117
Boyo v Lambeth London Borough
Council [1994] ICR 727   132
British Airports Authority v Ashton
[1983] IRLR 287; [1983] 1 WLR
1079   172
British Broadcasting Corporation v
Hearn [1977] IRLR 273; [1977]
ICR 685; [1977] 1 WLR 1004   165
British Home Stores v Burchell [1978]
IRLR 379   150
British Leyland UK Ltd v Ashraf
[1979] ICR 979   136–37, 144
British Leyland UK Ltd v McQuilken
[1978] IRLR 245   155
British Telecommunications plc v
Sheridan [1990] IRLR 27   16
Burdett-Coutts v Hertfordshire County
Council [1984] IRLR 91   86–87, 135
Burke v Royal Liverpool University
Hospital NHS Trust [1997]
ICR 730   53
Burton, Allton and Johnson Ltd v Peck
[1975] IRLR 87   138, 141

C. Czarnikow Ltd v Koufos, the Heron II
[1966] 2 QB 695   45
Cadoux v Central Regional Council
[1986] IRLR 131   56
Cairns v Visteon UK Ltd [2007] IRLR
175   51
Calder v H. Kitson Vickers Ltd [1988]
ICR 232   23

Campbell v Frisbee [2003] ICR 141   46
Carmichael v National Power plc
[2000] IRLR 43   14, 21–22
Carter v Bradbeer [1975] 3 All ER
158   27–28
Cassidy v Minister of Health [1951]
1 All ER 574; [1951] 2 KB 343   21
Chakki v United Yeast Co. Ltd [1982]
ICR 140   58
Cheall v United Kingdom (1986) 8
EHRR 74   193
City & Westminster Properties (1934)
Ltd v Mudd [1959] Ch 129   41
Clark v BET plc [1997] IRLR 348   77
Coleman v Attridge Law [2008] ICR
1128   110
Colen v Celerian (UK) Ltd [2004]
IRLR 210; [2005] ICR 568   59
Collier v Sunday Referee Publishing
Co. Ltd [1940] 2 KB 647; [1940]
4 All ER 234   39, 158
Collins v Hertfordshire County Council
[1947] KB 598   21
Consistent Group Ltd v Kalwak [2007]
IRLR 560   51
Corby v Morrison (t/a The Card
Shop) [1980] ICR 564; [1980]
IRLR 218   59
Council of Civil Service Unions v
United Kingdom (1988) 10 EHRR
269   194
Crown Agents for Overseas
Governments and Administration v
Lawal [1978] IRLR 542; [1979]
ICR 103   202
Croydon Health Authority v Jaufurally
[1986] ICR 4   202

Dacas v Brook Street Bureau (UK) Ltd
[2004] IRLR 358   4, 51–52
Davidson v Pillay [1979] IRLR 275   59
Davies v Presbyterian Church of Wales
[1986] IRLR 194; [1986] ICR
280   13–14

Davis v New England College of Arundel
[1977] ICR 6; [1976] ITR 278   22

Davis Contractors Ltd v Fareham UDC
[1956] 1 AC 696   56

Dekker v Stichting Vormingscentrum voor Jonge Volwassenen-Plus [1991]
IRLR 27   117

De Francesco v Barnum (1890) 43
ChD 165; 59 LJ Ch 151   53, 79, 174

De Lassalle v Guildford [1901] 2 KB
215   41

Denham v Midland Employers Mutual Assurance Ltd [1955] 2 QB 437   24

Derry v Peek (1889) 14 App. Cas. 337   10

Dimbleby & Sons Ltd v National Union of Journalists [1984] IRLR
161; [1984] ICR 386; [1984] 1
WLR 427   168

Doble v Firestone Tyre and Rubber Co. Ltd [1981] IRLR 300   130

Drake v Morgan [1978] ICR 56   179

Eastwood v Magnox Electric plc
[2004] IRLR 733; [2005] ICR
1064   81

Ebbw Vale Steel, Iron and Coal Co. v Tew (1935) 79 SJ 593   162

ECM (Vehicle Delivery Services) Ltd v Cox [1998] ICR 631; [1999]
IRLR 559   49

Edgington v Fitzmaurice (1885) 29
ChD 459   136

Edwards v Bairstow [1956] AC 14   17

Edwards v Halliwell [1950] 2 All ER
1064   179

Edwards v SOGAT [1971] Ch 354;
[1970] 3 All ER 689   184

Egg Stores (Stamford Hill) Ltd v Leibovici [1977] ICR 260; [1977]
IRLR 376   57

Enfield Technical Services Ltd v Payne
[2007] IRLR 840   59–60

Esso Petroleum Co. Ltd v Mardon [1976]
QB 801   41

Eweida v British Airways plc [2010]
IRLR 322   198

Express and Echo Publications Ltd v Tanton [1999] IRLR 367   22, 125

F.C. Shepherd & Co. Ltd v Jerrom
[1986] ICR 802; [1986] IRLR
358   58

Faccenda Chicken v Fowler [1986]
IRLR 69; [1984] ICR 589   19

Farr v Hoveringham Gravels Ltd
[1972] IRLR 104   88

Farrant v The Woodroffe School [1998]
ICR 184   88

Faust v Power Packing Casemakers Ltd [1983] IRLR 117   157

Ferguson v John Dawson & Partners (Contractors) Ltd [1976] IRLR 346;
[1976] 1 WLR 1213; [1976] 3 All
ER 817   14

FOCSA Services (UK) Ltd v Birkett
[1996] IRLR 325   77

Ford v Warwickshire County Council
[1983] IRLR 126   127

Foreningen af Arbejdsledere i Danmark v Daddy's Dance Hall [1988] IRLR
315   50

Foss v Harbottle (1843) 2 Hare 461   180

G.F. Sharp & Co. Ltd v McMillan
[1998] IRLR 632   56

Gannon v J.C. Firth Ltd [1976] IRLR
415   138

Gascol Conversions Ltd v Mercer [1974]
IRLR 155; [1974] ICR 420   85

Gate Gourmet London Ltd v Transport and General Workers Union [2005]
IRLR 881   170

General Billposting Co. Ltd v Atkinson
[1909] AC 118   46

George Wimpey & Co. Ltd v Cooper
[1977] IRLR 205; [1977] ITR 389   63

Gill and others v Cape Contracts Ltd
[1985] IRLR 499   41

Gisda Cyf v Barratt [2010] IRLR
1073   29, 62
Goring v British Actors' Equity
Association [1987] IRLR 122   180
Gray Dunn & Co. Ltd v Edwards
[1980] IRLR 23   55
Great Western Railway v Bater [1920]
3 KB 266   2
Griffiths v Buckinghamshire County
Council [1994] ICR 265   54
Grimmer v KLM Cityhopper Ltd
[2005] IRLR 596   201

Hadmor Productions Ltd v Hamilton
[1983] AC 191; [1982] IRLR 102;
[1982] ICR 114   165
Hall v Woolston Hall Leisure Ltd
[2000] IRLR 578   59–60
Hall (Inspector of Taxes) v Lorimer
[1994] IRLR 171; [1994] ICR
218   22
Hannen v Ryman (1975) unreported   59
Hardwick Game Farm v SAPPA
[1966] 1 WLR 287   45
Harper v Virgin Net Ltd [2004] IRLR
390; [2005] ICR 921   77
Harris (Ipswich) Ltd v Harrison
[1978] IRLR 382; [1978] ICR
1256   151
Heatons Transport (St Helens) Ltd v
Transport and General Workers'
Union [1973] AC 15; [1972] ICR
308   55
Hebden v Forsey and Son [1973] ICR
607; [1973] IRLR 344   57
Hewcastle Catering Ltd v Ahmed and
Elkanah [1992] ICR 626; [1991]
IRLR 473   60
Hewlett Packard Ltd v O'Murphy
[2002] IRLR 4   23
Heydon's Case 3 Co. Rep. Fa; 76 ER
637   28
Heyman v Darwins Ltd [1942] AC
356   44–45

Hill v C.A. Parsons and Co. Ltd
[1972] 1 Ch 305; [1971] 3 All ER
1345   80
Hillyer v Governors of St Bartholomew's
Hospital [1909] 2 KB 820   7, 24
Hilton International Hotels (UK) Ltd
v Protopapa [1990] IRLR 316   23
Hochster v de la Tour (1853) 2 E. &
B. 678   40
Holland v London Society of Compositors
(1924) 40 TLR 440   55
Hornby v Close (1867) 10 Cox CC
393   154, 177
Hotson v Wisbech Conservative Club
[1984] IRLR 422; [1984] ICR
859   82
Hubbard v Pitt [1975] ICR 308;
[1976] QB 142   171

Igbo v Johnson Matthey Chemicals Ltd
[1986] IRLR 215   137, 144
Industrial Rubber Products Ltd v
Gillon [1977] IRLR 389; [1978]
ITR 100   88
Initial Electronic Security Systems Ltd
v Avdic [2005] IRLR 671   202

J. Lyons & Sons v Wilkins [1899] 1
Ch 255   171
James v Eastleigh Borough Council
[1990] IRLR 288
James v London Borough of Greenwich
[2008] IRLR 302, [2008] ICR
545   119
Johnson v Unysis Ltd [2001] ICR
480; [2001] IRLR 279; [2001] 2
All ER 811   80–81
Johnstone v Bloomsbury Health
Authority [1991] ICR 269   81, 91

Kalac v Turkey (1999) 27 EHRR
522   198
Kallinos v London Electric Wire Ltd
[1980] IRLR 11   138

Kavanagh v Hiscock [1984] ICR 282;
[1974] QB 600; [1974] 2 All ER
177   170
Koodeswaran v Attorney-General for
Ceylon [1970] 2 WLR 456   65
Kopel v Safeway Stores plc [2003] IRLR
753   207
Kwamin v Abbey National plc [2004]
ICR 841   194

Lane v Shire Roofing Co. (Oxford) Ltd
[1995] IRLR 493   22
Lavarack v Woods of Colchester Ltd
[1966] 3 All ER 683; [1967] 1 QB
278   77
Lee v Chung and Shun Shing
Construction and Engineering Co.
Ltd [1990] IRLR 236   14, 22
Lee v GEC Plessey Telecommunications
[1993] IRLR 383   86
Lees v Arthur Greaves Ltd [1974] ICR
501   142
Lees v The Orchard [1978] IRLR 20   151
Lep Air Services Ltd v Rolloswin
Investments Ltd [1973] AC 331   45–46
Lewis and Britton v E. Mason & Sons
[1994] IRLR 4   156
Lindsey County Council v Mary
Marshall [1937] AC 97   7
London Borough of Southwark v Johnstone
EAT/641/97 (unreported)   42
London Transport Executive v Clarke
[1981] IRLR 166   131–32, 138
Lumley v Gye (1853) 2 E &
B 216   163, 165

Machine Tool Industry Research
Association v Simpson [1988] IRLR
212; [1988] ICR 588   202
MacLelland v National Union of
Journalists [1975] ICR 116   180
Mahmud v Bank of Credit and
Commerce International [1998]
AC 20   43

Malik v Bank of Credit and Commerce
International [1997] IRLR 462   19, 69
Mann v Nunn (1874) 30 LT 526   41
Market Investigations Ltd v Minister of
Social Security [1969] 2 QB 173;
[1968] 3 All ER 732   21
Marley v Forward Trust Ltd [1986]
IRLR 369; [1986] ICR 369   54
Marriott v Oxford and District Co-
operative Society Ltd (No.2) [1970]
1 QB 186   87
Marshall v Harland & Wolff [1972]
IRLR 90; [1972] ICR 101   56
Massey v Crown Life Assurance Co.
[1978] 2 All ER 576, [1978] 1
WLR 676   23
Martin v Automobile Proprietary Ltd
[1979] IRLR 64   88
Martin v Stout [1925] AC 359   40
McAlwane v Boughton Estates Ltd
[1973] ICR 470; [1973] 2 All ER
299   142
McClelland v Northern Ireland
General Health Services Board
[1957] 2 All ER 129   78
McFarlane v Relate Avon Ltd [2010]
IRLR 872   198
McGowan v Scottish Water [2005]
IRLR 167   196
McMeechan v Secretary of State for
Employment [1995] IRLR 461   17
McVitae v Unison [1996] IRLR 33   180
Merkur Island Shipping Corporation v
Laughton [1983] 2 AC 570; [1983]
IRLR 218   165
Mersey Docks and Harbour Board v
Coggins and Griffiths Ltd [1947]
AC 1   21
Midland Electric Manufacturing Co.
Ltd v Kanji [1980] IRLR
185   136, 144
Millam v Print Factory (London) 1991
Ltd [2007] IRLR 526; [2007] ICR
1331   48

Miles v Wakefield Metropolitan District
    Council [1987] AC 539; [1987]
    IRLR 193; [1987] AC 368   160
Monie v Coral Racing [1980] IRLR
    464; [1981] ICR 109   151
Morgan v Fry [1968] 2 QB 710;
    [1968] 3 All ER 452   160–61
Morgan v Manser [1948] 1 KB 184   58
Morrisens v Belgium (1988) 56 DR
    127   197
MS v Sweden (1997) 3 BHRC 248   196
Munro v United Kingdom (1987) 52
    DR 158   195

NACODS v Gluchowski [1996] IRLR
    252   184
Nagle v Feilden [1966] 2 QB 633;
    [1966] 1 All ER 689   184
National Association of Teachers in
    Further and Higher Education v
    United Kingdom (1998) 25 EHRR
    CD 122   194
National Coal Board v Galley [1958]
    1 WLR 16; [1958] 1 All ER
    91   55, 162
Nethermere (St Neots) Ltd v Taverna
    & Gardiner [1984] IRLR 240;
    [1984] ICR 612   14, 22
Niemitz v Germany (1993) 16
    EHRR 97   196
Norris v Southampton City Council
    [1982] IRLR 141   58
Norwest Holst Group Administration
    Ltd v Harrison [1985] IRLR 240;
    [1985] ICR 668   87

O'Kelly v Trusthouse Forte plc [1983]
    IRLR 369; [1983] 3 WLR 605   14,
                                16–17, 52
Ottoman Bank v Chakarian [1930]
    AC 277   19

Page One Records Ltd v Britton [1967] 3
    All ER 822; [1968] 1 WLR 157   80

Parr v Whitbread plc t/a Threshers
    Wine Merchants [1990] IRLR 39   151
Pepper v Hart [1992] 3 WLR 1032   12
Petrie v MacFisheries Ltd [1939] 4 All
    ER 281; [1940] 1 KB 258   90
Photo Production Ltd v Securicor
    Transport Ltd [1980] AC 827;
    [1980] 1 All ER 556   45–46, 131
Pioneer Aggregates (UK) Ltd v Secretary
    of State for the Environment [1984]
    2 All ER 358   28
Pitt v PHH Asset Management Ltd
    [1994] 1 WLR 327   41
Pointon v University of Sussex [1979]
    IRLR 199   104
Polkey v Dayton Sevices [1988] AC
    344; [1988] ICR 142; [1987]
    IRLR 503   82
Porter v Brandridge [1978] IRLR
    271   202
Powell v London Borough of Brent [1987]
    IRLR 466; [1988] ICR 176   80
Power v Regent Security Services Ltd
    [2007] IRLR 226   50
Prudential Assurance Co. v Lorenz
    (1971) 11 KIR 78   166

Quinn v Leathem [1901] AC 495   155,
                                    160

R v Arthur [1968] 1 QB 810   28
R v BBC ex parte Lavelle [1982]
    IRLR 404, [1983] 1 WLR 23,
    [1983] ICR 99   2
R v Secretary of State for Employment
    ex parte Seymour-Smith and Perez
    (No.2) [2000] IRLR 263   128
R.S. Components Ltd v Irwin [1973]
    IRLR 239; [1973] ICR 535;
    [1974] 1 All ER 41   88, 151
Radford v De Froberville [1977] 1
    WLR 1262   77
Radford v NATSOPA [1972] ICR
    484   180

Ready Mixed Concrete (South East) Ltd v Minister of Pensions and National Insurance [1968] 1 All ER 433; [1968] 2 QB 497   5, 21–22

Redfearn v Serco Ltd [2006] IRLR 623   114–15

Reigate v Union Manufacturing Co. Ltd [1918] 1 KB 892   69

Rhys-Harper v Relaxion Group plc [2003] IRLR 484; [2003] ICR 867   47

Richards v National Union of Mineworkers [1981] IRLR 247   178

Rigby v Ferodo [1988] ICR 29; [1987] IRLR 516   132

Robertson v British Gas Corporation [1983] ICR 351   56

Robinson v Flitwick Frames Ltd [1975] IRLR 261   88

Robinson v Tescom Corporation [2008] IRLR 408   135

Rock Refrigeration v Jones [1997] 1 All ER 1   46

Rookes v Barnard [1964] 2 AC 1129   159

Royal Crown Derby Porcelain Co. Ltd v Raymond Russell [1949] 2 KB 417   27

Sainsbury's Supermarkets v Hitt [2003] IRLR 23   150

Sarker v South Tees Acute Hospitals NHS Trust [1997] ICR 673   41–43

Schmidt and Dahlstrom v Sweden (1979–80) 1 EHRR 632   194

Scott v Coalite Fuels and Chemicals Ltd [1988] ICR 355   141, 143

Scott v Formica Ltd [1975] IRLR 104   143

Secretary of State for Employment v ASLEF (No.2) [1972] ICR 19; [1972] 2 QB 455   19, 68, 89, 160–61

Sheet Metal Components Ltd v Plumridge [1974] ICR 373; [1974] ITR 238   87

Sheffield v Oxford Controls Co. Ltd [1979] IRLR 133; [1979] ICR 396   143

Shields Furniture Ltd v Goff [1973] ICR 187; [1973] 2 All ER 653   87

Shirlaw v Southern Foundries (1926) Ltd [1939] 2 KB 206   68

Silvey v Pendragon plc [2001] IRLR 685   77

Singh v British Steel Corporation [1974] IRLR 131   55

Smith v Secretary of State for Trade and Industry [2000] ICR 69   195

Spring v Guardian Assurance plc [1994] IRLR 460; [1994] 3 All ER 129 (HL)   47

Stedman v United Kingdom (1977) 23 EHRR CD 168   198

Stenhouse Australia Ltd v Phillips [1974] AC 391; [1974] 1 All ER 117   44

Stevenson, Jordan and Harrison Ltd v Macdonald and Evans (1952) 1 TLR 101   5

Swedish Engine Drivers' Union v Sweden (1979–80) 1 EHRR 617   193

System Floors (UK) Ltd v Daniel [1982] IRLR 475; [1982] ICR 54   85

Taff Vale Railway Co. v Amalgamated Society of Railway Servants [1901] AC 426   155, 177

Tanner v D.T. Kean Ltd [1978] IRLR 110   130

Tarnesby v Kensington, Chelsea and Westminster AHA [1981] IRLR 369   58

The Moorcock (1889) 14 PD 64   69

Thomas v National Union of Mineworkers (South Wales Area) [1985] IRLR 136; [1985] 2 WLR 1081   167, 171, 179

Thomas Marshall (Exports) Ltd v Guinlé [1974] IRLR 236   131

Ticehurst v British Telecommunications plc [1992] IRLR 219; [1992] ICR 383   90

Torquay Hotel v Cousins [1969] 2 Ch 106   165

Tracey v Zest Equipment Co. Ltd [1982] ICR 481   144

Tramp Shipping Corporation v Greenwich Marine Inc. [1975] ICR 261; [1975] 2 All ER 989   156

Turriff Construction Ltd v Bryant [1967] ITR 292   85

Unger v Preston Corporation [1942] 1 All ER 200   58

W. Devis & Sons Ltd v Atkins [1977] AC 931; [1977] IRLR 314; [1977] ICR 662   148, 151

Walls Meat Co. Ltd v Khan [1978] IRLR 499; [1979] ICR 52   202

Wandsworth London Borough Council v D'Silva [1998] IRLR 193   88

Ward v Bignall [1967] 1 QB 534   45

Wardell v Kent County Council [1938] 2 KB 768   23

Warner Bros Pictures Inc. v Nelson [1937] 1 KB 209; [1936] 3 All ER 160   80

Western Excavating (ECC) Ltd v Sharp [1978] IRLR 27; [1978] ICR 221; [1978] QB 761   29, 62, 134

Whent v T. Cartledge Ltd [1997] IRLR 153   50, 56

Wickens v Champion Employment [1984] ICR 365   51

Wilson v St Helens Borough Council [1996] IRLR 320   50

Wilson and the NUJ; Palmer, Wyeth and the RMT; Doolan and others v United Kingdom [2002] IRLR 568   194

Wiltshire County Council v National Association of Teachers in Further and Higher Education and Guy [1980] IRLR 198; [1980] ICR 455   53, 133

Wiluszynski v Tower Hamlets London Borough Council [1989] IRLR 259; [1989] ICR 493   162

Wishart v National Association of Citizens Advice Bureaux Ltd [1990] IRLR 393   80

Withers v Flackwell Heath Supporters' Club [1981] IRLR 307   11, 17, 21

Wynes v Southrepps Hall Broiler Farm Ltd [1968] 3 ITR 407   127

Yeboah v Cropston [2002] IRLR 634   209

Yewens v Noakes (1880) 6 QBD 530   5, 21

Young and Woods Ltd v West [1980] IRLR 201   17, 22–23

Young, James and Webster v United Kingdom [1981] IRLR 408; (1982) 4 EHRR 38   181, 185, 193

TABLE OF LEGISLATION

UK

Agency Workers Regulations 2010   52

Combination Act 1799   61, 154
Combination Act 1800   61, 154
Combination Act 1824   61
Combination Act 1825   61, 154
Combination Act 1859   61
Combination Laws Repeal Act
    1824   154
Contempt of Court Act 1981
    s. 14   176
Contracts (Rights of Third Parties)
    Act 1999   35, 54
    s. 6   35
Criminal Justice Act 2003
    Sch. 3 Part 2   26
Criminal Justice and Court Services Act
    2000
    s. 42(2)   26
Criminal Law Amendment Act 1871   155

Disability Discrimination Act
    1995   110–111
Disability Discrimination Act 1995
    (Amendment) Regulations 2003   111

Employers and Workmen Act 1875   61
Employment Act 1988   180, 183
Employment Act 1990   183
Employment Act 2002
    s. 2   26

Employment Equality (Age) Regulations
    2006   110, 112
Employment Equality (Religion or Belief)
    Regulations 2003   110–112
    Reg 3   111
Employment Equality (Sexual
    Orientation) Regulations 2003   112
Employment Protection (Consolidation)
    Act 1978   149
Employment Rights Act 1996   19, 49, 87,
    124, 128–30, 137, 145, 149–50, 197
    s. 1   42, 65–66, 84, 90
    s. 4   87
    ss. 13–27   82
    ss. 40–43   198
    ss. 50–63   82
    ss. 86–87   52
    s. 94(1)   6
    s. 95   43, 141
    s. 95(1)(a)   130
    s. 95(1)(b)   52, 133, 142
    s. 95(1)(c)   62, 134
    s. 95(2)   130, 143
    s. 98   151
    s. 98(1)(b)   88
    s. 108   42, 46
    s. 108(3)   125
    s. 111(3)   203
    s. 111(4)   203
    s. 114   78
    s. 115   78, 146
    s. 118   147

s. 123(1)	148
s. 135(1)	6
s. 136(1)(a)	130
s. 136(1)(b)	52, 133
s. 136(1)(c)	62, 134
s. 136(3)	130, 143
s. 139(1)	145
s. 155	125
s. 203	144
s. 211(1)(a)	42
s. 212(1)	43
s. 216(1)	161
s. 230(1)	30–31, 43
s. 230(2)	124
s. 230(3)	124
s. 230(5)	124
s. 235	133
s. 236	192
Part II	95

Employment Tribunals Act 1996
s. 21	13

Employment Tribunals (Constitution and Rules of Procedure) Regulations 2004 — 205

Employment Tribunals (Extension of Jurisdiction) (England and Wales)
Order 1994	29
Article 3(c)	41

Employment Tribunals (Extension of Jurisdiction) (Scotland) Order 1994 — 29

Enterprise Act 2002
s. 128	26
s. 234	26

Equal Pay Act 1970 — 69, 95–98, 101, 103, 128

Equality Act 2006 — 187
s. 1	103
s. 77(2)	112

Equality Act 2010 — ix, 28, 82, 95, 101–03, 109–10, 116, 120
s. 4	102
s. 13	113
s. 39	6
s. 44	98

ss. 64–66	69
ss. 64–80	95–96
s. 64f	28
s. 66(2)(a)	70
s. 66(2)(b)	70
s. 83	31, 124
s. 108	47–48

Equality Act (Sexual Orientation) Regulations 2007 — 110

Financial Services and Markets Act 2000
s. 59	26

Fixed Term (Prevention of Less Favourable Treatment) Regulations 2002 — 52, 82

Health and Social Care Act 2001
Sch. 1 Part 3	26

Highways Act 1980
s. 137	171

Human Rights Act 1998 — 187, 191–192
s. 3	191
s. 6	191
s. 13	198

Income Tax (Earnings and Pensions) Act 2003
s. 4	26

Industrial Relations Act 1971 — 71, 78, 134, 180–81
s. 167(1)	24

Industrial Training Act 1964 — 200

Malicious Damage Act 1861
s. 2	28

Master and Servant Act 1823 — 61

Master and Servant Act 1867 — 2, 61

Maternity and Parental Leave
Regulations 1999	152
Reg 20(7)	152

Molestation of Workmen Act 1859 — 2

National Minimum Wage Act
1998	82, 104
s. 54	26

National Minimum Wage Regulations
1999   31, 149

Offences Against the Person Act 1861
    s. 18   28
Ordinance of Labourers 1349   2

Part-Time Workers (Prevention of Less
Favourable Treatment) Regulations
2002   52
Police Act 1996
    s. 89   171
Protection of Children Act 1999
    s. 12   26
Public Interest Disclosure Act
1998   82, 152
Public Order Act 1986
    s. 1   172
    s. 2   172
    s. 3   172
    s. 4A   171
    ss. 11–16   171

Race Relations Act 1965   98
Race Relations Act 1968   98
Race Relations Act 1976
    s. 1(1)   109–110, 115
Rehabilitation of Offenders Act 1974
(Exceptions) Order 1975   152

Sex Discrimination Act 1975   47, 101,
    109–110
    s. 1(1)   109–110
Sex Disqualification (Removal) Act
1919   98
Sexual Offences Act 2003
    s. 42(5)   26
Social Security Fraud Act 2001
    s. 15   26
Statute of Artificers 1562   2

Trade Dispute Act 1906   170
Trade Union Act 1871   61, 178
Trade Union Act 1913   178

Trade Union and Labour Relations
(Consolidation) Act 1992
    s. 1   31, 156, 178
    s. 10   177
    s. 10(1)   155
    s. 10(2)   54, 155
    s. 11   177
    s. 12   155, 177
    s. 15   179
    s. 20   157
    s. 71(1)   178
    s. 72(1)   178
    s. 82(1)   179
    s. 84(1)   178
    s. 137   180, 182
    s. 138   180
    s. 146   184
    s. 152   180, 183
    s. 152(1)   93, 152
    s. 174   185
    ss. 174–77   180
    s. 179   53
    s. 219   167
    s. 220   172
    s. 221(1)   175
    s. 221(2)   175
    s. 222   180
    ss. 226–34   169
    s. 236   53, 79, 162
    s. 237   132
    s. 237(1A)   157
    s. 238   132
    s. 238(A)   157
    s. 238(1)   156
    s. 238(2)   157
    s. 241   172
    s. 244(1)   168
    s. 244(2)   168
    s. 296   2
Transfer of Undertakings (Protection of
Employment) Regulations 2006
(TUPE)   47–50, 153
Reg 3   48
Reg 4(2)   49

Transport Act 2000
  s. 182   26
Tribunals, Courts and Enforcement Act
  2007   207

Unfair Dismissal (Variation of
  Qualifying Period) Order 1999   125

Wages Act 1986   95
Working Time Regulations 1998   31, 82
Workmen's Compensation Act
  1925   23

EU/International
Acquired Rights Directive   50

Equal Pay Directive (75/117) 97
  Art 1   110
Equal Treatment Directive (76/207) 97
  Art 2   110
Equal Treatment Framework Directive
  (2000/78/EC) 97, 100, 103
  Art 2(1)   110

European Convention on Human Rights
  1950   99, 181, 184, 187–196
  Art 3   197
  Art 4   192
  Art 6   194–95
  Art 8   196
  Art 9   197
  Art 10   196
  Art 11   181, 184–85, 193–94
  Art 14   192

International Labour Organization
  Convention No. 100 1951   98–99
International Labour Organization
  Convention No. 111 1958   98–99

Race Directive (2000/43)   110

Temporary Agency Work Directive
  (2008/104/EC)   52

United Nations International
  Convention on Social and Cultural
  Rights 1966   98–99

1

THE IDEA OF EMPLOYMENT

INTRODUCTION

In this chapter I consider the most fundamental issue of employment law – what is meant by the word 'employment'. I look first at what is involved in the process of defining 'employment'. Is it, for example, a matter of discovering what the word entails, in much the same way that a scientist uncovers facts about an identified physical phenomenon, or is it perhaps better seen as a process of constructing an idea in the most beneficial and logical way? I then turn to the idea that 'employment' is best seen as a conceptual tool, the meaning of which is determined by the purposes for which the concept is needed. This leads to an examination of the issue as to whether the question of what is meant by 'employment' is a matter of law or fact, and why that is important. I then examine the debate concerning whether employment can be seen as a unified concept, albeit sometimes viewed from different perspectives, or if the different definitions of employment in various parts of the law indicate that it is simply that the same word is used for convenience to cover a variety of closely-related yet nevertheless different ideas. Finally, I examine the idea that the concept of 'employment' should be abandoned altogether.

Debate 1

What is involved in defining a concept such as 'employment'?

It is clearly crucial to any consideration of the debates in employment law, as well as to the practice of employment law, to understand what is meant when we use the term 'employment'. This is for a number of reasons, of which I mention just two here. First, we need to delineate the subject matter of our enquiry – to make sure that we are all referring to the same fundamental idea, and not talking at cross-purposes. Secondly, we need to recognize that there are other concepts in this area that are similar and with which employment could be confused, or even thought of as synonymous. For example, employment is, of course, a relationship in which employees are parties on one side, but the law also recognizes (or has recognized) other ideas identifying those who are in a formal legal relationship working for another. So, people who have legal protection against the entity for whom they work so as not to be unfairly dismissed are described in law as employees. However, the law that applies to members of trade unions describes them as workers.[1] In the nineteenth century those who worked for others were generally referred to as servants.[2] Some people work for others as office-holders.[3] Other terms that have been employed in law are 'artificers',[4] 'workmen'[5] and 'labourers'.[6] These are not necessarily mutually exclusive ideas. For example, a worker is someone in law who has the characteristics of an employee, but has other characteristics too. In other words, the term 'worker' has been defined more widely than 'employee', and so an employee can at once be both an employee and a worker.[7] To add further confusion to this, some people who are often described as independent contractors are also referred to as 'self-employed'. It is often necessary to identify someone as an independent contractor precisely

---

[1] See Trade Union and Labour Relations (Consolidation) Act 1992, s. 296 which defines a worker as an individual who works under a contract of employment or who undertakes to do or perform personally any work or services for another who is not their professional client. See further G. Davidov, 'Who is a Worker?' (2005) 34 *Industrial Law Journal* 57; M. Freedland, 'From the Contract of Employment to the Personal Work Nexus' (2006) 35 *Industrial Law Journal* 1.

[2] See e.g. Master and Servant Act 1867 which attempted to decriminalize aspects of the working relationship. The use of the term 'servant' was used by the judges extensively even in the latter part of the twentieth century, although its use, other than in the domestic context, is now very rare.

[3] An office-holder was classically defined by Rowlatt J in *Great Western Railway v Bater* [1920] 3 KB 266 at 274 as 'a subsisting, permanent, substantive position which has its existence independently from the person who fills it, which continues and is filled in succession by successive holders'. It includes therefore, for example, company directors and police officers. However, the meaning of the term is by no means settled. For example, Woolf J in *R v BBC ex parte Lavelle* [1982] IRLR 404; [1983] 1 WLR 23; [1983] ICR 99 thought it was possible that it covered any employee who had legal protection against arbitrary dismissal. This proceeds on an entirely different basis to Rowlatt J's definition.

[4] See the Statute of Artificers 1562 which prohibited conspiracies to raise wages.

[5] See the Molestation of Workmen Act 1859 which allowed some freedom of association of working people, which had been severely curtailed after the Combination Acts earlier in the nineteenth century which were passed in the wake of fears of Jacobinism and revolutionary movements on the Continent.

[6] See the Ordinance of Labourers 1349 passed after the Black Death to introduce a system of wages fixed by local magistrates when labour was in great demand.

[7] See D. Brodie, 'Employees, Workers and the Self-Employed' (2005) 34 *Industrial Law Journal* 253 who introduces the useful term 'statutory workers' which includes those workers who agree to perform a service personally. This enables the term 'worker' to refer to all those who undertake work.

to establish that they are not an employee, and so to include the term 'employed' in their description is somewhat confusing.[8]

It is important to understand, however, that while it is often necessary to approach the definition of employment in this analytical and technical way, for general discursive purposes there is no objection to the word 'employment' being used to cover a variety of types of work relationships. I personally prefer the description 'the law of work' to 'employment law' simply because it does cover the panoply of work relationships and not just employment, but the idea has not, as yet, taken widespread root.[9] That is why the title of this book is as it is. That is, at least, a significant improvement on descriptions such as 'the law of master and servant' or even 'labour law',[10] both of which connote a rather narrower idea, even if the reality was somewhat different when these terms were in greater vogue than they now are.

I began above by referring to the importance of understanding what is meant when we use the term 'employment'. I could have written that differently. I could have said that it is important to understand what, in law, the term 'employment' means. It might be thought that there is little difference between the two ways of posing the issue. However, the first refers to the meaning of the concept of employment as understood by those who use, hear or read the word. The second connotes the idea that there is some objective, true, or correct meaning. These are very different ideas, and of course they raise issues not just for the legal concept of employment. They arise in the consideration of the meaning, or definition, of any term used in law and elsewhere. Nevertheless it is worth considering how this distinction impacts, or at least should impact, on how we understand the concept of employment in legal practice as well as in legal theory.

I would like to make one further introductory observation but before I do that it is increasingly important to identify 'employment', not to establish which individuals are employees – the traditional concern – but which are employers. This is particularly the case because of the growing fragmentation of types of work relationships with the growth of employment agencies, personal service contracts and so on. In these cases the person for whom the employee is working is not necessarily that person's employer.[11] Employment

---

[8] See further, H. Collins, 'Independent Contractors and the Challenge of Vertical Disintegration to Employment Protection Laws' (1990) 10 *Oxford Journal of Legal Studies* 353.

[9] Although Lord Wedderburn's seminal work, *The Worker and the Law* (Penguin, 3rd edn, 1986) dating from 1965, would suggest otherwise, as he favoured the term 'labour law' in the text.

[10] I have to admit that my own textbook in this area (now *Honeyball and Bowers' Textbook on Employment Law* (Oxford University Press, 11th edn, 2010) referred, until the 10th edition, to 'labour law' in its title.

[11] See S. Deakin, 'The Changing Concept of the "Employer" in Labour Law' (2001) 30 *Industrial Law Journal* 72.

law has grown up around the paradigm model of a person agreeing to work for another person or entity on a simple contractual basis. But the world of work has become much more complicated than that, with a variety of different types of work relationships often with an increasingly complex foundation. However, there are signs that the courts are beginning to be prepared to take a radical approach, and determine that, regardless of classical theory, an employment relationship may exist between parties between whom there is no direct express contractual nexus. So, for example, in *Dacas v Brook Street Bureau (UK) Ltd*[12] in 2004 an employment agency appealed against a decision of the Employment Appeal Tribunal, overturning the employment tribunal, to the effect that the defendant was employed by the employment agency. The Court of Appeal allowed the agency's appeal on the basis that the tests of employment, such as the requirement for a necessary degree of mutuality of obligation, had not been established. There was no cross-appeal against the tribunal's decision that the end-user (the Council) for whom the defendant worked was not the defendant's employer either, and so the Court of Appeal was not in a position to find that it was. However, two of the judges (Mummery and Sedley LJJ) gave strong indications that they would even have held the end-user to have been the defendant's employer, even though there was no express contractual relationship between them. The possibility existed that the contract could have been implied. The Court of Appeal retreated from this idea in the later case of *James v London Borough of Greenwich*[13] but this does show that the courts are at least willing to entertain the possibility of expanding the simple contractual explanation of employment into more complex areas.

In the present context it is also interesting to note (for reasons which will become clear below) that, not only was the identification of any employer the primary issue here, but the Court of Appeal assumed that a finding that the defendant was not employed for the purposes of her unfair dismissal claim entailed the idea that neither the employment agency nor the Council would have been vicariously liable for any torts she may have committed. In other words, it was impliedly accepted that the unified approach pertained.[14]

DOES THE MEANING OF 'EMPLOYMENT' INVOLVE A PROCESS OF DISCOVERY OR STIPULATION?

It would seem to follow from the idea that 'employment' has an objective meaning, quite independent of the way the word is used, that there is just one

---

[12] *Dacas v Brook Street Bureau (UK) Ltd* [2004] IRLR 358.
[13] *James v London Borough of Greenwich* [2008] IRLR 302; [2008] ICR 545.
[14] See the judgment of Mummery LJ at [2].

meaning of the term in law. That is an idea I will examine in a later Debate in this chapter. But it also involves the notion that, because of its independence from actual usage, there is a meaning of the term waiting to be discovered by those who want to apply it. So, when the courts develop tests for identifying who is an employee, what they are trying to do is to discover what the 'true' meaning of employment is. In developing the so-called 'control test' in the nineteenth century,[15] or the 'integration test' in the mid twentieth century,[16] or later the 'economic reality test' and 'multiple test',[17] they are on a voyage of lexicographical discovery. Rather like a scientist applying a litmus test, or a woman using a pregnancy test, the judges on this view are engaged in a process which they hope will inform them as to the correct legal position. As a scientist seeks to discover the presence or absence of acidity, or a woman seeks to discover whether or not she is in fact pregnant, the judges apply their tests in order to ascertain whether or not the party before them is an employee and therefore eligible to bring a claim, or belongs to some other category such as an independent contractor which might exclude them from doing so. This approach to the issue raises several further questions, such as how a word can come to have an objective meaning aside from that which is determinable from usage.

An alternative view is that the meaning of the term 'employment' has no objective meaning. The only meaning a word can have is that which has been assigned to it by human agency. As there is (in English at least) no formal mechanism by which meanings are attached to everyday words, such words when they are taken up by law are either specifically defined in law (for example, in the interpretation section of a statute) or are left to their own

---

[15] See e.g. *Yewens v Noakes* (1860) 6 QBD 530. This is the idea that there has to be a sufficient degree of control by one party over the other for there to be an employment relationship. If it can be directed not just what work is to be done, but also how and when it is to be done, that indicates an employment relationship. Otherwise the worker will probably be an independent contractor. This explains the difference between an employed chauffeur and a hired taxi driver.

[16] See *Stevenson, Jordan and Harrison Ltd v Macdonald and Evans* (1952) 1 TLR 101. The integration test concentrates on the extent to which the worker can be seen to be part and parcel of the other contracting party's enterprise. So, for example, if the worker provides their own tools and equipment that tends to suggest they aren't employed.

[17] These two tests can be traced to *Ready Mixed Concrete (South East) Ltd v Minister of Pensions and National Insurance* [1968] 1 All ER 433; [1968] 2 QB 497. However, they can be distinguished. The economic reality test involves the idea that the court or tribunal should go beyond a single technical test and apply a pragmatic approach, weighing all the factors on one side or the other. It emphasizes the pragmatic aspect of this method. The multiple test, however, whilst taking the same approach, emphasizes that no one test on its own can be determinative of employment status. It is rather a question of balancing all the factors on conceptual scales and seeing where the greatest collective weight is. This reflects an approach to definition which recognizes that any thing, or concept, is not defined by a single essence that no other thing or concept has (which is an approach to definition that derives from Plato's Theory of Forms discussed in, for example, his *Republic*) but is a matter of 'family resemblances' – see L. Wittgenstein, *Philosophical Investigations* (Oxford University Press, 1953).

devices, as it were, in the field of ordinary meaning. This is sometimes referred to as common usage. So, the meanings of words are simply those that are to be determined by how they are used. The question: 'what is the meaning in law of the term "employment"?' could elicit the answer: 'it means what the judges say it means'. In other words, when judges developed the tests for defining employment as described above, they were not developing tests to *inform* them whether someone is an employee or not, but to lay down rules as to who *should* be considered an employee. That, of course, is of great importance because, for example, whether someone is an employee is a gateway to claiming employment protection rights. Only an employee may claim for unfair dismissal,[18] or for redundancy,[19] or for certain discrimination rights[20] and so on. On this view, therefore, the judges – not the legislature or some other objective agency – are those who determine who should be eligible to claim. To some this might not seem surprising as the courts make such decisions every day. However, the important point here is that the judges are not simply applying tests that they have been given to see if a particular would-be claimant is eligible to claim, which everyone accepts as part of the role of the courts, but deciding as a matter of *policy* what categories of those in work should be eligible to claim. It is not difficult to see how this raises very important issues as to the political role of the judiciary, their accountability, their suitability for the task in hand, whether they have the necessary tools for that task, and a host of other issues.

To some extent this makes a great deal of sense as to why the tests have evolved when they have, and why they have changed over time. For example, in the nineteenth century[21] when the statutory employment protection remedies (such as for unfair dismissal and redundancy) that we have today were not in existence, determining whether someone was an employee (or a 'servant') was important for very different reasons. One was for establishing liability in tort. If person X harms person Y it is easy to see how it might be thought that X, and X alone, should be liable to Y. But if X were merely the mechanism by which harm to Y was occasioned – in other words that X was the agency by which Z harmed Y – there is a clear case that Z should be liable to Y by way of vicarious liability. Thus the extent to which Z controlled X would be highly significant in establishing liability. The degree to which, in an employment situation, the worker was under the *control* of Z as the work-giver

---

18 Employment Rights Act 1996, s. 94(1).
19 Employment Rights Act 1996, s. 135(1).
20 Equality Act 2010, s. 39.
21 The roots of vicarious liability for workers were in fact laid as far back as the seventeenth century – see G. Williams, 'Vicarious Liability and the Master's Indemnity' (1957) 20 *Modern Law Review* 220, at p. 228.

was thus clearly a highly significant factor. Therefore it would become natural to identify a category of workers (then referred to as servants and later referred to as employees)[22] who were distinguishable from others by the extent to which they were controlled in their work by their work-giver, and to whom liability could be transferred or shared. Hence the control test was applied to the level that it was in the nineteenth and early twentieth centuries.

Furthermore, in support of this idea, it is far less clear why the control test would have relevance in the modern world of work. It has been common to state that the reason why the test was thought in need of overhaul or replacement was that the nature of working relationships changed over the period after the late nineteenth century. Highly-skilled workers who are clearly employees to the natural eye, such as surgeons working for the National Health Service or airline pilots working for British Airways, are also clearly not under the type or degree of control that was to be seen in typical nineteenth century work relationships. Hence the absence of control was not a reliable indicator of the lack of an employment relationship.[23] Similarly some workers are under a great deal of control but are not regarded as employees of the person who controls them. A violinist in an orchestra is under the control of both the conductor and the orchestra's leader as to the manner of their work, but that does not mean that there is an employment relationship.[24] Indeed, some orchestral players are employed by the orchestra and some are not, but it is impossible to determine which is the case from the level of control they are subjected to during the course of their work. It is irrelevant.

However, whilst there is a certain amount of truth in this argument, it must not be overplayed. It is fanciful to think that, in the nineteenth century, typical gentleman owners of increasingly industrialized businesses were equipped, or even inclined, to control the manner in which their workers went about the specialized aspects of their crafts. The alternative, and arguably better, view is that employment in the later period was simply not characterized by the degree of control that was exercised over the worker in their work, but that the political necessity to inject control into the relationship was no longer there to the extent to which it once was, and thus less emphasis was placed upon it in the tests. In other words, the nineteenth century judiciary perhaps did not

---

22 The terms 'employee' and 'servant' are often considered to be synonyms, but Markesinis and Deakin state that this was not the case with judicial usage in the nineteenth century – see B. Markesinis and S. Deakin, *Tort Law* (Clarendon Press, 6th edn, 2008) p. 649. See too S. Deakin, 'The Contract of Employment: A Study in Legal Evolution' (2002) 11 *Historical Studies in Industrial Relations* 1.

23 This growing realization can be traced from *Lindsey County Council v Mary Marshall* [1937] AC 97. Compare the rigidity of the reasoning in the earlier case of *Hillyer v Governors of St Bartholomew's Hospital* [1909] 2 KB 820.

24 See *Addison v London Philharmonic Orchestra Ltd* [1981] ICR 261.

objectively identify control as being at the root of employment, but did all it could to ensure that employment relationships involved a great deal of control exercisable by the employer over their employees. The judges were thus stipulating the nature of the relationship, not discovering what it actually was.[25]

There is a particular difficulty from a theoretical point of view in seeing the process of establishing the meaning of employment as what I have described as a 'voyage of lexicographical discovery'. If this, contrary to the view just discussed, is what the judges have in fact been trying to do over the past two hundred years (perhaps in the light of their perceived traditional role as interpreters of the law rather than as law-makers) it is not surprising that they have failed to come up with a satisfactory test for determining employment status. This is because, on one view, it is not that they have failed to find the correct test but that the destination of their voyage of lexicographical discovery does not exist. It is quite simply that it is impossible to define employment in the manner in which the judges have attempted to do so. This is because employment is a concept and not a physical entity. It exists only in the non-physical world and has no corporeal existence. Of course, real human beings called employees and employers do exist, but it is rather that the *concept* of employment is used in respect of these physical entities. Similarly, on this view, it is nonsense to ask where a company exists (except of course in an analogous or ironical sense) because existence here connotes physical qualities which that concept, in fact by definition, does not and cannot have. The physical consequences of companies operating in the physical world (such as their headquarters, shareholders and warehouses) of course exist, but their corporate status does not.

If a concept *qua* concept does not exist in the physical world it naturally follows that it can have no physical properties. If one wants to know if something which physically exists has the properties that are required to make it something that it needs to be for the purposes of describing it in a particular way, one can simply take it apart and examine it for those properties, or indeed to see if it has unexpected properties. This is the method by which much of science is undertaken. For example, if it were to be questioned if an object were a fruit or a vegetable, a scientist would examine it to see if, amongst other things, its pericarp were on the outside or on the inside. It is also something that applies in everyday life. If I wanted to determine if something I see in a shop were a real hammer or a mere imitation, I need only examine it to see if it is made of hard metal – if it were

---

25 See J. Clark and Lord Wedderburn, 'Modern Labour Law: Problems, Functions and Policies' in Lord Wedderburn, R. Lewis and J. Clark (eds), *Labour Law and Industrial Relations* (Clarendon Press, 1983) p. 147.

made of rubber, I would not describe it as a hammer. These tests are physical – they are concerned with the physical properties the object in question has. With a concept, such as employment, this process cannot be undertaken. The only 'properties', or characteristics at least, that a concept can have are those that have been already given to it by human agency. On this view, no new properties can be discovered in a concept, precisely because it is a human mental construct and no more.[26]

There are several consequences of this which are important in the present context. One is that it would seem necessarily to involve the argument that, when the courts are confronted with a novel question about the concept of employment, they cannot discover what the answer is. The only way they can proceed is to stipulate an answer – in other words, in effect to legislate.

There is, however, a powerful counter-argument to this view. This is the argument that the law in effect consists of a type of map of statutory provisions, judicial decisions and other sources of law. Because of the nature of human frailty, limited imagination and resources of various types, the map is largely incomplete. It is as if only some of the towns and villages, roads and lanes, railway lines and rivers have been drawn. A novel question of law may be just that – novel – but on this view does not leave the judiciary free to fill the gaps in just where and how they will. It might be quite obvious (to pursue this analogy) that a drawing of a railway line between two towns, where only some of it has been drawn already, can easily be completed because, for example, it could continue on a straight line as there is nothing to impede it on perfectly flat terrain. Although no-one has ever drawn the line before, it is obvious that anyone who is charged with doing so would have no discretion, and would be impelled to complete it as a straight line. It is not that this is a process of discovery of where the line is, or even impeccable deduction as to an inevitable conclusion which, on empirical exploration, will be found to be true. Imagine it is a map drawn up as a *plan* as to how best to complete the railway line in reality. It would simply be unthinkable to suggest that the 'right' way to proceed would be anything other than to continue it in that way. Quite simply, it would be possible to say that someone who suggests a different route would reach a 'wrong' conclusion. If this, in the equivalent legal context, amounts to 'legislation', it does not do so in a way that connotes any discretion in any meaningful sense on the part of the judge making the decision. It is simply that here the judiciary is the mechanism by which the inevitable filling-in of the gaps is achieved. So, when the judges are asked to decide if someone fits the test of employment status, on this view they are not making new law

---

[26] See further, for the general idea explained here, H.L.A. Hart, 'Definition and Theory in Jurisprudence' [1954] 70 *Law Quarterly Review* 37, also to be found as Ch.1 in his book *Essays in Jurisprudence and Philosophy* (Clarendon Press, 1983).

but articulating an inevitable conclusion that exists already – if logical conclusions are to be reached – because they are inevitable. In a field of law like employment, which is so often rooted in political ideology, controversy and dispute, this is a very attractive idea to the judiciary, particularly in the light of their undemocratic authority to reach such conclusions. It is another matter, however, whether that idea is at all realistic.[27]

Debate 2

Should policy determine employment status?

Closely linked to the issue of whether the courts in determining the meaning of 'employment' are discovering its meaning or deciding what it should be, is the issue of the role of policy in this process. I have alluded to this already, but the idea should be explored further.

An argument that policy has, or should have, an important role to play in this definitional process could run like this. The reason why the word 'employment' is used, particularly in statutory claims, is purposive. It is to decide who should have a remedy and who should not. Or rather, it reflects the idea that some workers (in the broad sense) should have a particular obligation or right attached to them, and that this category of workers should be identified by a particular term. It might therefore be a good idea to invent a term so that its meaning cannot be tainted by extra-legal usage.[28] Alternatively, a common word could be used which, generally speaking, covers the type of workers one would normally expect to see in that category. In the latter case, one has to bear in mind that, in using the common term, one is using it in context with a particular meaning. So, although most people have a fair idea as to what an employee is, when the word 'employee' is used in a statutory context, for example, to determine the category of people who are eligible to claim under a provision, it must be remembered that the meaning is particular and technical. It is for this reason that it would make no sense to refer to common usage to determine the meaning of

---

[27] See further, R. Dworkin, *Law's Empire* (Harvard University Press, 1986).

[28] A.W.B. Simpson has written of the effect that terms in ordinary discourse can have on words or phrases which are not legal terms of art but which have a peculiar legal meaning (see A.W.B. Simpson, 'The Analysis of Legal Concepts' (1964) 80 *Law Quarterly Review* 535). He has found that where the word or phrase is a term of art, with no meaning at all to the layman, such as 'tenant in tail after possibility of issue extinct', the concept behind the word or phrase is not amenable to change. However, where a word is current in ordinary language outside the law as well as within the law, the extra-legal concept may react upon the legal concept in a variety of different ways. He gives the example of *Derry v Peek* (1889) 14 App. Cas. 337 where the legal concept of fraud was made to conform with the ordinary, moral, concept though previously the two had been distinct. This is not so only with moral terms but others too, such as trespass and consideration (see Simpson, p. 547).

employment in a particular context, as was suggested in *Withers v Flackwell Heath Supporters' Club*.[29]

The role of 'employment' and related terms, on this view, is therefore akin to a type of shorthand to designate a category of workers, rather than to leave them as unidentified, which involves having to make an argument out in each case. Imagine that a new claim is to be introduced under statute, and that it is decided that 'employees' should be those who are eligible to claim for it. It is not that it has been decided that employees, as understood by definition, have been designated to be the group who are entitled to the new protection. Rather, it is that a category of workers has been determined which should be entitled to the new protection, and that those particular workers, for this reason and in this context, are to be given a particular description – namely, employees as defined.

The reason why this approach might be adopted could be to give effect to the policy behind the legislation, rather than to be definition-driven. What I mean by that is this: Imagine again that the government minister who is responsible for introducing the new legislation is asked by a newspaper reporter whether apprentices will be included in the workers who are protected. The minister might reply that this has yet to be decided. If the approach to determining the definitional employment question – who is an employee? – were one of lexicographical discovery, as I described it above, the minister's answer would have to be construed as meaning that they are not sure whether apprentices could properly or correctly be defined as employees. That is highly unlikely. What they would be much more likely to mean is that they have not yet decided whether apprentices should be given the protection the government intended to introduce. If the decision were that they should have such protection, the definition of 'employee' in the interpretation section of the statute would be drawn so as to include apprentices. If they were to decide that apprentices should not have the protection, the definition would be drafted differently. In other words, the meaning of employment (and related terms) in legislation is driven by policy, not definitionally objective, considerations.

That policy should be at the root of such a consideration would seem to be a clearly powerful view, and has unsurprisingly had strong adherents. We have already seen how Clark and Wedderburn argued that policy drove much of the nineteenth century case-law on this point.[30] However, as Hugh Collins has written:

---

[29] *Withers v Flackwell Heath Supporters' Club* [1981] IRLR 307.
[30] Clark and Wedderburn, 'Modern Labour Law: Problems, Functions and Policies', n 25, p. 147.

'It is always tempting to urge the courts to adopt a purposive approach, and indeed this was attempted for a brief period in the USA. But without additional guidance this seems highly indeterminate and vulnerable to judicial misconceptions of purpose'.[31]

This, of course, is the main difficulty with such a policy-based approach. Although legislation may have been drafted for policy reasons, with a particular end in view, that policy is not articulated in the legislation itself. For the judges to be charged with ascertaining the policy behind provisions would involve them getting into very difficult territory, both politically and practically. Of course, it has long been a part of judicial statutory interpretation that purposive approaches can and should be adopted but, despite authority to examine Hansard,[32] the courts have generally attempted to do this by restricting themselves to clues from within the text being interpreted.

There are indeed some, such as Ronald Dworkin, who have argued that judges in fact do not, nor should, refer to policy in reaching their decisions.[33] His reasons for arguing this are that, whereas arguments about principles are arguments about a standard to be observed because it is a requirement of justice or some other dimension of morality, arguments about policies are (by definition) ones about the attainment of some economic, political or social feature of the community. As such, they are not arguments about rights with which the courts should be concerned, but about community objectives, which should be in the political domain. Even if it were thought legitimate as a matter of principle for the courts to be involved in such matters, they are not equipped to do so. The courts can hardly determine public views by, for example, conducting opinion polls.

An alternative view is that, instead of seeking to ascertain the common view, the courts should attempt themselves to come to legal decisions based

---

31 Collins, 'Independent Contractors and the Challenge of Vertical Disintegration to Employment Protection Laws', n 8, p. 378.

32 *Pepper v Hart* [1992] 3 WLR 1032.

33 R. Dworkin, *Taking Rights Seriously* (Harvard University Press, 1977) and *Law's Empire* (Harvard University Press, 1986). The statement in the text is true of the common law, but Dworkin takes a different approach when it comes to statutory interpretation. Those readers familiar with Dworkin's work will be aware of the mythical super-judge Hercules and the function he performs within Dworkin's theory. Unlike his approach to a case at common law, Hercules will look at policy, and this may involve looking at policy broader than that suggested by the statute. A policy behind a particular statutory provision may be competing with other policies which will also have to be examined. If, for example, large sums of public money have been spent on building a dam, and an environmental group seeks to prevent its completion by bringing an action to protect an endangered species which is threatened by the building project, the policy of protecting endangered species may be balanced against the policy that public funds should not be wasted. In deciding to look at wider policy considerations Hercules may be guided by the Act itself, in that it may, for example, contain a number of qualifications. Even if he is minded to come to a particular view, and the text of the statute supports it, he may for reasons of fairness (in the sense of a fair political structure) come to a different conclusion.

not on interpretation of the law but the most just outcome. In other words, they should 'legislate'. On this view, workers should be classified as 'employees' when it is *right* (whether they *have* the right or not) to give them the entrance ticket to the tribunal to have it hear their employment law claims. This is obviously a highly controversial and complicated area, involving a major jurisprudential debate which space and the particular focus of this work do not allow me to explore further. But that, of course, is not to deny its relevance and importance to the present Debate and the jurisprudentially-minded reader is encouraged to do so.[34]

Debate **3**

Is employment status a matter of fact or law?

A question at the heart of what is involved in determining employment status in law is the issue as to whether such a question is one of law or one of fact. It is an important question because, in general, an appeal can be made from an employment tribunal to the Employment Appeal Tribunal only on a question of law.[35] That it is one of law might suggest that there is a correct answer that is best determinable or determined by judges and which applies across the board through the application of rules or principles. That it is one of fact might suggest that the law recognizes that the question is one which is subject to tests of empirical truth, about which reasonable people could disagree if they had insufficient knowledge of the empirical data. So, this issue is closely linked to the central problem I have been considering in the previous Debates, namely whether employment status in law is one which is capable of being correct (determined by reference to objective criteria) or which is the product of stipulated (posited) decision-making.

This issue has proved to be an analytical question of great complexity. It has been complicated for many reasons, not least because discussions of it are not always entered into, one might suspect, for purely analytical reasons. There is a very practical aspect that needs to be borne in mind, and that is that it is an important issue because of the lack of the right to appeal on questions of fact as I mentioned above. A cynic might even argue therefore that, if the courts are to keep the appeal lists as light as possible, it would therefore be helpful if difficult questions were considered to be questions of fact and not of law.

---

[34] See e.g. S. Honeyball and J. Walter, *Integrity, Community and Interpretation* (Ashgate, 1998).
[35] Employment Tribunals Act 1996, s. 21. The Employment Appeal Tribunal has some original jurisdiction, but it is very limited.

THE APPROACH OF THE COURTS

The story of the courts' deliberations of this issue is a winding and confused one. I will describe it briefly here and attempt to state the basics of the present legal position.

In *Ferguson v John Dawson & Partners (Contractors) Ltd*[36] Browne LJ took the view that this question was an issue of fact and thus not open to challenge on appeal. The later decision of the Court of Appeal in *O'Kelly v Trusthouse Forte plc*[37] suggested that the question was one of law but that it involved matters of degree and fact which were essentially for the employment tribunal to determine. In *Nethermere (St Neots) Ltd v Taverna & Gardiner*[38] the same court held that the Employment Appeal Tribunal could not interfere with a tribunal's decision unless it had misdirected itself in law or its decision was one which no tribunal properly directing itself on the relevant facts could have reached. The House of Lords in *Davies v Presbyterian Church of Wales*[39] disagreed. It felt that, if a tribunal erred in deciding the question whether the applicant was an employee, the decision must be reversed. It did not matter that other tribunals might have reached a similar erroneous conclusion. However, in *Lee v Chung*[40] the view of the Privy Council was that *Davies* was exceptional in that it was concerned *only* with the situation where the relationship was dependent solely upon the construction of a written document. Where the relationship has to be determined by the investigation and evaluation of the factual circumstances in which the work is performed, the question was one of fact and degree. But it does not follow that investigation and evaluation of the factual circumstances involves restricting *Davies* to the situation where there is a written document. A construction of a written document can be a question of fact within the meaning assigned to those terms in *Davies,* as it may involve evaluating matters relating to just the parties in the case and may not be applicable generally. Support for this view can now be found in the decision of the House of Lords in *Carmichael v National Power plc.*[41]

WHY IS THE DEBATE SO COMPLEX?

One of the reasons this debate has proved to be so complex is the range of arguments and distinctions that have been employed. It cannot be said that many of them have received the rigorous analysis in the courts that a

---

[36] *Ferguson v John Dawson & Partners (Contractors) Ltd* [1976] IRLR 346; [1976] 1 WLR 1213; [1976] 3 All ER 817.
[37] *O'Kelly v Trusthouse Forte plc* [1983] IRLR 369; [1983] 3 WLR 605.
[38] *Nethermere (St Neots) Ltd v Taverna & Gardiner* [1984] IRLR 240; [1984] ICR 612.
[39] *Davies v Presbyterian Church of Wales* [1986] IRLR 194; [1986] ICR 280.
[40] *Lee v Chung and Shun Shing Construction and Engineering Co. Ltd* [1990] IRLR 236.
[41] *Carmichael v National Power plc* [2000] IRLR 43. See particularly the speech by Lord Hoffmann.

professional philosopher would bring to the topic, and many false trails have been laid. Partly this is because the issue as far as the courts are concerned is not always an analytical one. Their main purpose has not necessarily been to provide a rigorous analysis of the distinction between fact and law, but to reach a pragmatic solution to a practical problem. One such problem is to decide which forum is best in order to decide a particular type of issue. Courts and tribunals trying cases at first instance have a very different role to those trying cases on appeal. The system needs a test to determine what type of cases should be determined by each court. On the whole (but not universally so) issues of fact are thought to be best determined by courts at first instance, and issues of law by courts on appeal. Therefore, it seems natural to say that issues best considered at first instance alone are generally issues of fact and those considered in the higher courts are issues of law. That may seem axiomatic, but it is not when it converts to the idea that *by definition* issues that can be appealed are to be described as questions of law and those that cannot are issues of fact. In other words, it is not that an analytical distinction is drawn in law between issues of fact and issues of law which, according to their type, are thereby determinable in their respective forums, but rather that the law/fact distinction is dependent upon whether it is deemed to be an appealable issue or not. The latter may not be so much an analytical question as possibly a practical one, or one rooted in policy. It is not necessary to take the cynical view I posed above (that an issue might be deemed one of fact in order to reduce the appeal waiting lists) but this could be for many other reasons. One might be that the best forum to determine whether an act was reasonable is a forum with a predominantly lay membership – but that does raise the question as to why the appeal tribunal, which may only (with minor exceptions) consider questions of law, has a predominantly lay membership in the way that an employment tribunal does.[42]

A further problem (before I consider the particular arguments that have been raised) is that the courts are in the position of having to make a distinction between issues of fact and issues of law. It is inherent in the system that a question has to be one or other, or a mixture of both, as we have seen. It is not at all clear that this should be the case. I am not suggesting that there are further categories that could be employed – that an issue arising in court might be one neither of law nor of fact. It would be difficult to see what such an issue could be. Instead, it might be that this is simply not the best way to divide the issues. Fact and law simply might not be the most relevant categories in a given instance like the present. To take a simple (and possibly

---

[42] The lay members of the Employment Appeal Tribunal indeed have the power to out-vote the judge even though the issue will be purely one of law.

unnecessary) analogy, I am not suggesting that the courts are confronted with the equivalent of having to place a pear in either a basket labelled 'oranges' or another labelled 'apples' when it clearly is neither. But it might be irrelevant for the task in hand to have to divide them into baskets labelled 'larger' and 'smaller', or 'brighter' and darker', both of which distinctions would be applicable to all the fruit. It might be irrelevant because relative sweetness is the issue. Likewise, whether something is best labelled as an issue of fact or law might be irrelevant to determining the best forum to have the final say on that matter. It might be better to divide the issue in some other way. I will return to this in my conclusion below. In the meantime, let us consider the various interlocking complex of questions and distinctions that have surrounded this question.

I will begin by identifying those considerations that could be thought by the courts (and several have) as relevant to considering the issue as one of law, and some problems associated with them –

▸ The Employment Appeal Tribunal is superior to employment tribunals in deciding such matters as employment status. This includes issues of empirical fact as well as law because it also has two lay members, with greater experience and judgment than those sitting in employment tribunals. The difficulty with this is that, in general, only questions of law may be appealed to the Employment Appeal Tribunal. It is therefore necessary to label such issues as questions of law.

▸ If this were a question of fact, employees working for an employer on identical terms and conditions on the same grade could have contradictory and non-appealable decisions as to their legal status made by different tribunals.[43]

▸ The Employment Appeal Tribunal has the power to overturn a decision of an employment tribunal on the grounds that its findings were unsupported by law or were so perverse that no reasonable employment tribunal could have come to that decision.[44] However, this entails that the Employment Appeal Tribunal should consider questions of fact in some instances.

▸ That the issue is appealable as a question of law does not entail that findings of fact are not in point – the Employment Appeal Tribunal's task may be to make a decision of law based upon the findings of fact reached by the employment tribunal.

▸ Questions of fact should be restricted to empirically verifiable data. The secondary interpretation of such data can be a matter for appellate

---

[43] See the views of Ackner LJ, dissenting, in *O'Kelly v Trusthouse Forte plc*, n 37.

[44] See e.g. the decision of the Court of Appeal in *British Telecommunications plc v Sheridan* [1990] IRLR 27.

jurisdiction. This may be true, but it is difficult to see how the interpretation of facts pertinent to individual cases should be classifiable as questions of law, essential to the Employment Appeal Tribunal's jurisdiction.

However, there are also several counter-arguments for the idea that employment status should be viewed as a question of fact –

▶ The question is one of degree, and therefore one of fact.[45] However, this implies that questions of law cannot be ones of degree, which is a rather strange argument in that legal arguments tend to involve questions of interpretation compared with the ascertainment of empirical truth.

▶ Different tribunals are usually unaware of the decisions of other employment tribunals on identical facts. Strain would be placed on the system if such inconsistencies could always result in appeals. However powerful this may be from a bureaucratic point of view, it does not seem sustainable from the viewpoint of justice.

▶ Questions of interpretation are often better viewed not as questions of law which are thereby appealable, for that might undermine the particular expertise the employment tribunal has in assessing, for example, the reasonableness of the actions of the parties and witnesses who appear before them which the appellate courts cannot assess.

▶ The employment tribunal has particular local knowledge which the Employment Appeal Tribunal does not have, and which may be relevant, for example, to how the parties would have understood their legal relationship. However, the understanding of the parties and how they describe their employment relationship is considered by an employment tribunal only when all other factors are evenly balanced.[46]

▶ 'Employee' and 'employer' are not just legal terms but, in common ordinary usage, are understandable by the person in the street. The issue is therefore not one of law.[47] However, this would seem to ignore the point which I will consider in greater detail in the next Debate that these terms are merely shorthand to ideas with a purely legal meaning, which differ from legal context to legal context.

---

[45] See *O'Kelly v Trusthouse Forte plc*, n 37. The idea derives from Lord Radcliffe's speech in *Edwards v Bairstow* [1956] AC 14. However, it has been argued that Lord Radcliffe was using the phrase in an unfortunate sense, only to mean those cases in which the question on the facts warrants a decision either way – that is to say, in cases in which the tribunal cannot be said to be wrong. See T.A.O. Endicott, 'Questions of Law' (1998) 114 *Law Quarterly Review* 292, at p. 301.

[46] See e.g. *Young and Woods Ltd v West* [1980] IRLR 201 and *McMeechan v Secretary of State for Employment* [1995] IRLR 461.

[47] See e.g. *Withers v Flackwell Heath Supporters' Club*, n 29.

A CONCLUSION

As I mentioned above, I will not attempt here to provide a reasoned argument through all the distinctions and questions. That would not be possible in the space available (although perhaps the courts and tribunals should have a theoretical framework to guide them on this important question) but it is also a debate that goes far outside this area of employment law. It affects all law.

However, I will simply suggest for present purposes what appears to me to be the most sensible conclusion. That the issue is one of law would seem to make sense in principle as well as in policy. The policy behind non-interference in first instance decisions is based on the idea that matters which are peculiar to a particular case (such as facts which are personal to a particular party, or an event) are best determined by the tribunal or court that has heard the witnesses and all the evidence that arise out of those particular circumstances. But matters of fact which are relevant not just to the instant case, but are of wider application, seem in principle to be subject matter properly reviewable by a higher court in order to achieve a desirable uniformity. It therefore seems that the issue should consequently be deemed one of law, regardless of the meaning of that word in other contexts. To do otherwise has rather odd-looking consequences. To treat the question as one of fact would involve the idea that different tribunals may come to different conclusions on the same set of facts, as Gwyneth Pitt has pointed out.[48] So a nationwide company could dismiss all its workers in a particular grade, doing exactly the same work, with the possibility that only some of them may claim statutory employment protection as different tribunals may legitimately come to opposite conclusions as to their employment status. It is true that they might legitimately do so for geographically-based reasons, but the argument is not rooted in that idea. It might be that *all* relevant comparisons are identical. It is surely not correct to argue that there has been no mistake by at least one tribunal, which it should be within the competence of an appellate tribunal to correct.

Debate **4**

Is employment a unified concept?

The legal contexts in which the word 'employment' is used are many. I have referred to a few already. It is, to take some important examples, used in

---

[48] G. Pitt, 'Law, Fact and Casual Workers' (1985) 101 *Law Quarterly Review* 217. This is an excellent piece, on which I draw substantially here. See too, by the same writer, 'Deciding Who is an Employee – Fact or Law?' (1990) 19 *Industrial Law Journal* 252.

employment law to identify those who are entitled under statute to employment protection rights such as those in unfair dismissal and redundancy law, as well as to rights to a written statement as to particulars of employment, to an itemized pay statement, not to have unauthorized deductions from wages made by the employer, guarantee payments on not being provided with work and so on.[49] It is also necessary to identify those who are under the correlative liabilities. The term 'employment' is used at common law to indicate the nature and extent of obligations under different types of work contracts, for example by the incorporation of different types of implied terms.[50] In the law of tort it is used primarily in the context of establishing whether there is vicarious liability on the part of one party for the torts committed by those who work for him or her.[51] In revenue law, 'employment' identifies, for example, those who are liable to particular income tax liabilities.[52] In public law it is relevant in, for example, the context of establishing rights to natural justice.[53] The very multiplicity of contexts would suggest that there is not one simple concept of employment that is in play here.

I have also mentioned in previous Debates in this chapter that the concept of employment is defined differently in different Acts and case-law and that there are several ways of viewing why this might be. One is that the drafters of legislation and the courts could not agree on how employment should have been defined, either because they did not agree on what the relevant terms meant or because there were differing policy considerations behind those differing definitions. Another is that the term 'employment' (and related terms such as 'employer' and 'employee') is, in different contexts, referring in fact to different concepts. This is why someone who finds that they are not an employee for the purposes of claiming unfair dismissal might find they are an employee when it comes to claiming, for example, sex discrimination. The definitions for these purposes are simply different, even though the same terms are used as a form of legal shorthand to signify that in this employment context a particular type of worker is entitled to claim.

I want to introduce a third possibility here. This is that, although the

---

[49] See primarily the Employment Rights Act 1996.

[50] So, for example, if a contract is found to be a contract of service, there will be implied terms of co-operation (*Secretary of State for Employment v ASLEF (No.2)* [1972] ICR 19; [1972] 2 QB 455), obedience (*Ottoman Bank v Chakarian* [1930] AC 277), confidentiality (*Faccenda Chicken v Fowler* [1986] IRLR 69; [1984] ICR 589) and mutual trust and confidence (*Malik v Bank of Credit and Commerce International* [1997] IRLR 462) that are not to be found implied in contracts for services. Thus the contract and the relationship are not characterized by virtue of the content of the contract, but the content of the contract is determined, at least in part, by the nature of the relationship.

[51] See e.g. W.V.H. Rogers, *Winfield and Jolowicz on Tort* (Sweet and Maxwell, 18th edn, 2010) ch.20.

[52] See e.g. J. Tiley, *Revenue Law* (Hart Publishing, 4th edn, 2000) p. 201f.

[53] See e.g. W. Wade and C. Forsyth, *Administrative Law* (Oxford University Press, 9th edn, 2004) p. 539f.

definition of employment in different legal contexts may be different, this does not mean that this is good evidence that the concept of employment referred to in each instance is different. On the contrary, it may be that there is but one concept of employment that is merely being viewed from different angles. In other words, despite varying definitions, for legal purposes 'employment' is a unified concept. Another way of putting it is that there are different ideas as to what employment is that can be unified into a single conceptual whole. This might be called the 'argument of perspective'. In much the same way that one woman may be correctly described by different people as an employee, a manager, a mother, a daughter and a sister, varying descriptions may not necessarily indicate that the object or thing being described connotes anything other than just one example of what it is.[54]

There would seem to be one further competing reason why there are different definitions in different statutes. This is because there may have been a change in understanding of the concept. This might be called the 'argument of perception'. Inadequacies in previous legislation might have been identified and thus the opportunity has been taken to take remedial action. So, on this viewpoint, the definition of employment for sex discrimination protection purposes is therefore somewhat wider than that for unfair dismissal and redundancy (as I have already mentioned) because, perhaps, when the sex discrimination legislation was drawn up (later than that for unfair dismissal and redundancy) it was realized that the definition of employment was deficient. It was therefore altered to account for the previous error in understanding.

These differing approaches signify that there is some confusion as to whether or not the legal idea of employment is a 'unified' one, with different definitions arising out of alternative viewpoints or misunderstandings, or whether there are in reality several ideas simultaneously at work here, each going under the shorthand terms which indicate who may or may not be a claimant in an employment law case.

THE 'UNIFIED' ANALYSIS AND THE COURTS

How have the courts viewed the idea that there is only one concept of employment in law? Initially it might appear that they have consistently adopted a 'unified' analysis.[55] One factor suggesting that this is the case is

---

[54] Readers with interests in Christian theology might have thought about this in the context of the biblical description of the Holy Trinity as God the Father, Son and Holy Ghost being Three in One and One in Three. This might be a concept that is not quite so mysterious as it is sometimes made out to be.

[55] Some academic writers also seem to assume that a unified approach is the more preferable – see e.g. Deakin, 'The Changing Concept of the "Employer" in Labour Law', n 11, p. 72.

that the tests in employment law are also those that have been employed in, for example, tort and tax cases.[56] The oldest test, which is retained as an element in later tests, was that of control. The greater the degree of control over the worker by the other party, the greater the likelihood that the relationship would be considered to be one of master and servant. The leading case in the nineteenth century was *Yewens v Noakes*,[57] a decision of the Court of Appeal concerning the issue of whether or not 'habitable house duty' was payable. Most obviously, perhaps, the element of control is applicable in tort cases, especially with regard to vicarious liability when it would seem clear that the test should be whether liability should attach to someone who controls the negligent acts of another[58] but the idea is still considered to be an important element to be considered in more sophisticated tests for employment protection remedies.[59]

Various factors contributed to the demise of the control test as a single-factor test, as I have already mentioned. It was considered to be increasingly inadequate and was replaced by a number of other judicial approaches. The so-called integration (or organizational) test was explored in the early 1950s whereby the extent to which the worker was assimilated into the business was considered to be the best determinant. The important point for present purposes is that this test was not confined to employment protection liabilities but found its way into a variety of areas of law. The test was also used in tort cases, such as the decision of the Court of Appeal in the negligence case of *Cassidy v Minister of Health*[60] as well as tax cases such as *Bank voor Handel en Scheepvaart NV v Slatford*.[61]

When the economic reality test first appeared, enunciated in the High Court decision in *Market Investigations Ltd v Minister of Social Security*[62] in 1969, the area of law in point related to National Insurance.[63] But, again, the

---

[56] See E. McKendrick, 'Vicarious Liability and Independent Contractors – A Re-examination' (1990) 53 *Modern Law Review* 770, at pp. 782–84 where the author states, in an argument that accepts the existence of the unified approach of the common law, that a contextual approach was urgently required for the purposes of the law on vicarious liability.

[57] *Yewens v Noakes* (1880) 6 QBD 530.

[58] See e.g. *Mersey Docks and Harbour Board v Coggins and Griffiths Ltd* [1947] AC 1 and *Collins v Hertfordshire County Council* [1947] KB 598.

[59] Control continues to play an important part in the multiple test, dating from the decision of the High Court in *Ready Mixed Concrete (South East) Ltd v Minister of Pensions and National Insurance* [1968] 2 QB 497; [1968] 1 All ER 433 expressly approved more recently by the House of Lords in *Carmichael v National Power plc* [2000] IRLR 43.

[60] *Cassidy v Minister of Health* [1951] 1 All ER 574; [1951] 2 KB 343. It was because of this case that the demise of the control test to be replaced by the integration test was predicted by Sir Otto Kahn-Freund in his case note 'Servants and Independent Contractors' (1951) 14 *Modern Law Review* 504. This proved to be greatly exaggerated.

[61] *Bank voor Handel en Scheepvaart NV v Slatford* [1953] 1 QB 248; [1954] 2 WLR 867.

[62] *Market Investigations Ltd v Minister of Social Security* [1969] 2 QB 173; [1968] 3 All ER 732.

[63] On a similar point see *Withers v Flackwell Heath Football Supporters' Club*, n 29.

test was utilized in other areas of the law. In *Young and Woods Ltd v West*,[64] for example, the Court of Appeal applied it in a case concerning unfair dismissal. It was applied in a decision on liability for compensation for injury in the Privy Council case of *Lee v Chung*[65] in 1990.

More recently, the courts have not looked for any particular identifying characteristic of employment but rather have adopted a so-called multiple approach which is more concerned with an exercise which balances factors on the one hand indicating employment and on the other those that do not.[66] In *Ready Mixed Concrete*[67] it was stated that the test was three-fold. First, the employee agrees that in consideration of a wage or other remuneration he (sic) will provide his own work and skill for the employer. Secondly the employee expressly or impliedly agrees that he will be subject to the employer's control. Thirdly, the other provisions of the contract have to be consistent with a contract of employment. This can be broken down into a great number of relevant considerations such as the extent to which the employee provides his own tools or clothing, the extent to which he is free to do the work at a time of his own choosing, or where he chooses to do so, the manner in which it is done, the extent to which he can sub-contract, if at all, the work delegated to other workers, whether he bears any financial risk, insurance responsibilities and so on. No one factor is determinative but each is placed on the theoretical scales which will dip one side or another. If this does not happen the description of the relationship made by the parties could be considered relevant.[68] The *Ready Mixed* case was one to do with National Insurance liabilities. But, the important point here is that, as with the other tests, this test has also been applied in other areas of the law. So, in *Hall (Inspector of Taxes) v Lorimer*[69] the Court of Appeal applied it in a case concerning liability for income tax. It has been applied in negligence cases, such as *Lane v Shire Roofing Co. (Oxford) Ltd*[70] as well as, of course, to employment law situations.[71]

There are also indications that the courts view the concept of employment as unified, not just because they apply the same tests in different contexts, but also because, in general, they do not allow different definitions in the same

64 *Young and Woods Ltd v West* [1980] IRLR 201.
65 *Lee v Chung* [1990] IRLR 236.
66 See e.g. *Nethermere (St Neots) Ltd v Taverna & Gardiner* [1984] ICR 612, [1984] IRLR 240.
67 *Ready Mixed Concrete (South East) Ltd*, n 59.
68 *Davis v New England College of Arundel* [1977] ICR 6; [1976] ITR 278.
69 *Hall (Inspector of Taxes) v Lorimer* [1994] IRLR 171; [1994] ICR 218.
70 *Lane v Shire Roofing Co. (Oxford) Ltd* [1995] IRLR 493.
71 For examples of employment law situations see *Express and Echo Publications Ltd v Tanton* [1999] IRLR 367 and the House of Lords' decision in *Carmichael v National Power plc* [2000] IRLR 43.

situation. Take, for example, *Massey v Crown Life Assurance Co.*[72] where the Court of Appeal would not allow a man who had been classified as self-employed for the purposes of his status for income tax purposes to be classified as employed for the purposes of claiming unfair dismissal. In the later case of *Young and Woods Ltd v West*[73] the Court of Appeal did allow a re-classification, but it still did not countenance different classifications in different circumstances. It felt that the Inland Revenue should re-coup the advantage the employee had received by way of the earlier mis-classification. In *Calder v H. Kitson Vickers Ltd*[74] Ralph Gibson LJ was clear, without argument, that the unified theory was correct. He concluded that, referring to the issue as to whether a worker was an employee, his decision did not depend upon the circumstances in which the question is raised, that is to say, for example, whether it were a claim for damages for personal injury or an issue as to the obligation to deduct National Insurance contributions.

In the Employment Appeal Tribunal case of *Hilton International Hotels (UK) Ltd v Protopapa,*[75] the employee claimed that she was constructively dismissed by her employer because her employment was in fact terminated by her superior who had no authority to do so. Knox J stated that the Employment Appeal Tribunal saw no reason to draw the line in any other place than that applied by the general law of vicarious liability of the employer, even though this was in the context of a statutory claim for unfair dismissal in circumstances where vicarious liability would never be an issue.

However, sometimes the courts are prepared to accept different classifications in the same situation. For example, in *Hewlett Packard Ltd v O'Murphy*[76] the Employment Appeal Tribunal held that, even though a claimant had been characterized as an employee for tax purposes, it was right not to classify him as such for unfair dismissal purposes. Nevertheless, it did not consider, nor does it seem it was invited to consider, the implications of differing characterizations of one status in different areas of law. In *Airfix Footwear Ltd v Cope*[77] the Employment Appeal Tribunal held that someone was an employee for the purposes of unfair dismissal protection even though he was treated as an independent contractor for tax purposes. Likewise, in *Wardell v Kent County Council*[78] the Court of Appeal stated that a person could be a servant for the purposes of the Workmen's Compensation Act 1925 even

---

[72] *Massey v Crown Life Assurance Co.* [1978] 2 All ER 576; [1978] 1 WLR 676.
[73] *Young and Woods Ltd v West* [1980] IRLR 201.
[74] *Calder v H. Kitson Vickers Ltd* [1988] ICR 232 at 254.
[75] *Hilton International Hotels (UK) Ltd v Protopapa* [1990] IRLR 316.
[76] *Hewlett Packard Ltd v O'Murphy* [2002] IRLR 4.
[77] *Airfix Footwear Ltd v Cope* [1978] ICR 1210; [1978] ITR 513.
[78] *Wardell v Kent County Council* [1938] 2 KB 768.

though they were not for the purposes of the law of negligence.[79] A similar decision was reached by the Court of Appeal again in *Denham v Midland Employers Mutual Assurance Ltd*.[80]

PROBLEMS WITH THE 'UNIFIED' ANALYSIS

If it is correct to view the courts' approach as proceeding on the basis that employment is a unified concept, it does not follow that it is in fact. There are several difficulties with it. Take, for example, what I have termed above, the 'argument of perspective'. This, it will be remembered, is the idea that there is a unified concept of employment, with varying definitions consequential on differing standpoints. One thing, or idea, can remain constant but can be perceived differently according to the angle from which it is viewed. There is a problem with this idea insofar as the meaning of 'employment' is concerned in that it is not merely that different wording is used in differing contexts, but that the employees who are covered by a particular definition differ in each instance. Sometimes a definition can be wider, or narrower, than others. That sometimes someone might find that they are an employee for one purpose and not for another is different from their status as an employee being *described* in different ways. This is strong evidence against the argument of perspective.

Similarly, examine what I have referred to above as the 'argument of perception'. This is the argument that varying legal definitions are the result of changing understandings of what the legal concept of employment amounts to. However, that is not at all a convincing explanation. The definition under the Employment Rights 1996 Act (covering unfair dismissal and redundancy protection) is actually to be found in earlier legislation[81] pre-dating the original sex discrimination legislation, and yet it has been re-adopted. If it were thought to be an incorrect or inadequate definition of a unified concept of employment, one would expect it to have been altered when the opportunity presented itself. But it was not.

There are further difficulties associated with the unified approach, not least

---

[79] Greer LJ (dissenting) made the different but related point that it is possible to be a servant for some of the tasks involved in a position whilst being an independent contractor for others. So, a nurse in performing nursing duties was not, he thought, a servant, but whilst performing administrative duties, she was (see too *Hillyer v Governors of St. Bartholomew's Hospital* [1909] 2 KB 820). Whilst the majority disagreed with Greer LJ on the facts, they did not question the logic of his argument. The court does not appear to have given any thought to the daunting complications this gave rise to regarding the employee's tax status. See too A.L. Goodhart, 'Hospital and Trained Nurses' (1938) 54 *Law Quarterly Review* 553 and C. Grunfeld, 'Recent Developments in the Hospital Cases' (1954) 17 *Modern Law Review* 547.

[80] *Denham v Midland Employers Mutual Assurance Ltd* [1955] 2 QB 437.

[81] Industrial Relations Act 1971, s. 167(1).

on the grounds of public policy.[82] Some writers have suggested, as I have mentioned already, that the reason why the control test came to be seen as unsatisfactory as the single determinant of employment status was that many relationships the courts wanted to recognize as such simply did not have the necessary degree of control. Modified analyses, attempting to retain the pivotal role of control – such as the idea that, even if there were not actual control of the worker in their tasks, the residual capacity of the other party to exert that control if they so desired was enough – did not work either. Some employers clearly did not have this expertise. It was not that they chose not to exercise it – the element of control was simply missing. It is thus thought by these writers that the move to other tests was brought about by changing social factors together with changing ways in which work was done, and the evolving nature of that work. As Markesinis and Deakin put it:

> 'The control test was more appropriate to the social conditions of an earlier age ... As specialist skills of employees increased, the unskilled employer was less and less able to control their work ... The increasing subtlety of the employment relationship makes the control test, however modified, inadequate'. [83]

However, this is not an entirely satisfactory analysis. What makes the control test increasingly inapplicable, at least for a unified concept of employment, is that it is not based upon sound policy grounds when taken away from the area of vicarious liability and utilized elsewhere. To extend vicarious liability to A (an employer) where B (an employee) does a negligent act would seem to be justified if there is a sufficient degree of control by A over B, at least while B does the act over which A has control. In effect, the person really committing the tort is the employer. The employee to all intents and purposes is the tool, or the medium, by which the negligent act is brought about. As Lord Chelmsford L.C. put it in *Bartonshill Coal Co. v McGuire*:[84]

> '... every act which is done by a servant in the course of his duty is regarded as done by his master's orders, and consequently is the same as if it were the master's own act'.

On the other hand, it is not at all clear why the element of control should be considered to be important in determining whether there should be statutory liability for the manner in which a working relationship is brought to an end,

---

[82] My argument here is taken from S. Honeyball, 'The Conceptual Integrity of Employment' (2005) 36 *Cambrian Law Review* 1.

[83] Furthermore, as Markesinis and Deakin also point out, the move to a test that requires an examination of the issue, not as to whether there is control, but if there is a right to so control, presupposes that the relationship has already been characterized as an employment relationship – see Markesinis and Deakin, *Tort Law*, n 22, p. 574.

[84] *Bartonshill Coal Co. v McGuire* (1858) 3 Macq. 300 at 306.

or for acts which are, for example, sexually discriminatory. Different policy considerations surely there come into play and a contextual approach seems necessarily more appropriate.

Professor Patrick Atiyah felt able to state in 1967, in an argument that supported the unified thesis, that Parliament approached legislation in a manner consistent with it. He sought to illustrate that by showing that the phrase 'contract of service' appeared in legislation, as it not infrequently did, without definition. He said: 'it is a reasonable assumption that it intends to attract the existing body of law on the subject',[85] that is to say, it would be right to assume, the whole body of case-law on the matter, whatever the context. However, even if that were true then, it would not appear to be true today. It is still the case that Parliament continues to use the phrase 'contract of service' without further definition, such as in section 2 of the Employment Act 2002 concerning rights to statutory paternity pay and statutory adoption pay. However, the phrase generally tends to appear within a definition of employment, and these are quite varied. So, to take some recent examples, in section 42(5) of the Sexual Offences Act 2003, 'employment' means any employment, whether paid or unpaid and whether under a *contract of service* or apprenticeship, under a contract for services, or otherwise than under a contract. This can be contrasted with section 4 of the Income Tax (Earnings and Pensions) Act 2003, which states that 'employment' includes:

(a) any employment under a *contract of service*,
(b) any employment under a contract of apprenticeship, and
(c) any employment in the service of the Crown.

Note that this is not, unlike others, an exclusive definition. Compare this with section 42(2) of the Criminal Justice and Court Services Act 2000 on provisions relating to the protection of children where 'employment' means paid employment, whether under a *contract of service* or apprenticeship or under a contract for services. So, even if the phrase 'contract of service' is generally undefined in modern statutes, it generally appears within a definition of the concept of employment that is defined in a wide variety of ways.[86]

Atiyah was conscious of the two views examined here as to the meaning of 'employment', but nevertheless continued to prefer the unified approach. He said the purposive approach 'has the merit of emphasising that legal concepts are tools to be used intelligently for the purpose in hand and not to be applied

---

85 P. Atiyah, *Vicarious Liability in the Law of Torts* (Butterworths, 1967) p. 32.
86 For other examples, see Criminal Justice Act 2003, Sch. 3 Part 2; Enterprise Act 2002, ss. 128 and 234; Social Security Fraud Act 2001, s. 15; Health and Social Care Act 2001, Sch. 1 Part 3; Financial Services and Markets Act 2000, s. 59; Transport Act 2000, s. 182; Protection of Children Act 1999, s. 12; National Minimum Wage Act 1998, s. 54.

blindly to a variety of uses'.[87] However, he argued that where the law does recognize fundamental legal concepts it seems pointless not to use them. They at least provide 'valuable sign posts'.[88] But this surely begs the question. It is only if the field in question is unified that this would be the case. There is also the danger with this view of falling into the trap when dealing with concepts of allowing definitions to determine solutions to problems instead of definitions following on from purposive analysis.[89]

Professor Simon Deakin puts forward an argument that creates difficulties for those advocating a unified approach. He states that the prevailing attitude towards statutory interpretation regards reasoning by analogy from one statutory context to another as illegitimate, and he gives examples in support of this thesis.[90] If he were right, it would be a significant impediment to the argument I have presented. However, perhaps he overstates his case. For example, in the decision of the House of Lords in *Carter v Bradbeer*[91] in 1975 Lord Diplock said:

> 'The ratio decidendi of a judgment as to the meaning of particular words or combination of words used in a particular statutory provision can have no more than a persuasive influence on a court which is called on to interpret the same words or combination of words appearing in some other statutory provision'.[92]

So it is clear that, although the practice of, if you like, translation of interpretation is not required, it is by no means viewed as 'illegitimate'.[93] Indeed, if the statutes are on the same subject matter (*in pari materia*) the approach of the courts is that the same meaning will usually be given, with exceptions being made in cases, for example, where a prior interpretation is obviously erroneous, as in the Court of Appeal's decision in *Royal Crown Derby Porcelain Co. Ltd v Raymond Russell*.[94] Sir Rupert Cross states that what amounts to an 'obligation' exists on the judge to consider other statutes *in pari materia*.[95] Even in cases where statutes are not *in pari materia* Cross shows that reasoning by analogy is by no means illegitimate. He states:

---

[87] Atiyah, *Vicarious Liability in the Law of Torts*, n 85, p. 32.

[88] Ibid, p. 32.

[89] As H.L.A. Hart famously wrote: 'though theory is to be welcomed, the growth of theory on the back of definition is not' (See Hart, 'Definition and Theory in Jurisprudence' in *Essays in Jurisprudence and Philosophy*, n 26, pp. 21, 25.

[90] Deakin, 'The Changing Concept of the "Employer" in Labour Law', n 11, p. 79.

[91] *Carter v Bradbeer* [1975] 3 All ER 158.

[92] Ibid, at 161.

[93] See further, C. Manchester, D. Salter, P. Moodie and B. Lynch, *Exploring the Law: The Dynamics of Precedent and Statutory Interpretation* (Sweet and Maxwell, 2nd edn, 2000) p. 49.

[94] *Royal Crown Derby Porcelain Co. Ltd v Raymond Russell* [1949] 2 KB 417.

[95] R. Cross, J. Bell, and G. Engle (eds), *Statutory Interpretation* (Butterworths, 3rd edn, 1995) pp. 151–52. This contains a useful analysis of the circumstances in which statutes will be considered to be in *pari materia* – see p. 150f.

'In a statutory area, reasoning by analogy within the statutory "code" is perfectly acceptable by application of the general rule permitting the use of other statutes on the same subject as a guide to interpretation'.[96]

A good example of this is R v Arthur[97] in 1968 when the words 'any person' in section 18 of the Offences Against the Person Act 1861 were given the same meaning, contrary to the initial inclination of the court, as those same words in section 2 of the Malicious Damage Act 1861.[98]

As Lord Diplock pointed out in Carter[99] the undoubted move towards a greater degree of purposive interpretation by the courts[100] will mean that similar words in different statutes will result only in a persuasive argument at most that they should be interpreted similarly. Different contexts will mean the potential at least for identical words to be given different interpretations. However, it is not always necessary in the context of a purposive approach for the interpretations to be different in that such an approach recognizes that even identical concepts may be treated differently in different contexts. It is not dependent on varied definitions but on a varied application in different situations.

Deakin states, however, that the reluctance of the courts to reason by way of analogy from statute to the common law is now decreasing, and that this is facilitative of a unified analysis of employment.[101] It is certainly true that there has not been a unified approach with regard to the conceptual relationship between statute and the common law historically. Statute tends to provide additional, alternative remedies and conceptual frameworks to the common law. It does not, on the whole, attempt to amend the common law. Even on those occasions when it strays into common law territory, it does so very tentatively. So, for example, the equality provisions in the Equality Act 2010 seek to remedy the deficiencies of the common law that do not require equal treatment between the sexes in the terms and conditions of employment. It does so by stating that, where a contract does not already contain one, an equality clause shall be deemed to be included.[102] And yet the remedy is not in contract at all but is a stand-alone statutory claim under the Act with the

---

96 Ibid, p. 44. See further Pioneer Aggregates (UK) Ltd v Secretary of State for the Environment [1984] 2 All ER 358.
97 R v Arthur [1968] 1 QB 810.
98 See further Z. Bankowski and N. MacCormick in N. MacCormick and R.S. Summers (eds), Interpreting Statutes (Dartmouth, 1991) p. 369.
99 Carter v Bradbeer [1975] 3 All ER 158 at 161.
100 Of course, there is nothing new in purposive approaches in interpreting statutes which goes back at least as far as 1584 – see Heydon's Case 3 Co. Rep. Fa; 76 ER 637, 638. See D. Miers and A. Page, Legislation (Sweet and Maxwell, 2nd edn, 1990) p. 170f.
101 See particularly S. Deakin, 'Private Law, Economic Rationality and the Regulatory State' in P. Birks (ed.), The Classification of Obligations (Clarendon Press, 1997) p. 283.
102 Equality Act 2010, s. 64f.

consequence that, for example, normal contract limitation periods do not apply. Also, cases were brought in an industrial tribunal even when it did not have jurisdiction to hear contract claims.[103]

However, I have argued elsewhere that there are many examples where the courts, in interpreting employment legislation, have found it difficult to abandon their common law roots and have injected common law ideas into statutory claims.[104] I referred to what I considered to be a particularly striking illustration of this in the case of *Western Excavating (ECC) Ltd v Sharp*.[105] This was a case concerning the definition of 'constructive dismissal', now in section 95(1)(c) of the Employment Rights Act for the purposes of claiming unfair dismissal. Professor Deakin was later to use the same case in point.[106] This provision states that the employee will be taken to have been dismissed if they resign in circumstances such that they are entitled to do so by reason of the employer's conduct. Entitlement here was originally thought to arise where the employer had acted unreasonably – this is, after all, in the context of a statutory claim that seeks to provide remedies where the common law does not for the unfairness of a dismissal. However, the Court of Appeal held that this was not correct. The test to apply was whether the employer had committed a repudiatory breach of contract. The common law had crept in through the back door.

Perhaps this, after all, should not be so striking as it first appears, for several reasons. First, the scheme of the unfair dismissal claim is such that the issue of reasonableness has its part to play in that stage of the proceedings where the fairness or unfairness of the dismissal is examined. To introduce the concept of reasonableness at the earlier point when determining whether there has been a dismissal at all may make the later issue redundant and at best may cause confusion. Secondly, the legislation is not so divorced from the common law as it might appear. For example, the unfair dismissal remedy does not apply where an employee is dismissed from his or her employment, but upon the termination of a contract of employment, and one employment may consist of a number of contractual periods. Furthermore, it should be remembered, employment under the legislation is still defined in terms of the existence of contractual relationships.

---

[103] This has now changed by virtue of the Employment Tribunals (Extension of Jurisdiction) (England and Wales) Order 1994 (SI 1994 No. 1623) and the Employment Tribunals (Extension of Jurisdiction) (Scotland) Order 1994 (SI 1994 No. 1624).

[104] See S. Honeyball, 'Employment Law and the Primacy of Contract' (1989) 18 *Industrial Law Journal* 97. See for an indication that the Supreme Court is willing to reverse this process, *Gisda Cyf v Barratt* [2010] IRLR 1073.

[105] *Western Excavating (ECC) Ltd v Sharp* [1978] IRLR 27; [1978] ICR 221; [1978] QB 761.

[106] See Deakin, 'Private Law, Economic Rationality and the Regulatory State', n 101, pp. 283, 297.

CONCLUSION

The picture is thus a confusing one. Whilst the unified approach does seem to be the one favoured by the judiciary and the legislature, consistency is lacking. Furthermore, whether the unified or multiple approach is adopted, it is not clear that this is as a result of a fully-reasoned working out of the considerations involved, or whether it is a consequence of more fortuitous factors. Neither is it certain that it is the approach that should be adopted.

Although there are clear difficulties associated with the unified approach, as we have seen, to move to a multiple approach, perhaps policy-focussed, would in any event not be straightforward. There would be a price that it might not be possible or desirable to pay. To take but one example, a multiple approach would probably best be served by an attendant change in nomenclature, particularly in legislation, in order to make clear that different concepts were in point. It would seem that much of the confusion has arisen in this area because, if different concepts have been in issue, the same term has been used to apply to them. If different terms were to be adopted this result would largely be avoided. But the consequence of that in turn would be that the law would appear more technical to those to whom it applies, and more divorced from reality. The familiarity of the lay person with the terms 'employment', 'contracts of employment', 'contracts of service' and so on mean that the law is more accessible than it would be were neologisms to abound, as would otherwise be required. Neither, purely on a practical and political level, is such a change likely to be brought about. I can discard it as a serious possibility.

However, there is one improvement that could be made which, though modest and limited in scope, would I suggest be a move in the right direction. Matters are made unnecessarily confused at present because the limited terminology that is used is employed in a definitionally cross-referencing manner that is unhelpful. To define an employee as one who works under a contract of employment, for example, is not only generally unenlightening but opens up the definitional approaches that have been adopted in other areas with regard to those phrases.[107] Be it good or bad, this invites a unified approach. On the other hand, if an approach were to be adopted that sought to identify the concept without reference to other concepts in law, this would, I suggest, be both more enlightening and less of a temptation to stray into areas that have not been fully worked through. But this would merely be a beginning. What is fundamentally required is a thorough understanding of the theoretical complexities involved in the definition of concepts which is not substantially evident at the moment.

---

[107] As with the heavy case-law on section 230(1) of the Employment Rights Act 1996.

Debate 5

Should the concept of employment be abandoned?

An approach to the problems I have considered in the previous Debates might be to say that the concept of employment should be abandoned, at least as the main reference point for the legal foundation of work relationships. There are simply too many definitions of employment in the legislation (in addition to the understanding of the idea at common law) and other terms that are used in contradistinction to those, such as 'self-employed' and 'worker'. The latter term in particular has been used in a highly confusing manner because it, like the concept of employment, has been used to identify those who are entitled to certain work-based claims. So, for example, workers are entitled to protection under the minimum wage[108] and working time regulations,[109] and the concept of 'worker' is relevant in several collective employment law contexts, such as the definition of a trade union.[110] More confusingly still, the definition of 'worker' often appears closer to some definitions of employee than some definitions of employee to other definitions of employee. So, for example, the Equality Act 2010, s. 83 defines 'employment' principally as 'employment under a contract of employment, a contract of apprenticeship or a contract personally to do any work'. It is the latter that takes the definition further than, for example, that of 'employee' under the Employment Rights Act 1996, s. 230(1). And yet it is much closer to the definition of worker in s. 230(3) as referring to an individual who works under a contract of employment or any other contract to do or perform personally any work or services for the other party to the contract, not being their client or customer. However, the latter part of this definition is in fact missing from that of employee in the Equality Act 2010, and so is somewhat narrower rather than, as is usual, wider than the idea of employment.

There would thus appear to be a 'crisis of fundamental concepts' in employment law, with too many definitions of too many concepts clashing with each other. An alternative to the present situation has been put forward by Professor Mark Freedland.[111] He suggests that there should be a unification

---

[108] National Minimum Wage Regulations 1999 (SI 1999 No. 584).

[109] Working Time Regulations 1998 (SI 1998 No. 1833).

[110] Trade Union and Labour Relations (Consolidation) Act 1992, s. 1 defines a trade union as an organization (whether temporary or permanent) which consists wholly or mainly of workers of one or more descriptions and whose principal purposes include the regulation of relations between workers of that description or those descriptions and employers or employers' associations. It also includes constituents of affiliated organizations.

[111] M. Freedland, *The Personal Employment Contract* (Oxford University Press, 2003). The term 'crisis in fundamental concepts' is Freedland's (see e.g. p. 26) and Lewis and Clark's – see J. Clark and Lord Wedderburn, 'A Crisis in Fundamental Concepts', in Wedderburn, Lewis and Clark, *Labour Law and Industrial Relations: Building on Kahn-Freund*, n 25.

of the work concepts employed in this area of law, to result in what he terms 'the personal employment contract'. The idea would cover both employment contracts as presently understood and other contracts to which workers are party. This would remove what he sees as the false distinction between the employed and the self-employed. But he would also go further by simply extending the category of employment to include the self-employed worker, even those who work for clients or customers where there is some economic dependence on the other party. This particularly includes providing a body of law to explain the nature of workers who are economically semi-dependant but not employees, such as casual workers. In addition, he argues, a more coherent analysis is required to cater for more modern forms of working, quite different from that for which the older[112] employment concept was devised, based as it is on the paradigm of relationships between individuals. Whilst, of course, many working relationships are based on this model many are not. Large numbers of people work in organizations, some very large, which require a very different legal analysis of working relationships in them.[113] In addition, patterns of the creation of work relationships have changed so that often there is not a simple bilateral contractual exchange. This has come to the fore in recent years with the difficulties the courts have encountered in attempting to provide a workable analysis of agency relationships, as we have seen, whereby workers may obtain work through an employment agency but work on a day-to-day basis as if they were employees, not of the agency, but of the 'end-user'.

Freedland's work in this area has proved to be thought-provoking, and refreshingly provocative. It encapsulates much that has been dimly understood as to the changing nature of work relationships in the past half-century and beyond. A broader conception of employment that encapsulates wider ideas is much to be welcomed and reflects modern realities. Old distinctions are shown to be irrelevant and new complexities embraced. Having said that, it is debatable how extensive an alteration of approach this entails. Having a wider unified concept of employment in this sense does not entail that the need for a plethora of distinctions will be done away with, but merely that the distinctions drawn will be more modern and relevant to today's world of work. This is because the contexts in which employment (however defined) appears are many and varied, and particularly so having their own policy

---

[112] Simon Deakin has often argued convincingly that the importance of the legal distinction between employee and self-employed is much more recent than is commonly supposed – see particularly his 'The Comparative Evolution of the Employment Relationship' in G. Davidov and B. Langille (eds), *Boundaries and Frontiers of Labour Law: Goals and Means in the Regulation of Work* (Hart Publishing, 2006), and also 'Does the "Personal Employment Contract" Provide a Basis for the Reunification of Employment Law?' (2007) 36 *Industrial Law Journal* 68.

[113] See also Collins, 'Independent Contractors and the Challenge of Vertical Disintegration to Employment Protection Laws', n 8.

considerations. It will continue to be necessary to distinguish between types of work relationships if rights and duties are to remain dependent upon a definition of these relationships. There will continue to be different classes of workers, however their work relationships are defined, precisely because they are defined to give effect to different policy considerations in different areas. There will continue to be one group of workers who should be entitled to protection against discrimination who are not thought to be entitled to unfair dismissal protection; there will continue to be workers who have the right to rest breaks who are not thought entitled to a redundancy payment; and there will continue to be workers whose actions found tortious liability in their other contracting parties who will nevertheless not be considered to be employees for numerous other reasons. This being the case, perhaps all that can be striven for in this context is to make the categories of working we employ up-to-date, effective and relevant.

Further Reading

D. Brodie, 'Employees, Workers and the Self-Employed' (2005) 34 *Industrial Law Journal* 253.

H. Collins, 'Independent Contractors and the Challenge of Vertical Disintegration to Employment Protection Laws' (1990) 10 *Oxford Journal of Legal Studies* 353.

G. Davidov, 'Who is a Worker?' (2005) 34 *Industrial Law Journal* 57.

S. Deakin, 'The Changing Concept of the "Employer" in Labour Law' (2001) 30 *Industrial Law Journal* 72.

S. Deakin, 'The Contract of Employment: A Study in Legal Evolution' (2002) 11 *Historical Studies in Industrial Relations* 1.

T.A.O. Endicott, 'Questions of Law' (1998) 114 *Law Quarterly Review* 292.

M. Freedland. 'From the Contract of Employment to the Personal Work Nexus' (2006) 35 *Industrial Law Journal* 1.

H.L.A. Hart, 'Definition and Theory in Jurisprudence' [1954] 70 *Law Quarterly Review* 37.

E. McKendrick, 'Vicarious Liability and Independent Contractors – A Re-examination' (1990) 53 *Modern Law Review* 770.

G. Pitt, 'Law, Fact and Casual Workers' (1985) 101 *Law Quarterly Review* 217.

G. Pitt, 'Deciding Who is an Employee – Fact or Law?' (1990) 19 *Industrial Law Journal* 252.

A.W.B. Simpson, 'The Analysis of Legal Concepts' (1964) 80 *Law Quarterly Review* 535.

K.W. Wedderburn, R. Lewis and J. Clark, *Labour Law and Industrial Relations* (Clarendon Press, 1983).

G. Williams, 'Vicarious Liability and the Master's Indemnity' (1957) 20 *Modern Law Review* 220.

2

THE EMPLOYMENT CONTRACT
AND THEORY

INTRODUCTION

In this chapter I will concentrate on the contractual aspects of employment from a theoretical point of view. In other words, I will be concerned with the nature of employment and whether it is best analysed in its present state in terms of the law of contract. I will leave until the next chapter normative, or prescriptive, issues regarding the extent to which, if employment is contractual, contract provides the best model for employment from the point of view of the parties to the relationship, and particularly if it allows employees to be given the degree of job security that is thought suitable in the modern world of work.

A great deal has been written on the topic of the first Debate which lays down the arguments why employment may be best analysed as contractual in nature. It has been for good reason, as the issue lies at the root of the employment relationship. It defines what type of legal relationship employment is. It is for this reason that I will devote a far greater amount of space to this Debate than to others. I will examine, first, what the basic position might appear to be, and then examine several reasons why this may not be as clear as it would seem on first inspection. Several reasons why the contract model seems not to fit as well as it would at first blush from an analysis of the birth and the death of the relationship will be examined, followed by a discussion of other reasons arising from how contract works during the life of the relationship. The second Debate will consider, if employment is not best explained from a theoretical point of view as contractual in nature, what alternative candidates exist. Finally, the third Debate will examine to what extent the judiciary might be said to retreat to contractual analysis in providing a theoretical foundation for employment because it is naturally conservative in this regard.

Before I begin, however, it is important to strike a note of caution. As with many issues relating to theory, the perspective of a debate can be crucial. The construction of an argument can skew the way any conclusion is reached. Further, the historical development of ideas can affect how one views the outcome. Let me give one example here to illustrate what I mean by this. The historical position relating to the issue as to who could sue in contract has been determined by the doctrine of privity, whereby only the parties to the contract could do so. No other party had given consideration for the agreement and that, amongst other things, means that third parties could not sue. This was changed in 1999 with the passage of the Contracts (Rights of Third Parties) Act of that year. Under section 1 the general rule is that an identifiable third party to a contract may, in their own right, enforce a term of the contract if the contract expressly so provides or if the term purports to confer a benefit on them. However, this does not apply if, on a proper construction of the contract, it appears that the parties did not intend the term to be enforceable by the third party. Nevertheless, this does not apply under section 6 of the Act with regard to any term of a contract of employment against an employee. So third parties, such as customers of suppliers in a contractual relationship with an employer, may not sue an employee for breaking their contracts of employment with that employer. There are several ways this could legitimately be viewed in terms of theory. It could show that employment contracts are paradigm contracts in that the classical doctrine of privity applies to them despite modern changes to the idea. Alternatively, it might be thought that, as employment contracts have not been treated under the 1999 Act in the same way as most other contracts,[1] this illustrates that they are not typical contracts. If the historical starting point of contractual theory had been that laid down in the 1999 Act, then it would have readily been seen that employment contracts would not be typical contracts in that they differ from most types of contracts. But because the position with employment contracts now reflects classical theory it is easier to argue that they are paradigmatic contracts. And yet the position of contracts under the 1999 Act as well as those not under the Act are exactly the same on either view. The chronology of the development of the analysis and hence the perspective adopted has a part to play in the characterization of the concept which would have been the same however it had been devised.

---

[1] There are, however, other exceptions under the Act, such as workers (including home workers and agency workers), negotiable instruments, bills of exchange and promissory notes.

Debate **1**

Is contract the best theoretical foundation for the employment relationship?

FIRST IMPRESSIONS

At first sight, it might seem that the debate as to whether the employment relationship is primarily contractual has little substance. If one were to ask any lawyer who had no particular knowledge of employment law what the employment relationship consisted in, the reply would probably be that it was contractual. This is because the manner in which an employment relationship comes about fits, at first sight, very neatly into the contractual model with which all lawyers are thoroughly familiar. An employer, after perhaps a lengthy advertising, shortlisting and interviewing process will begin putting into place what it recognizes as a legal relationship. This begins with the employer choosing the applicant it thinks would be most suitable for the position and communicating that fact to them. The applicant might go away and think about it for a while and then inform the employer that they would like to work for it. There might be some more discussion as to the terms of the post, but eventually the two parties will agree upon the terms under which the relationship will be regulated, at least at this stage as to its most basic terms. These will include the work the employee is to do, or be willing to do, for the employer, and for what remuneration. The employee might then, or at some later point, sign a written statement laying out the terms of the relationship, but this will be in pursuit of an agreement already reached orally. The agreement is recognized by both parties as being formal in nature, with any disputes capable of being settled, if all else has failed, in the courts or an employment tribunal. In short, there will have been an offer by the employer which has been accepted by the would-be employee, accompanied by consideration moving from both parties coupled to an intention by both parties to create a legal relationship. In other words, a contractual relationship will have been created, and a rather paradigm contract at that. It might be thought, then, that it would seem surprising to our lawyer unversed in employment law that it is not at all so clear in reality. However, any lawyer trained in contract (and all, of course, have been) would comprehend after only a little thought that the contractual analysis of the employment relationship bears only a degree of weight, and that there are some clear difficulties with it.

One reason why contract might seem ill-suited to employment is that what might be called the 'agreemental' aspect of contract is not so much the case in employment as in other contractual relationships. If I agree to sell you my car we operate on an entirely obvious equal footing. Of course, sometimes contractual relationships are entered into which are not equal in one sense.

You and I entering into a contract with a large utilities company or high street chain will not feel equal with them, having to take the terms on offer which might be contained in a good deal of small print. But that is equality (or the lack of it) in the sense of equality or inequality of bargaining power there is even less with contracts we make with vending machines or parking meters. In employment there is certainly a lack of equality of bargaining power in most (but by no means all) relationships, but there is an additional feature of inequality that exists that sets employment relationships apart from other contractual relationships. This is the hierarchical aspect of employment. One does not enter into employment, whatever level of bargaining power one might have enjoyed in doing so, expecting to be on a level footing with the employer during the course of the relationship. One signs up to a place within the institutional hierarchy, somewhat subordinate to the place of the employer within it. Indeed, the employer will be co-terminous with the institution, or at least a major element of it. Those offering the post to you will, in large organizations, themselves be employees acting on authority given to them within the bureaucracy to appoint you. They will, in all probability, remain superior to you in the hierarchy and could well be your line manager once appointed to the post. That employment is entered into in a manner which is highly indicative of a contract does not entail that a typically contractual relationship ensues. The agreement that is made is for employees to place themselves within a hierarchical relationship involving a degree of subservience to the organization and those within it. The word 'subservience' here is a pertinent one, because the terminology of employment law makes it clear that this is fundamental to the employment relationship, in that it is often referred to as a contract 'of service' to be contrasted with a contract 'for services' which is entered into by independent contractors working on their own account.

Professor Hugh Collins has argued powerfully against the idea that employment should be seen as primarily contractual, pointing out the bureaucratic features of much employment that militate against this.[2] For him, 'the simple characterization of employment as a contract fails to grasp the nature of the social relations involved' he writes.[3] For example, the ordinary nexus between managers and employees cannot be described as contractual in that they have never made a contract between them. Managers further up the hierarchy will have determined the relationship between them. The line manager's means of redress against employees will be through disciplinary measures, not through law for monetary compensation.

[2] See H. Collins, 'Market Power, Bureaucratic Power and the Contract of Employment' (1986) 15 Industrial Law Journal 1.
[3] Ibid, at p. 3.

Furthermore, an employee does not suffer in terms of their wage packet for defective or tardy performance. This is all, of course, true. However, how far does it take us? Collins seems to have correctly pointed out that the relationship between employees and their immediate managers in bureaucratic organizations is not based in law. That of course is true, but only serves to highlight more, I would suggest, that the legal relationship that employees have is with the business as a whole. That the former is not contractual does not mean that the legal relationship is not contractual. Of course, Collins is presumably making a different point, and that is that lawyers should not feel that a legal, contractual, analysis of the employment relationship cannot be a full explanation of the work relationships involved as a whole. However, that is a point that can be cheaply conceded for my purposes here.

FURTHER ANALYSIS

It thus seems, even on this cursory additional thought, less clear than might immediately appear that the employment relationship is a simple contractual one. It is important, therefore, to examine in considerably more detail further reasons why the contractual analysis of employment turns out to be inadequate in a number of respects.

In suggesting above that the natural legal characterization of the employment relationship is contractual I did so only from the viewpoint of the creation of the relationship – an offer which is accepted and supported by consideration intended to have legal consequences. When one delves further into the life of the employment relationship it is then that we see standard contractual ideas being stripped away from the relationship. This partly flows from the bureaucratic nature of employment in many instances but also is the case where there is no sophisticated bureaucratic structure, particularly with employers employing just a few people. I will consider further difficulties with the contractual analysis during the lifetime of the employment relationship below. However, before doing so, I will examine in more depth other occasions when contractual analysis does not seem to capture the nature of the employment relation. I will take examples here from both the period before the relationship begins and after it has been terminated.

Pre-employment contractual analysis

One difficulty with the contractual analysis of the employment relationship is that employment generally consists of one or a series of employment contracts. If an employee has one job that lasts for a period of time it might be that their employment consists of just one contract of employment. However, there might be several contracts, for example if the employee is promoted. Nevertheless there is but one period of employment the duration of which is determined by the contracts. So, an employer might bring an employment relationship to an end by terminating the employee's only or final contract or the employee might do so by resigning. In each case, the employment terminates when any notice period expires, whether or not the employee works during that period, or on the date of resignation or dismissal as the case may be if there is no notice period given. This gives rise to some difficulties as I shall shortly explain, but I will leave those to one side for now.

However, the most obvious difficulty with the contemporaneity of employment and contracts of employment lies at the other end of the relationship. Sometimes applicants start work immediately after they are offered a job, and become employees straightaway. But it is extremely common for applicants to accept a position, continue to work for their present employer whilst working out a period of notice and begin work for their new employer some weeks or even months later. The law views the employment relationship in these latter instances as starting, not when the employer's offer is accepted and the contract formed, but on the date on which the employee begins work. There is thus no contemporaneity of contract and employment. The contract may pre-date employment by some time. This is a major stumbling block for the simple contractual analysis of employment.

This difficulty could, in theoretical terms, be overcome very easily. The consideration moving from the employee to the employer on a contract of employment is the willingness to do the work. It is not actually performing the work.[4] So, if for some reason or another the employee does not do any work, that does not mean that there is no contract of employment during that period. It might be simply that the employer does not require the employee to work, but nevertheless the employment relationship continues unbroken. In a striking phrase, the judge in one case stated that, so long as he paid his cook her wages, she could not complain if he took any or all of his meals out.[5] There are, of course, exceptions to this rule, such as where the employee given work is part of the consideration understood by the parties to move from the employer. Sales staff working on a basic income supplemented by commission, or actors hired to appear in a play, are good examples. The former needs the extra work to provide them with a reasonable income, and the latter requires work not only to secure an income but also to give them a platform to acquire a reputation so that they can advance in their careers. But these are the exceptions. The point here is that there is little to prevent, in theoretical terms, the law from stating that the employment begins when an offer is accepted. It is true that one stumbling block might be that the employee could be in two full-time employments at once for a period, but that would not be

---

[4] See B. Napier, 'Aspects of the Wage-Work Bargain' [1984] *Cambridge Law Journal* 337.
[5] *Collier v Sunday Referee Publishing Co. Ltd* [1940] 2 KB 647.

insurmountable. The terms of the new contract would entail that the employee was not obliged to work for their employer during the period of notice to be served out for their present employer. The obstacles rather are ones of policy. For example, certain employment rights, such as for unfair dismissal and redundancy require that the employee has a period of service with their employer before they are eligible to claim. The basis of this is that a period of working for that employer entitles them to the new claim. It is difficult to see how a period when the employee is not obligated to work for their new employer, when they are perhaps working full-time for another employer, should count towards this entitlement. (Of course, it is arguable that no employment claim should be dependent on continuity having been accrued, but I must leave that debate aside for now).

There are arguments, however, that there ought, in principle, to be rights and obligations between the parties once an employment contract has been entered into but before the employment has actually begun. (Some of these can also be applied to the reasons why continuity should not be required, just mentioned). For example, an employee who accepts an offer of a new post could well be making a significant life-changing decision, which has financial and other consequences. To move oneself and one's family from (say) Durham in the north to Truro in the far south-west may involve a major upheaval for the employee and their family, entailing changes of schools and their spouse's or partner's job, loss of previously-enjoyed employment protection and so on. That the rights and duties that will exist in the employment contract once the employee starts work do not exist in the hiatus between the employee accepting the employer's offer and the employee actually beginning work is to place the employee in a very vulnerable position. Even if there should be no statutory employment protection during this period – and I would argue that that is not at all clear – it would seem at least arguable that the employer should do nothing to undermine the trust and confidence between the parties during that period that is necessary to exist once the employee has started work, and which is part of the contractual obligations of the parties by way of an implied term. It perhaps should also be the case that, depending on the particular circumstances, employees should have a level of obligation to co-operate with their new employees during this period, which is also an implied term of employment contracts.

That contractual rights and duties exist after an offer is accepted but before employment starts is supported by the fact that a 'dismissal' of the employee in the period between the date of the contract and the date on which the employee is to start work may amount to a breach of contract.[6] But the

---

[6] See e.g. *Hochster v de la Tour* (1853) 2 E. & B. 678 and *Martin v Stout* [1925] AC 359.

question arises, a breach of what type of contract? If it were the employment contract itself that would mean an employment relationship were already in existence, which at first sight appears not to be the case. Most obviously, of course, this would seem to suggest that whereas a contractual relationship exists between the parties prior to work beginning, the contract is not an employment contract. It would follow that the pre-work and work phases are governed by distinct, sequential contracts, the earlier being a collateral contract, one *for* rather than *of* employment.

The possibility of sequential contracts was raised in *Sarker v South Tees Acute Hospitals NHS Trust*.[7] The claimant was offered a job with the respondents but the respondents subsequently withdrew their offer of employment. The tribunal dismissed the claim for wrongful dismissal[8] on the basis that it did not arise 'on the termination of the employee's employment' and as such the tribunal had no jurisdiction to hear the claim.[9] Before the Employment Appeal Tribunal (EAT) the respondents argued that, while the correspondence between the parties gave rise to a contract, it was 'merely a contract *for* employment and not a contract *of* employment'.[10] While it may be that the concept of a contract for employment requiring the parties subsequently to enter into a contract of employment is not a familiar one, there seems no obstacle in principle to the parties so arranging their affairs. The collateral or preliminary contract is well-established in general contract law.[11] There was also a previous employment law decision of the Northern Ireland Court of Appeal to support the two-contract idea, but not referred to in *Sarker* in the judgement or in argument. In *Gill and others v Cape Contracts Ltd*[12] in 1985 the claimants were induced to give up their existing employment by a representation that they would be employed by the defendants at much higher wages. They were awarded substantial damages when the defendants cancelled the offer of employment due to a threat of industrial action. Lord Justice O'Donnell stated that the representations led to a collateral contract which was independent of the contract of employment and that the representation was a warranty which the defendants had failed to honour. However, the EAT in *Sarker* were not

---

[7] *Sarker v South Tees Acute Hospitals NHS Trust* [1997] ICR 673.
[8] The tribunal chairman failed, on the face of the decision, to deal with the unfair dismissal claim; see *Sarker* above at 682E.
[9] See Article 3(c) of the Employment Tribunals (Extension of Jurisdiction) (England and Wales) Order 1994.
[10] *Sarker* at 678A (emphasis added).
[11] See, e.g.. *Pitt v PHH Asset Management Ltd* [1994] 1 WLR 327; *Blackpool & Fylde Aero Club v Blackpool Borough Council* [1990] 1 WLR 1195; *Mann v Nunn* (1874) 30 LT 526; *De Lassalle v Guildford* [1901] 2 KB 215; *City & Westminster Properties (1934) Ltd v Mudd* [1959] Ch 129; *Esso Petroleum Co. Ltd v Mardon* [1976] QB 801.
[12] *Gill and others v Cape Contracts Ltd* [1985] IRLR 499.

persuaded by the two-contract approach because no further contract between the parties was required. As and when the appellant turned up for work on the agreed date, she would have been performing the contract already entered into, not making a fresh offer which the respondents would then accept by allowing her to work and paying her. The EAT preferred the idea that there was a single contract, of which there may be an anticipatory breach if unequivocal notice is given that there is no intention to perform the contract.[13] It concluded that the tribunal had been wrong in its determination that it had no jurisdiction and remitted the case to the tribunal to deal with both the wrongful and unfair dismissal claims.[14]

According to *Sarker*, therefore, the employment relationship does come into existence at the same time as the contractual relationship. An employee is employed from the moment that the contract is made, notwithstanding that they may not begin work for several months. *Sarker* is a significant decision because, by adopting the single contract approach, it opens up the possibility that the employee may enjoy much wider rights in the pre-work phase than is commonly recognized.[15] Indeed, in *Sarker* itself, the EAT clearly felt that Ms Sarker would have been able to claim unfair dismissal had her contract been terminated before the start date for an inadmissible reason, such as pregnancy or union membership.[16]

The single contract approach in *Sarker* suggests that other rights, in addition to the right not to be unfairly dismissed, may be acquired in the pre-work phase. Section 1 of the Employment Rights Act 1996 provides for an employee to be given a written statement of particulars of employment not later than two months after the beginning of the employment. Whether this entitles the employee to the statement within two months of the start of the pre-work phase does not appear to have been considered. Non-statutory rights may also

---

[13] *Sarker,* n 7 at 678.

[14] The approach in *Sarker* was adopted by the EAT in *London Borough of Southwark v Johnstone* EAT/641/97 (unreported).

[15] Mark Freedland has suggested that a personal employment contract can be said to exist in 'pre-employment mode' (M. Freedland, *The Personal Employment Contract* (Oxford University Press, 2003) p. 107). He prefers this analysis to the idea that a contract *for* employment may be entered into to commit the parties to enter into a future employment contract, or the idea that the contract of employment does not come into existence at all until the later date. During this period, however, even though there is a contract of employment in existence, the worker would not yet be described as being in the employment of the employing entity.

[16] *Sarker,* n 7 at 681G. It is less clear, however, that a claim for unfair dismissal lies in the pre-work context where the employee must demonstrate a qualifying period of continuous employment. s. 108, Employment Rights Act 1996 states that the right not to be unfairly dismissed generally does not apply unless the dismissed employee has been continuously employed for a period of not less than one year. s. 211(1)(a), Employment Rights Act 1996 provides that the period of continuous employment 'begins with the day on which the employee starts work'. See further, S. Honeyball and D. Pearce, 'Contract, Employment and the Contract of Employment' [2006] *Industrial Law Journal* 30.

arise in the pre-employment phase: it may be that both parties are subject to duties implied at common law.[17] It is perhaps difficult to conceive of most of the terms commonly implied in an employment contract extending to the pre-work stage. For example, the employee would not, subject to any contrary arrangement, be under a duty to be ready and willing to work, nor would the employer be under a duty to make work available. The term which would appear most likely to have an impact is that as to trust and confidence. For instance, where the employee has given up their existing employment to work for their new employer or where the fact of the agreement to join the new employer is in the public domain, there appears little to justify denying the existence of the duty established in *Mahmud v BCCI*.[18] Other duties may exist, for example, restraining the disclosure of confidential information which the employee may already have gained concerning their new employer.[19] Nor in principle would the fact that the employee is in the pre-work phase appear, of itself, to preclude the employer from being vicariously liable for some torts or breaches of the statutory duty of the employee.[20]

I have sought to demonstrate that the implications of the finding in *Sarker*, that the employee dismissed during the pre-work phase had had her contract of employment terminated, may be more far-reaching than commonly supposed.[21] But such an outcome does not, I suggest, undermine the *Sarker* approach. Rather, the consequences which may arise from that case do so to a large extent because of the reliance in the legislation on the concept of the employment contract. Thus an employee is defined as an individual who has entered into a contract of employment;[22] an employee is dismissed for unfair dismissal purposes when their contract is terminated;[23] and, weeks will count for continuity purposes when an employee's relations with their employer are governed by a contract of employment.[24] That an employee who is dismissed before starting work may be able to claim unfair dismissal, whether or not that

---

[17] According to Freedland, the contract in pre-employment mode 'probably does not impose any current obligations on either party, other than those of, respectively, keeping the employment opportunity available on the appointed date and remaining available for employment on the appointed date' (Freedland, *The Personal Employment Contract*, n 15, p. 107).

[18] *Mahmud v Bank of Credit and Commerce International* [1998] AC 20.

[19] Of course, such a duty may not be contractual in origin.

[20] Generally, see W.V.H. Rogers, *Winfield & Jolowicz on Tort* (Sweet & Maxwell, 18th edn, 2010) ch.10.

[21] Cf. Freedland who states that the EAT in *Sarker* was conscious that it was resolving a difficult point 'and that the law was being stretched in a purposive way' (Freedland, *The Personal Employment Contract*, n 15, p. 99). Consider further the position of the candidate at a job interview who accepts an offer of employment there and then who is injured on her way out of the building. Would it be possible for that enmployee to sue under the contract (not simply in tort) for failing to provide a safe system of work?

[22] Employment Rights Act 1996, s. 230(1).

[23] Employment Rights Act 1996, s. 95.

[24] Employment Rights Act 1996, s. 212(1).

claim requires a period of continuous employment, may not have been the intention of Parliament. However, it may not be undesirable.

Post-employment contractual analysis

There are also difficulties with the contractual analysis of employment at the other end of the employment relationship. An employment relationship may be terminated by several means, such as resignation, dismissal, performance of specific contractual obligations, agreement and (rarely) frustration. Common to any termination of employment is that it is brought about by way of the termination of the only or latest contract of employment regulating the relationship. If a contract is terminated, it might be thought that it necessarily follows that all the rights and obligations under the contract are thereby extinguished. If, for example, an obligation were to continue under the contract, capable of being enforced in the courts, it could hardly be said, it would seem, that the contract has been terminated.

Restrictive Covenants

The difficulty with the argument just put forward is that some terms of contracts of employment do survive the termination of the employment relationship. A restrictive covenant is a term of a contract of employment that places restrictions on the employee's immediate employment opportunities with other employers, or the ability to work for themselves in the same type of activity. These restrictions may be temporal or spatial. The restrictive covenant may, for example, indicate a period after the termination of the original employment during which the employee may not undertake the same type of work as they were previously doing, and within a particular geographical area. These types of contractual terms are interpreted very narrowly by the courts. They must go no further than is necessary for the employer to preserve its business, and must be in the public interest.[25] The important point for the present purposes, however, is that the courts recognize them at all, given that the employment relationship that they regulate has been terminated in virtue of the termination of the contracts that contains them. Indeed, they are of significance, and come into operation, *only* once the termination of the contract that contains them has occurred.

It is clearly necessary for the courts to provide a coherent explanation for how this can be. The idea that a term of a contract can survive the contract's termination would not appear to be exclusive to restrictive covenants in employment contracts.[26] For example, in *Heyman v Darwins Ltd*[27] the House of

---

[25] See e.g. the decision of the House of Lords in *Stenhouse Australia Ltd v Phillips* [1974] AC 391; [1974] 1 All ER 117.

[26] I am greatly indebted in this section to the views of David Pearce. See Honeyball and Pearce, 'Contract, Employment and the Contract of Employment', n 16, p. 39f.

[27] *Heyman v Darwins Ltd* [1942] AC 356.

Lords confirmed that an arbitration clause in a commercial contract remains effective despite the acceptance by one party of the other party's repudiation of the contract. Lord Diplock classified contractual rights into primary and secondary rights.[28] He stated that 'each promise that a promisor makes to a promisee by entering into a contract with him creates an obligation to perform it owed by the promisor as obligor to the promisee as obligee'.[29] Such an obligation is a primary obligation.[30] A general principle of English law is that the parties are 'free to determine for themselves what primary obligations they will accept'.[31] These may be stated in express terms, but in practice many are implied. Subject to some statutory exceptions, the parties are free to reject or modify primary obligations which would otherwise be so incorporated. Secondary obligations, on the other hand, are obligations which arise on breaches of primary obligations. Secondary obligations arise by implication of law, generally common law, but sometimes statute. The 'most important'[32] secondary obligation is to pay monetary compensation or damages to the injured party. Lord Diplock labels this the 'general secondary obligation'.[33] Generally, where there is a failure to perform any primary obligation the remaining primary obligations of both parties, in so far as they are not fully performed, remain unchanged, even if the obligation to perform the contract has been removed because of the fundamental nature of the breach by one of the parties.

However, on closer analysis it would not seem that Lord Diplock's views do support the idea that a term can survive the termination of a contract. His comments may go no further than to suggest that obligations to perform the contract may have come to an end, but that does not mean that other obligations under the contract may continue. Acceptance of a breach going to the root of the contract brings an end to performance of the contract[34] but the contract itself is not rescinded.[35] In *Lep Air Services v Rolloswin Investments Ltd*[36] Lord Diplock referred to ancillary obligations which continue to exist notwithstanding that *performance* of the contract has come to an end following a repudiation.[37]

---

[28] Lord Diplock developed his classification in a series of judgments. See, e.g. *Belmar v Denny* [1958] 1 Lloyd's Rep 112; *Hardwick Game Farm v SAPPA* [1966] 1 WLR 287; *C. Czarnikow Ltd v Koufos, the Heron II* [1966] 2 QB 695; *Ward v Bignall* [1967] 1 QB 534; *Lep Air Services Ltd v Rolloswin Investments Ltd* [1973] AC 331; *Photo Production Ltd v Securicor Transport Ltd* [1980] AC 827. Generally, see B. Dickson, 'The Contribution of Lord Diplock to the General Law of Contract' (1989) 9 *Oxford Journal of Legal Studies* 441.

[29] *Lep Air Services Ltd v Rolloswin Investments Ltd*, n. 28 at 347.

[30] Ibid, at 347.

[31] *Photo Production Ltd v Securicor Transport Ltd*, n 28 at 848.

[32] *C. Czarnikow Ltd v Koufos (The Heron II)* [1966] 2 QB 695 at 730.

[33] *Photo Production Ltd*, n 28 at 849.

[34] *Heyman v Darwins Ltd* [1942] 356 at 367 per Viscount Simon LC.

[35] Ibid, at 373, per Lord Macmillan.

[36] *Lep Air Services Ltd*, n 28.

[37] Ibid, at 350.

The essential characteristic of these obligations is that they are 'ancillary to the main purpose of the contract', that purpose being that 'the parties should perform their primary obligations voluntarily'.[38] A restrictive covenant in a contract of employment may be seen as a classic example of an ancillary obligation. However, in *General Billposting Company Ltd v Atkinson*[39] the House of Lords held that an employee who was wrongfully dismissed was thereby released from all of the other obligations under the contract. Restrictive covenants in the contract of a wrongfully dismissed employee will be discharged even though the contract might make plain the parties' intention that the covenants should remain binding however the employment ends. Although there is no reference in *General Billposting* to ancillary duties, it is consistent with the idea. The decision in that case is problematic, however, in that it ignored the intentions of the parties. It also imposes a non-pecuniary penalty on the employer for wrongfully dismissing its employee.

The existence of contractual rights in the post-work phase clearly suggests a lack of contemporaneity between contract and employment. One view of ancillary obligations entails that substantive primary obligations, albeit ones ancillary to the main purpose of the contract, may remain to be performed after the employment relationship has terminated and that the contract of employment lives on after the employment has ended. But ancillary duties aside, the ending of the employment relationship would in all other circumstances appear to be contemporaneous with the ending of the contractual relationship. The start of the post-work phase implies that any dismissal for unfair dismissal purposes will have occurred. There appears no possibility of any week in the post-work phase counting for continuity purposes, even though during those weeks the employee's relations with their now former employer may be said to be governed by a contract of employment, as s. 108 of the Employment Rights Act 1996 states that the continuity period ends with the effective date of termination. Further, given that the duty to perform the main primary obligations under the contract of employment will have been discharged on entry to the post-work period, either through performance or breach, it seems that neither party will owe the

---

[38] *Lep Air Services Ltd*, n 28 at 350. Lord Diplock defines the main purpose of the contract in terms of the parties performing their promises voluntarily. This appears a fairly abstract approach. The main purpose of an employment contract would generally be viewed as the employee's agreement to be willing to work for the employer in return for payment.

[39] *General Billposting Company Ltd v Atkinson* [1909] AC 118. In *Rock Refrigeration v Jones* [1997] 1 All ER 1, a majority of the Court of Appeal was content to assume that the *General Billposting* principle remained good law, and that accordingly 'in cases of repudiatory breach by the employer, the employee is on that account released from his obligations under the contract and the restrictive covenants, otherwise valid against him, accordingly cannot be enforced' (at 8). However, this is doubtful following several other cases. See e.g. *Photo Production Ltd*, n 28; *Attorney-General v Blake* [2001] 1 AC 268 and *Campbell v Frisbee* [2003] ICR 141.

other any implied contractual duties in this period.[40] The beginning of the post-work phase marks the end both of employment and of the duty to perform those primary obligations relating to the main subject-matter of the contract, which is, of course, the employment of the employee. Other duties, including ancillary contractual ones, may however remain.

Perhaps an explanation for this which accounts for the various difficulties is the following. The employment relationship is defined by contracts of employment. So long as a contract of employment exists, an employment relationship between the parties exists. However, once the duties to perform the contract have terminated, it is no longer a contract *of employment* but one which could be labelled in some other way – perhaps simply as a post-employment contract. It is not that the contract after the employment has ended is a new contract. This would create difficulties in theory as clearly the terms of the contract derive from the contract of employment, and the parties simply have not entered into a new contract by way of a new agreement in fact. It is perhaps that the nature of the contract has changed and it – the same contract – can no longer be called a contract of employment. Therefore, the employment no longer exists. But that is not to say that the contractual obligations contained in the contract when it was one of employment have ceased to be. The contract of employment (and employment with it) has metamorphosed into something else.

Transfers of undertakings
A further instance in which it does not appear that the contractual analysis of employment fits well on the termination of employment is where there has been a transfer of an undertaking. The normal contractual analysis of the situation where an employer and an employee have entered into an employment relationship, but where the employer gives the employee lawful notice to terminate it because it is transferring the business to another business on a sale, seems clear. This is that the original contract has come to an end. Any new employment relationship between the second business and the employee is entirely for them, and it begins completely afresh.

However, matters are not so simple as that, due to the Transfer of Undertakings (Protection of Employment) Regulations 2006,[41] commonly

---

[40] Clearly, other duties may arise in the post-work phase. Thus in *Rhys-Harper v Relaxion Group plc* [2003] IRLR 484; [2003] ICR 867 the House of Lords held that an employee's complaint of sexual harassment could be brought under the Sex Discrimination Act 1975 even though it occurred after her employment had ended because it arose out of, or was attributable to, the employment relationship (see now s. 108, Equality Act 2010). Similarly, the law has no difficulty in seeing obligations owed by an employer when writing references for an ex-employee, notwithstanding that the employment has ended. A duty of care exists by reason of that previous employment which can lead to a claim in negligence: see *Spring v Guardian Assurance plc* [1994] IRLR 460; [1994] 3 All ER 129 (HL).

[41] SI 2006 No. 246.

known as the TUPE Regulations.[42] These state that, given certain conditions, the employment with the first employer is taken as carried over to the second and that, if there is a dismissal of the employee where there is such a transfer and because of it, that is an unfair dismissal. Furthermore, the dismissal is one that does not need to be tested for fairness in order to be considered unfair – it is automatically unfair.

These are important provisions in the defensive armoury of an employee. They apply ostensibly in a wide range of employment contexts, where there is a relevant transfer of an undertaking, business or part thereof situated in the United Kingdom. Regulation 3 provides that the Regulations apply where there is a transfer of 'an economic entity which retains its economic identity, in turn defined as 'an organised grouping of resources which has the objective of pursuing an economic activity, whether or not that activity is central or ancillary'. It is not a requirement for the Regulations to apply that undertakings are operating for gain, so long as they are engaged in economic activities. They apply to both public and private undertakings. The Regulations also now apply where there is a 'service provision change' (an SPC). This is defined as occurring where activities cease to be carried out by a person on his own behalf and are carried out instead by another person on the client's behalf; where activities cease to be carried out by a contractor on a client's behalf (whether or not those activities had previously been carried out by the client on his own behalf) and are carried out instead by another person on the client's behalf; or activities cease to be carried out by a contractor or a subsequent contractor on a client's behalf (whether or not those activities had previously been carried out by the client on his own behalf) and are carried out instead by the client on his own behalf.

Nevertheless, there are some limitations. It is necessary for the employer to retain its identity. Therefore, where there has been a transfer of shares only this will not amount to a transfer as in that event identity is retained unless the purchaser assumes subsequent control of the company.[43] In addition it is necessary to show that, immediately before the transfer, there is 'an organised grouping of employees' situated in Great Britain which has as its principal purpose the carrying out of the activities concerned on behalf of the client but there would seem to be no reason why a grouping should not include just one employee. The client must also intend that the activities will, following the SPC, be carried out by the transferee other than in connection with a single specific event or task of short duration. Buying in services on a 'one-off' basis

---

[42] For detailed commentary on the Regulations see J. Bowers et al., *Transfer of Undertakings* (Sweet & Maxwell), updated service. See too J. McMullen, 'An Analysis of the Transfer of Undertakings Regulations (Protection of Employment) Regulations 2006' (2006) 35 *Industrial Law Journal* 113.

[43] *Millam v Print Factory (London) 1991 Ltd* [2007] IRLR 526; [2007] ICR 1331.

will not therefore be included. Neither is there an SPC where the activities consist wholly or mainly in the supply of goods for the client's use, nor is an administrative reorganization of a public administrative authority or the transfer of such functions between such bodies a relevant transfer. Highly significant in terms of the limitations of the TUPE Regulations is where there is a labour-intensive undertaking which is being transferred. It has been argued here that the transferee is in the surprising position of being able to choose whether or not the Regulations apply.[44] This, of course, would be surprising in that it might be thought that the right of the employees to be retained should be dependent upon whether the Regulations do or do not apply, not the other way round. It also means that the position remains questionable after the event of a transfer whereas the employees need to be aware of the position before the transfer occurs. For this reason, the approach in *ECM (Vehicle Delivery Services) Ltd v Cox*[45] is to be preferred as there it was emphasized that retention of staff was merely one of several factors to be weighed in the balance.

So, it is clear how important these Regulations are. But it might be thought that they need not affect contractual analysis of employment relationships. This is for a number of reasons. The first is that they are concerned with a statutory scheme of employment protection rights. The preservation of continuity of employment from one employer to another is relevant to claims such as unfair dismissal and redundancy which are contained in the Employment Rights Act 1996, but they do not appear to affect the contractual basis of employment. Indeed, they work on the basis that the employment relationship is contractual. Such is the argument. However, the contrary view is that the Regulations are very important in this context because they also have some consequence on the parties' contractual position. Whilst a basic contractual analysis is assumed, the employment relationship is transformed into something quite different to that which is produced by contract at common law. The effect of any transfer under the Regulations is a statutory novation of the contract of employment. The transferee of the business then stands in the shoes of the transferor as far as the latter's contractual employment responsibilities are concerned. This happens automatically and the transferee need do nothing. More specifically, the transferee of the undertaking takes over all 'rights, powers, duties and liabilities under or in connection with any such contract'.[46] It is only in relation to the contract that these rights are transferred. So non-contractual occupational pension

---

[44] See *Betts v Brintel Helicopters Ltd and KLM ERA Helicopters (UK) Ltd* [1997] IRLR 361; [1997] ICR 792.

[45] *ECM (Vehicle Delivery Services) Ltd v Cox* [1998] ICR 631; [1999] IRLR 559.

[46] Regulation 4(2).

schemes are not transferred and neither is the transferee employer under any obligation to provide them.[47]

However, there are caveats that should be made here. Not all aspects of contractual analysis are retained where there is a transfer. So, it would not normally be open to an employer to avoid its obligations under an employment contract by simply terminating it. Nevertheless, it has been held by the European Court of Justice that the effect of the Acquired Rights Directive, which the TUPE Regulations seek to implement, is that the transferor is discharged from all obligations, whether or not the employees agree.[48] Further, in a case under the TUPE Regulations themselves,[49] the House of Lords held that transfer-related changes to the terms and conditions of employment were void, even if for good consideration and with employee consent.[50]

Contractual analysis of the duration of employment

Atypical Workers

It would seem, from the previous two sections that, even if the contractual analysis seems to fit the creation of the employment relationship, it does not fare well during the period after the contract has been entered into, but before the employee starts work, and neither does it easily satisfy policy requirements for the post-employment period. There are further types of difficulties with the contractual analysis of employment. In this section I will examine the position of workers who do not fit the normal employment model, but who might be thought to be, at first blush, indistinguishable from employees and therefore working under contracts of employment.

The most topical category of workers in this position is agency workers. These are workers who may be doing the same type of work as employees, in the same place, under the direction of the same line manager, with the same length of continuity of employment and the same work obligations. However, the means by which they obtained their position may mean that they are not employees, and so do not have many of the rights and protections that the law affords employees, such as those in relation to unfair dismissal, redundancy, discrimination and so on. On the other hand, they may not be under exactly the

---

[47] See *Adams v Lancashire CC and BET Catering Services Ltd* [1997] IRLR 436; [1997] ICR 834. However, contractual entitlements arising from a collective agreement made by the transferor will also bind the transferee employer, even if that transferee is not a party to the collective bargain, according to the EAT in *Whent v T. Cartledge Ltd* [1997] IRLR 153.

[48] See *Berg and Busschers v Besselsen* [1989] IRLR 447; [1990] ICR 396.

[49] *Wilson v St Helens Borough Council* [1996] IRLR 320.

[50] However, the Employment Appeal Tribunal has stated that the employee may take advantage of favourable changes effected by the transferee even though the transferee has no such equivalent right – see *Power v Regent Security Services Ltd* [2007] IRLR 226 but compare the earlier decision of the ECJ in *Foreningen af Arbejdsledere i Danmark v Daddy's Dance Hall* [1988] IRLR 315 and C. Wynn-Evans, 'The Ongoing Saga of TUPE and Contractual Variations' (2007) 36 *Industrial Law Journal* 480.

same obligations either. The reason for this is that agency workers obtain their position, not from an employer directly, but from an intermediary. The agency brings the worker and the 'end-user' (as it is somewhat quaintly described) together. More importantly, the contract the worker has is with the agency, not with the end-user. Because there is no contractual nexus between the worker and the end-user, it would be difficult in theory to see the worker as an employee of that end-user. This is despite every other similarity between the worker and their co-workers who are categorized as employees. That leaves open the possibility, of course, that the worker is nevertheless an employee of the agency. There are several difficulties with that analysis, however, for some obvious reasons. One is that the worker does not work for the agency, but for the end-user, is under the end-user's direction and so on. Nevertheless, it has been thought possible to find an employment relationship between the worker and the agency if there were a sufficient degree of control.[51] However, that would certainly seem to exclude any possibility of the worker being employed by the end-user, on the principle that one cannot at the same time serve two masters.[52]

Is there any possibility, therefore, of finding a means by which an employment relationship can be found between the worker and the end-user that satisfies contract theory? It is, after all, the position that seems most close to reflecting reality to the objective observer. The Court of Appeal in *Dacas v Brook Street Bureau (UK) Ltd*[53] thought so, as long as there were an obligation on the agency's part to find work for the worker and for the employee to perform it, together with a sufficient degree of control.[54] In other situations those would be the criteria necessary in order to establish an employment relationship. This view has the additional merit that it means that, in the absence of an employment relationship between a worker and the end-user, the worker is not left in legal limbo with no employment relationship with anyone. The Court of Appeal's further comments, however, that the longer the relationship the more likely it would be considered to be one of employment would not seem to be correct. It is the nature of the relationship that matters, not how long it has lasted. The Court of Appeal so decided in *James v London Borough of Greenwich*[55] in 2008 in a regressive decision when it also said that there would have to be a necessity to find an employment relationship, in that case between the worker and the end-user. It is difficult to see many cases falling within that description.

---

[51] See the decision of the Employment Appeal Tribunal in *Consistent Group Ltd v Kalwak* [2007] IRLR 560. This was reversed by the Court of Appeal at [2008] IRLR 365, but on a different point.

[52] See *Cairns v Visteon UK Ltd* [2007] IRLR 175.

[53] *Dacas v Brook Street Bureau (UK) Ltd* [2004] IRLR 358.

[54] This had proved to be an important stumbling block to employee status in earlier cases – see e.g. *Wickens v Champion Employment* [1984] ICR 365.

[55] *James v London Borough of Greenwich* [2008] IRLR 302; [2008] ICR 545.

The position remains, therefore, that it is quite possible, in fact normal, for an agency worker to be an employee of neither the agency nor the end-user. This is an unsatisfactory state of affairs which the Court of Appeal in *Dacas* were most keen to avoid, and which seems contrary to common sense. Fortunately, to some extent the effects of this position are vitiated by the EC Council Directive on Temporary Agency Work[56] and the Agency Workers Regulations 2010[57] which will provide some statutory protection to agency workers. However, these work on the premise that agency workers are temporary workers. Most are, of course, but there is nothing in the nature of agency work that prevents the worker from working for one end-user on a permanent basis.[58]

In any event, that legislation is required to provide protection to workers who are otherwise denied it highlights the inadequacies and inflexibility of a contractual analysis of the employment relationship.[59] Other atypical workers have found themselves in the same boat, such as temporary workers and casual workers. The former have received a degree of legal protection by way of Regulations,[60] but the latter have not where there is a lack of mutuality of obligations.[61]

Fixed term employment contracts and limited term contracts[62] are further types of atypical working that present problems for contractual analysis. The common law contractual rule is that an employment contract may be terminated by notice, to be determined by a term in the contract or, if there is no such express term, an implied term of reasonableness. This is supplemented by statute requiring any term to be subject to certain minima depending upon length of continuous service.[63] With fixed term contracts, however, a theoretical difficulty arises. How can it be that a contract of employment which is to terminate at a particular point in time agreed between the parties can terminate earlier on the decision of just one of the parties? Notice, after all, seems to be dependent upon the idea that the contract is open-ended and, to prevent it being

---

[56] Council Directive 2008/104/EC.

[57] SI 2010/93. These come into force on 1 October 2011.

[58] See further N. Contouris and R. Horton, 'The Temporary Agency Work Directive: Another Broken Promise?' (2009) 38 *Industrial Law Journal* 329.

[59] It might be argued, on the other hand, that *Dacas* shows that contract is capable of providing protection for agency workers, but only in a way that perhaps should be left to Parliament.

[60] See the Fixed Term (Prevention of Less Favourable Treatment) Regulations 2002 (SI 2002 No. 2034).

[61] See *O'Kelly v Trusthouse Forte plc* [1983] IRLR 369; [1983] 3 WLR 605.

[62] See Employment Rights Act 1996, ss. 95(1)(b), 136(1)(b). Limited term contracts cover fixed term contracts (which terminate when a particular term expires) and those that terminate by performance of a specific task (however long that takes) or the occurrence (or non-occurrence if that is relevant) of an identified event. In other words, limited term contracts cover contracts of employment that are not open-ended, by whatever means. I use 'fixed term contracts' here to cover both types of contracts which reflects common usage.

[63] See Employment Rights Act 1996, ss. 86 and 87.

a permanent contract into which both the parties are forever locked, rules as to notice need to be applied. But, by definition, this is not the case with fixed term contracts. To be able to terminate a fixed term contract early would appear to drive a coach and horses through the idea of what it is to be a contract of fixed duration. How can a fixed term contract be unfixed, even by notice? Against this, however, is the idea that has been abhorrent to the common law for many years[64] – that employees can be tied into a contract without prospect of release. To be so would amount to a contract of slavery.[65] The common law rules, in their normal application, are simply not robust enough to provide an answer in both rational or normative terms to this conundrum. Such contracts have been held to be subject to earlier termination, despite the violence this does to the idea of what it is for something to be describable as 'fixed'.[66]

Collective agreements

A particularly interesting area where classical contractual analysis does not easily cope with the employment relationship is in the field of collective agreements, or collective bargains. To the unsuspecting observer, these might appear to be agreements between employers and trade unions that, although not having all the hallmarks of a contract drawn up by a lawyer,[67] are intended to be formal and have legal force. They are the product of formal and serious negotiations on matters that are highly significant to employees. However, the legal situation is somewhat different. On the whole, collective agreements are not legally enforceable. Unions and employers are not entitled to sue each other for a breach of a collective agreement, except in rare cases where the parties have stipulated in the agreement that the terms are enforceable at law.[68] This, at common law, was because one of the essential elements of a legally binding contract is usually missing in collective agreements, namely the intention to create a legal relationship. Usually, however, the agreement will make it specifically clear that there is no such intention, and will include a TINALEA (or the anthropomorphic TINA LEA) clause – meaning 'this is not a legally enforceable agreement'.

---

[64] See *De Francesco v Barnum* (1890) 43 ChD 165 for a clear exposition of this view.

[65] It is often suggested that the prospect of slavery is the reason why specific performance is not available for contracts of employment (see s. 236, Trade Union and Labour Relations (Consolidation) Act 1992) but the more prosaic reason is probably that open-ended contracts of employment, being executory in nature, are almost impossible in practice for the courts to supervise. This is not the case where a specific act constituting a full performance of a party's contractual obligations can be determined by the court to have been satisfactorily executed.

[66] See *Allen v National Australia Group Europe* [2004] IRLR 847. For the position on other types of limited term contracts see e.g. *Wiltshire County Council v NATFHE and Guy* [1980] ICR 455; [1980] IRLR 568.

[67] Collective agreements do not require the same precision of language as would be expected of commercial contracts for incorporation into individual contracts of employment to occur – see *Burke v Royal Liverpool University Hospital NHS Trust* [1997] ICR 730.

[68] Trade Union and Labour Relations (Consolidation) Act 1992, s. 179.

It is thus somewhat striking that the terms of a collective agreement may become incorporated into contracts of employment. It is striking for a number of reasons. The first is that it is an unusual state of affairs for the terms of an agreement that is specifically stated not to be legally enforceable between the parties to become legally enforceable in other agreements. Their unenforceability in one contract does not prevent their enforceability in another. In *Marley v Forward Trust Ltd*[69] it was held by the Court of Appeal that the usual clause to the effect that the collective agreement was not enforceable did not affect the issue of incorporation into the employee's contract of employment. This would seem to be a pragmatic solution. As Hazel McLean has stated, if the decision had gone the other way, trade unions would have had to consider removing TINALEA clauses from collective agreements.[70]

A second reason it is striking is that one of the parties (the employee) is not party to the unenforceable agreement. (The employees cannot be equated with the trade union). This seems to go quite contrary to the basic common law principle in contract that contracts are enforceable only between the parties to the contract because it is their bargain, they have agreed to it, and third parties should not be bound by it or, indeed, not take advantage of it contrary to the wishes of the parties to the contract. A term of a bargain conferring rights or imposing duties on a person other than employer and employee cannot, in the absence of express agreement of the parties,[71] be incorporated into an individual contract of employment because of the constraints of the doctrine of privity. Ultimately whether a term is appropriate for incorporation turns on the construction of the clause in context. If the clause is set out in the context of other primarily procedural matters this may make it more likely that the term will also be regarded as inappropriate for incorporation.[72]

It might be thought that there should be little difficulty in identifying employees with their union, even if they are not to be equated with it. However, in that unions are unincorporated associations and are not, and cannot be treated as if they were, corporate bodies (except for certain purposes specified in statute),[73] they do not have a legal identity in the same way that their members do. Even if they were able to be corporate bodies, they would by definition have a legal identity separate from their members. So, they cannot be equated with their members, and neither can they be particularly identified with them. However, there is a much more significant reason for present purposes why trade unions cannot be equated or identified with their

[69] *Marley v Forward Trust Ltd* [1986] IRLR 369; [1986] ICR 369.
[70] H. McLean, 'The Contract of Employment' (1987) 16 *Industrial Law Journal* 59.
[71] See the Contracts (Rights of Third Parties) Act 1999.
[72] See *Griffiths v Buckinghamshire County Council* [1994] ICR 265.
[73] Trade Union and Labour Relations (Consolidation) Act 1992, s. 10(2).

members, and that is that terms of a collective agreement may become incorporated into contracts of employment of employees even if they do not belong to the trade union that is party to the collective agreement. Incorporation may be readily implied from the universal observance of the collective bargain in the employee's workplace, even though the individual employee may neither know of it nor be a member of the union which negotiated it.[74]

A third reason why it is striking that the terms of a collective agreement might be incorporated into contracts of employment is that one obvious legal technique by which this could be achieved has been one which the courts have been somewhat reluctant to utilize. This is the concept of agency. It might seem clear that the employee could be a principal in an agency agreement and the trade union their agent. In fact, there is no reason union representatives should not be agents of employees to make a contract, or to receive a notice, or otherwise effect a binding transaction on the employees' behalf. But that agency would not stem from the mere fact that the agents were union representatives and members of the union. There must be a specific act of creation of the agency relationship in the ordinary way. The main difficulty with this, however, would arise if a union member as principal purported to withdraw authority from the union to act as their agent.[75] The courts have thus been reluctant to find an agency relationship except when the numbers involved are small. In fact, in one case it was held that the union acts as a principal and not its members' agent in bargaining.[76]

So, on what theoretical basis might collective agreements become incorporated into individual employment contracts? Clearly only certain terms will become incorporated. Some terms of the collective bargain are not susceptible to incorporation into the individual contract because they relate to obligations entered into by the union collectively, such as union recognition or redundancy procedures.[77] There must be some sort of connection between the collective bargain and the individual contract for its incorporation and this is often by way of express reference in the actual contract or in the employee's written statement of terms – the so-called 'section 1 statement'.[78] The advantage of this is that the contract need not be amended every time negotiations take place. Knowledge of the terms is usually not necessary for incorporation. However, once there has been incorporation, the terms will become enforceable.

---

[74] *Gray Dunn & Co. Ltd v Edwards* [1980] IRLR 23.
[75] *Heatons Transport (St Helens) Ltd* v *Transport and General Workers' Union* [1973] AC 15; [1972] ICR 308; *Singh v British Steel Corporation* [1974] IRLR 131.
[76] *Holland v London Society of Compositors* (1924) 40 TLR 440.
[77] See *British Leyland UK Ltd v McQuilken* [1978] IRLR 245.
[78] See *National Coal Board v Galley* [1958] 1 WLR 16; [1958] 1 All ER 91.

It should not be thought that in this area all the rules of contract law disappear. For example, once incorporated into individual employment contracts, some of the features of classic contract theory clearly apply. Contracts create obligations, and are not open to unilateral action to avoid them. Release from contractual duties requires consent from the other contracting party. So, where a collectively bargained term has been incorporated into the individual contract of employment, the employer cannot unilaterally terminate it.[79] Neither can termination of a collective agreement have an effect on terms of remuneration incorporated into an individual's contract of employment.[80] It follows that any unilateral power of variation must be included in the contract of employment itself. In this way it is not in reality a unilateral right of one party, but derives from an agreement made between the parties expressly provided for in the contract.[81] It thus resembles the powers of the employer in the managerial prerogative to make works rules unilaterally.

Frustration

If employment contracts were typical contracts one would expect that all the normal doctrines of the common law of contract would apply, as a matter of contract law. However, there are clearly some areas of contract law that do not, from a point of view of principle, morality or policy provide the solutions that the law is required to provide to enable, for example, the degree of employment protection thought minimal in the modern world. (I will consider this aspect of the issue in the following chapter). But there is also the point (and the important one for the present purposes) that, as a matter of contract theory, the contract of employment does not fit with the classical doctrines of contract law. One such example is the doctrine of frustration.

The general contractual position is that frustration occurs whenever the law recognizes that, without fault in either party, a contractual obligation has become incapable of being performed because the circumstances in which performance is called for would render it a thing radically different from that which was undertaken by the contract.[82] A frustrated contract is at an end, and there is therefore, in employment cases, no entitlement either to notice or to pay in lieu of notice.[83]

Donaldson P in the EAT formulated the appropriate test in employment cases in *Marshall v Harland & Wolff*.[84] Tribunals should take account of such

---

[79] *Robertson v British Gas Corporation* [1983] ICR 351.

[80] *Whent v T. Cartledge Ltd* [1997] IRLR 153.

[81] *Cadoux v Central Regional Council* [1986] IRLR 131.

[82] See the decision of the House of Lords in *Davis Contractors Ltd v Fareham UDC* [1956] 1 AC 696, particularly the speech by Lord Radcliffe.

[83] *G.F. Sharp & Co. Ltd v McMillan* [1998] IRLR 632.

[84] *Marshall v Harland & Wolff* [1972] IRLR 90; [1972] ICR 101.

matters as the terms of contract including provisions as to sickness pay; how long the employment was likely to last in the absence of sickness; the nature of the employment; the nature of the illness or injury and how long it has already continued and the prospects of recovery; and the period of past employment. A relationship which is of long standing is not as easily destroyed as one which has but a short history. In *Egg Stores (Stamford Hill) Ltd v Leibovici*[85] Phillips J thought it might also be important to consider the need of the employer for the work to be done together with the need for a replacement to do it; the risk to the employer of acquiring obligations in respect of redundancy payments or compensation for unfair dismissal to the replacement employee; whether wages have continued to be paid; and the acts and statements of the employer including the dismissal of, or failure to dismiss, the employee. The judge stated that the questions should be asked whether, as a matter of common sense, the time had arrived when the employer could no longer be expected to keep the absent employee's place open.

So far it would appear, then, that the courts in theory and approach apply the doctrine of frustration to employment contracts in a fairly classical fashion. However, the principles on which they would do so are fairly classical and so does not entail that in practice the courts apply the doctrine. They are in fact very reluctant in practice to find that frustration applies. Take for example *Hebden v Forsey and Son*.[86] The respondents ran a small factory employing two men, including the applicant. The latter had worked for the business for many years when he had to undergo an operation on an eye. Due to a lack of available necessary surgical equipment his return to work was likely to be in two years time. The employer agreed with the employee that it would be better if he waited on the sick list, drawing state benefits until his eye was fully recovered.[87] There was insufficient work for him to do when he was completely fit, so that he could not return. It was held that the employer had not discharged the burden resting on him to prove frustration but had in fact dismissed him.

It may clearly be beneficial to the employee to have a finding of dismissal rather than that the employment contract has been frustrated because that would then leave open the possibility of claiming for statutory remedies of unfair dismissal and redundancy, or even wrongful dismissal at common law if the employer has dismissed without sufficient notice. It may be for these reasons that the courts are reluctant to find that the contract has been

---

[85] *Egg Stores (Stamford Hill) Ltd v Leibovici* [1977] ICR 260; [1977] IRLR 376.
[86] *Hebden v Forsey and Son* [1973] ICR 607; [1973] IRLR 344.
[87] Tony Blair, in his autobiography, *A Journey* (Hutchinson, 2010) makes the point that it may be in governments' best interests to have workers on the incapacity register when the alternative is that they move off and become unemployed – at pp. 122–123.

frustrated. But there is also the technical difficulty that statute requires for a variety of purposes that an 'effective date of termination' (EDT) is identifiable. This may be required, for example, to determine whether sufficient notice under statute has been given, when the employee has become unemployed for the purposes of claiming benefits, and whether the employee has sufficient continuity of employment for the purposes of claiming the unfair dismissal and redundancy remedies. The difficulty here is that a frustrated contract does not have a clearly identifiable EDT. By its nature the doctrine of frustration tends to terminate the contract by a gradual and lengthy period after which it may be possible to say that the contract has terminated because it no longer is capable of being performed, although it would be difficult to identify exactly at what point that occurs. There is 'open texture'[88] here in the same way that a man's baldness may be clearly identifiable, but not from a specific number of hairs that no longer remain on his head.

Most difficult have been the cases involving imprisonment of employees.[89] One of the tenets of the doctrine of frustration is that the frustrating event should not be self-induced as that would mean that the contract would not be brought to an end by operation of law but by way of a volitional act or omission of one of the parties. The courts have come to differing views on this.[90]

Illegality
I began the previous discussion by stating that it might be expected that, if employment were fully contractual, all the common law contractual doctrines would apply to it. We saw there that there is some doubt about this with regard

---

[88] The term is taken from H.L.A. Hart, *The Concept of Law* (Clarendon Press, 2nd edn, 1994).

[89] Although illness is the most common frustrating event, contracts have also been frustrated when the employee was called up to the army (*Morgan v Manser* [1948] 1 KB 184; [1947] 2 All ER 666); interned as an enemy alien (*Unger v Preston Corporation* [1942] 1 All ER 200); suspended from medical practice for 12 months and his name temporarily removed from the register (*Tarnesby v Kensington, Chelsea and Westminster AHA* [1981] IRLR 369).

[90] In *Norris v Southampton City Council* [1982] IRLR 141 the EAT held that imprisonment was a self-induced event. In *Chakki v United Yeast Co. Ltd* [1982] ICR 140 the EAT stated it is essential to determine precisely when it had become commercially necessary for the employer to decide whether or not to employ a replacement, to have regard to what, at that time, a reasonable employer would have considered the probable duration of the employee's absence to be and to consider whether the employers had acted reasonably in employing a permanent rather than a temporary replacement. In *F.C. Shepherd & Co. Ltd v Jerrom* [1986] ICR 802; [1986] IRLR 358 a four-year apprenticeship was held not to be frustrated by a sentence of six months because a prison sentence is no more than a potentially frustrating event. The important consideration here was that there was an agreed and detailed termination procedure and in such circumstances the courts should be slow to hold that a particular set of circumstances lies outside its scope so as to frustrate the contract. This would seem to make sense where the alternative to frustration is a claim for, for example, unfair dismissal (see further R. Fentiman, 'Frustration of Contract of Employment' (1986) 15 *Industrial Law Journal* 54), but there would not seem to be a justification for the approach in *Shepherd* where this was not the case.

to the doctrine of frustration. I will now examine another area of classical contract law that by contrast is subject to a particularly common law approach, and largely to the detriment of employees, namely illegal contracts.

The standard approach to illegal contracts is that they are void and therefore of no effect. There are obviously very good grounds of public policy why this should be at least the starting point for any approach in this area. However, if the doctrine were to apply in such a stark way, that would be particularly harsh on employees because they would lose not only their contractual rights but also much statutory protection. This is so because, not only are contractual remedies dependent upon the existence of a contract of employment, but many statutory remedies are too. In order to have employment status – the gateway to much statutory employment protection – it is necessary to be employed on a contract of employment. Indeed, the status of other workers is also dependent upon the existence of a contract of some sort. So, of course, if there is no contract, the statutory protection too is lost. It has been suggested that, in so far as the statutory rights are concerned, they should not be lost because of the avoidance of the contract,[91] but this solution has not been taken up. However, what has happened is that in recent years the courts have been willing to be more flexible and allow claims where the illegality is nothing to do with the reason for the employee's claim[92] and to require an element of misrepresentation or lack of good faith.[93]

It certainly seems harsh, or at least potentially so depending on the facts of each individual case, for the common law rule to be transported into statutory remedies and to deny an employee not just their rights in contract (as would be the case under contract law for any other type of contract) but statutory protection too. In other words, the denial of a statutory remedy is entirely dependent upon the lack of contractual status regardless of whether or not the employee is deserving of losing their statutory protection. This is evidenced by, for example, the fact that there does not appear to be a *de minimis* rule whereby very minor infringements may be overlooked. In one case,[94] involving tax evasion over a four-year period, the amount in issue was the same number of pounds, but the illegality doctrine was nevertheless applied to deny the employee a remedy. It is also evidenced by the fact that the courts were not willing to give quarter to workers who were unaware of the illegal nature of their employment. Ignorance of the law is no excuse.[95] However, later cases

---

[91] See C. Mogridge, 'Individual Employment Law' (1981) 10 *Industrial Law Journal* 23.
[92] *Hall v Woolston Hall Leisure Ltd* [2000] IRLR 578; *Colen v Celerian (UK) Ltd* [2004] IRLR 210; [2005] ICR 568.
[93] *Enfield Technical Services Ltd v Payne* [2007] IRLR 840.
[94] *Hannen v Ryman* (1975) unreported.
[95] *Corby v Morrison (t/a The Card Shop)* [1980] ICR 564; [1980] IRLR 218. Cf *Davidson v Pillay* [1979] IRLR 275.

have indicated that lack of knowledge of the illegality might affect whether the employee is to be denied a remedy.[96]

It cuts across the argument to the effect that the courts' approach to illegality shows that contract law is unsuited to the employment relationship that other contractual ideas may come to the aid of employees here. One is that illegal terms of a contract may be severed and discarded in order to retain the other provisions and therefore the employment status of the worker. Obviously, if the contract is one which is illegal by its very nature (such as an agreement between thieves to divide their spoils) the whole contract must fall. But if it is merely that a small part of an otherwise legal contract is performed illegally, the principle would seem to be different.[97]

Debate 2

Is the judiciary 'contract-reactionary' in employment cases?

The Debate just considered was concerned with the best analysis of employment from a theoretical point of view. As a matter of analysis, does contract provide the explanation of the employment relationship that best fits? This leaves open the question as to whether from a normative, or prescriptive, point of view, contract provides the best analysis. In other words, does it provide the solutions to the analytical problems of the nature of the employment that we want from the point of view of such ideas as morality, fairness and justice, workability and policy? I will consider this aspect of the employment relationship in the next chapter. However, before I examine that question, I will take a brief detour into two further debates that may be had about the progress of judicial interpretation of the employment relationship. One concerns the alternatives to contractual analysis of employment. The first concerns what might be viewed as a conservative and reactionary approach of the courts when it comes to contract law and its application to employment.

A number of ideas can very easily be assumed about the way the judiciary have approached this in the past and do now. Most particularly it might be thought that the judges are firmly rooted in common law ideas, particularly in

---

96 This perhaps began with *Hewcastle Catering Ltd v Ahmed and Elkanah* [1992] ICR 626; [1991] IRLR 473. (See S. Honeyball, 'The Enforceability of Illegal Contracts' (1992) 21 *Industrial Law Journal* 143). See too the later decision of the Court of Appeal in *Hall v Woolston Hall Leisure Ltd* [2000] IRLR 578; and most recently *Enfield Technical Services Ltd v Payne* [2008] ICR 30 and *Blue Chip Trading Ltd v Helbawi* [2009] IRLR 128.

97 See generally M. Pilgerstorfer and S. Forshaw, 'A Dog's Dinner? Reconsidering Contractual Illegality in the Employment Sphere' (2008) 37 *Industrial Law Journal* 279.

contractual doctrines, and that they have interpreted, and continue to interpret, work relationships from the viewpoint that they are predominantly contractual and, even in the context of statutory claims, cling to notions of contract. I will hope, by way of just a short excursion, to show that this attitude towards the judiciary must be treated with a deal of caution, even if there may be some element of truth in it.

The applicability of common law doctrines of the law of contract to the employment relationship, some examples of which I have just examined, to some extent go further than simply that but also indicate the approach of the judiciary on the issue. The common law is not written in stone, after all, but is the product of judicial thinking. It would be a mistake to think of the common law unfolding through history, slowly working out a Grand Idea, somewhat on the lines of a Hegelian view of the development of dialectic synthesis of thesis and antithesis. Rather, it was developed in a much more piecemeal, even accidental, way. As S.F.C. Milsom has written, one must think of the common law as the product of cases where lawyers arguing cases before judges are doing nothing more than seeking to get their present day clients out of present day difficulties.[98] Those judges nevertheless have fashioned the law, to a large extent before the last century, unencumbered by the extent of statutory overlay in many areas of the law with which the present day judiciary have to contend.

The common law idea of contract was fundamental to much judicial thinking in the nineteenth century in particular. It is then that many of its foundations were laid and built upon. It is therefore natural, with twenty-first century eyes, to think that the employment relationship was almost inevitably seen as having its roots in contract in the nineteenth, and to think of it as a virtually statute-free zone. This would be a mistake, however. There was a good deal of legislation in the nineteenth century governing the relationship of master and servant. Most obviously, of course, there were the Master and Servant Acts of 1823 and 1867, the Employers and Workmen Act of 1875 and the Combination Acts (as they are now known in essence) of 1799 (if I can be forgiven a little latitude here in my concept of the nineteenth century), 1800, 1824, 1825 and 1859. Much of this, along with the Trade Union Act of 1871, was to do with collective labour relations, but not all of it. There were some common ideas behind the legislation aimed at the collective and individual aspects of employment, of course, most particularly a concern to ensure that the workforce did not get ideas above their station. It is thus really only with higher-status workers in the managerial and equivalent classes that were afforded anything that could be described as close to the modern-day notion

---

[98] S.F.C. Milsom, *Historical Foundations of the Common Law* (Butterworths, 1969) p. 7.

of a contract of employment. The roots of the common law idea of contract were very much concerned with *laissez-faire* and freedom of contract, which were reflected in the idea that the courts would not be concerned with the contents of a bargain but merely with enforcing it. This is most notably shown in the rule of the doctrine of consideration that the courts are not concerned with the adequacy but merely the sufficiency of consideration – in other words, that there must be consideration, but whether the agreement is a good bargain is of no concern to the courts. To apply this to the common man in his working relationships with his master was clearly a very unpalatable idea to the nineteenth century judiciary. Thus it was that a distinction grew up between the managerial and similar classes and workmen which went further than degree – the very legal nature of their working relationships were put on a different footing. So, the concept of a contract of employment was reserved for the higher-status employees whereas those lower down the hierarchy had contracts of service regulated not by bargains, volition and agreement, but by status, hierarchy and command.[99] This was the difference between employment and service.

This approach to work relationships continued into the twentieth century, and was largely replaced by an employment model that extended to all workers with the growth of social legislation.[100] However, the incidences of legal control of the employment relationship and the preservation of bureaucratic structures and hierarchical relationships through the method of large-scale incorporation of implied terms into the contract of employment can be traced. I will explore this in the next Debate. But an interesting feature of the role of contract in work relationships in the nineteenth century is this. It would be easy to see in more recent times the (perhaps over-reliance) on contractual doctrines, even in the statutory context, as being reactionary and a hangover from a contractual approach in the nineteenth century. I have argued that some years ago myself.[101] But it would not be correct. Let us take one, but an important, example. In 1978, in *Western Excavating (ECC) Ltd v Sharp*[102] Lord Denning in the Court of Appeal seemed to betray just this sort of approach. The issue concerned the test for constructive dismissal. The test then, as now,[103] for there

---

99 See A. Merritt, 'The Historical Role of the Law in the Regulation of Employment – Abstentionist or Interventionist?' (1982) *Australian Journal of Law and Society* 1, at p. 56.

100 See the work of Simon Deakin in this area, particularly his 'The Evolution of the Contract of Employment 1900–1950: the Influence of the Welfare State' in N. Whiteside and R. Salais (eds), *Governance, Industry and Market Relations in Britain and France* (Routledge, 1989).

101 See S. Honeyball, 'Employment Law and the Primacy of Contract' (1988) 17 *Industrial Law Journal* 97.

102 *Western Excavating (ECC) Ltd v Sharp* [1978] ICR 221; [1978] IRLR 27. The Supreme Court has recently stated that there is a need to separate traditional common law contract principles from statutorily conferred rights, see *Gisda Cyf v Barratt* [2010] IRLR 1073.

103 Employment Rights Act 1996, ss. 95(1)(c), 136(1)(c).

to be a constructive dismissal required that the employee resigned in circumstances such that they were entitled to do so by reason of the employer's conduct. The claim the employee was making in that case was for unfair dismissal, this being a remedy that seeks to redress the unfairness that is possible at common law in that the law of contract is not interested in the fairness of a dismissal, but merely whether the employer has abided by the terms of the contract in dismissing employees. So, very often, a breach of contract claim on dismissal turns on whether the employer has given the employee sufficient notice under the contract. The relevant statute had the purpose of alleviating this unfairness and providing a remedy for the employee that was built on fairness, at least the issue whether the employer could be said to have acted unfairly in dismissing the employee, even if it did not focus on any injustice done to the employee.[104] One might have thought, therefore, that the employee would have been 'entitled' to resign in virtue of the employer's conduct and for this to amount to a constructive dismissal through the application of a test of fairness. In other words, the question that would need to be asked was whether the employer had acted unfairly. This indeed was the test prior to 1978, and it was called the 'industrial test'.[105] However, the Court of Appeal in *Western Excavating* applied a contractual test. It thought that the question to be asked was whether the employer in dismissing the employee had committed a fundamental breach of contract. Not only does this appear to go against the purpose of the legislation in that it was to provide a remedy because of the deficiencies of the common law of contract, but it also appeared to be reactionary, reverting to the judicial approach of the nineteenth century. But it would be wrong to identify the Court of Appeal's reasoning as reactionary in that to apply the industrial test was illogical in the context of the scheme of an unfair dismissal claim. Then, as now, unfair dismissal claims are schematic. One stage of the process involves examining whether the employee has been dismissed, and a later stage involves an examination of the fairness of that dismissal. So, to conflate the two and bring in the concept of fairness to the earlier stage when examining whether there had been a dismissal would pre-empt the finding as to fairness at the latter stage. This is but one example, but an important one of the importance of examining the evidence closely. It would be a mistake to suppose that this case is evidence of judicial contractual conservatism.

---

[104] It is important to recognize this distinction in the law of unfair dismissal. It is perhaps best explained by an example. Imagine that the employer, in dismissing the employee, relied on false information given to it by another employee, and that it was reasonable to rely on this. There would clearly be injustice suffered by the employee here, but no unfair dismissal in consequence. The focus is on the reasonableness of the employer's acts, not on the employee.

[105] See *George Wimpey & Co. Ltd v Cooper* [1977] IRLR 205; [1977] ITR 389.

Debate 3

What are the alternatives to contractual analysis?

IS EMPLOYMENT A CATEGORY 'SUI GENERIS'?

If the employment relationship is not best viewed from a theoretical point of view as contractual in nature, the question inevitably arises as to what any alternative might be. One is that it is a category *sui generis* in law, unique and not definable in terms of other existing legal category concepts. This has been propounded from a prescriptive point of view – that it would be better for employment relationships to be so constructed – and so I will leave that until the next chapter when I will consider other similar normative arguments. Here, however, I will look at the main alternative to contract as an explanation of employment in terms of existing legal ideas, and that is that it is best viewed as a status relationship.

IS EMPLOYMENT A STATUS RELATIONSHIP?

It is certainly true that employers and employees do, in virtue of them having a legal relationship, have rights and duties that are, and which they intend to be, justiciable in the courts. Indeed, that aspect of their relationship has been instrumental, as we have seen, in the courts applying a contractual analysis to employment as the law of contract requires an intention to create a legal relationship. It is thus not a legal vacuum, and requires a legal explanation.

Many relationships recognized by law do attract rights and obligations without the existence of a contractual relationship, or indeed any other founded upon agreement. Most obviously, familial relationships arise in that way – I have legal duties towards my six-year-old daughter even though she and I have entered into no contract. Historically, of course, it is well-known that work relationships consisted to a large extent outside contract, particularly with regards to such notions as serfdom. In fact, the latter was also rooted in family status in that a serf was such in virtue of birth – it was hereditary. The natural characterization of such legal relationships is that they are or were rooted in status. Status can be viewed as distinct from contractual relationships. Indeed, it is possible to define status in terms of the absence of contract. Whereas contract determines rights and obligations between the parties as arising out of an agreement which has the consequence of creating a relationship between them, status sees rights and duties as existing *because* of the relationship between the parties, to which their agreement or lack of it is irrelevant.

Put this way the distinction between contract and status looks clear. Some have even seen the mark of a civilized society as the move from status towards contract.[106] It would thus seem natural to decry the idea that, with the notion of employment having moved away from status to contract and having become well-established over one hundred years ago, the reality should be that employment is a status relationship, or that there has been a move back towards status as characterizing it. After all, to enter into employment is a volitional act. In the absence of slave labour in modern Britain the idea of status seems misplaced in the world of work, even if it is an idea that we accept in other areas of our lives. Indeed, in the one example of where working without volition has occurred in relatively recent times – namely conscription into the armed services – it is acknowledged that no employment relationship there exists. Service under the Crown is still not one of employment, even if some sort of contractual relationship could be said to exist.[107]

Nevertheless an argument can be made out for the idea that employment displays many of the vestiges of status. Some of these can be seen to be predominantly social in nature, such as the deference that is sometimes accorded by employees further down a work hierarchy to those above them, although the extent to which hierarchy is post-feudal in nature or a necessary characteristic of organizations can be a matter of debate. But there is also the argument that the law perpetuates the status nature of the relationship, particularly by according rights and obligations to the parties that are both heavily weighted towards the employer's advantage on the one hand and also by according rights and obligations that are not discernible by reference to any agreemental (as I have termed it in Chapter 1) aspect of the relationship. Furthermore, and this is the paradoxical quality of this approach, the law does this by a subtle use of classical contractual analysis. Let me explain these points in turn.

Written statement of terms

It is possible to see the law leaning towards advantaging the employer in the way it views the bureaucratic nature of the employment relationship in a number of ways. I will give but one example here. Some of the rights and obligations of the employee clearly derive directly from the express terms of the contract. Section 1 of the Employment Rights Act 1996 explicitly places an obligation on the employer to provide the employee with a statement (the 'written statement', or the 'section one statement' as it is frequently known) detailing the important terms of the agreement between them. Under a classical contract analysis the written statement would not add to the terms agreed by the parties which would have become fixed at the point the

---

[106] See H.J.S. Maine, *Ancient Law* (John Murray, 1861) ch.5.
[107] *Koodeswaran v Attorney-General for Ceylon* [1970] 2 WLR 456.

employer's offer (usually) was accepted by the employee. This will often be a verbal agreement. Of course, to avoid any future dispute as to the content of the agreement, it makes sense for the parties to reduce their agreement to writing. It also makes sense for the law to require them to do this, and to place the obligation on the employer who not only has the resources to do so but who will wish to ensure consistency between the terms of all its employees. So much is obvious. However, in reality what happens is that the written statement will include a great deal more detail than has in fact been agreed between the parties, and in fact s. 1 requires that the written statement includes details that may not have been agreed between the parties.[108] It thus can no longer be described as a record of what has been agreed between the parties but an opportunity for the employer to place additional obligations (and rights too, admittedly) on the employee. This is particularly the case because the employee is now hardly in a position to refuse to agree to what, in effect, has become a proposed variation of terms given that, in most instances, rights to such employment protection regarding unfair dismissal will not accrue for a further year[109] and for a further two years for redundancy protection. It is true that the semblance of contractual analysis is maintained throughout this process in that it is always open to the parties to agree a variation in terms, but it does not reflect the lack of agreement that in fact exists between them and upon which contractual theory is based.

---

[108] The details required by s. 1 include the following: the names of the employer and employee; the date when the employment began; the date on which the employee's period of continuous employment began (taking into account any employment with a previous employer which counts towards that period); the scale or rate of remuneration or the method of calculating remuneration; the intervals at which remuneration is paid (that is, weekly, monthly or other specified intervals); any terms and conditions relating to hours of work (including any terms and conditions relating to normal working hours); any terms and conditions relating to any of the following – entitlement to holidays, including public holidays, and holiday pay (the particulars given being sufficient to enable the employee's entitlement, including any entitlement to accrued holiday pay on the termination of employment, to be precisely calculated); incapacity for work due to sickness or injury, including any provision for sick pay, and pensions; the length of notice which the employee is obliged to give and entitled to receive to terminate his contract of employment; the title of the job which the employee is employed to do or a brief description of the work for which he is employed; where the employment is not intended to be permanent, the period for which it is expected to continue or, if it is for a fixed term, the date when it is to end; either the place of work or, where the employee is required or permitted to work at various places, an indication of that and of the address of the employer; any collective agreements which directly affect the terms and conditions of the employment including, where the employer is not a party, the persons by whom they were made; and, where the employee is required to work outside the United Kingdom for a period of more than one month – (i) the period for which he is to work outside the United Kingdom, (ii) the currency in which remuneration is to be paid while he is working outside the United Kingdom, (iii) any additional remuneration payable to him, and any benefits to be provided to or in respect of him, by reason of his being required to work outside the United Kingdom, and (iv) any terms and conditions relating to his return to the United Kingdom.

[109] At the time of writing the Coalition Government has announced its intention to increase the qualifying period for unfair dismissal to two years.

Works rules

Likewise, the employer is also in a position to place further obligations on its employees by way of another technique. This is the idea of works rules. Works rules contain obligations placed by the employer on its employees to which the employee is not free to reserve assent. They are often contained in a booklet which the employer gives to the employee, but it is possible for them to be contained in another paper or web document to which the employee is referred. They appear to be less important in some respects than the written statement, or at least more fundamental, but it is not necessarily the case in practical terms. They might contain such matters as the company's dress code, vehicle inspection requirements, mode of performance of particular job tasks, and so on. It would be very costly for the employer to have to include all of these details in the written statement. It would also be impracticable in a long-term contractual relationship, requiring a degree of prescience on the employer that would be unrealistic. The important point for present purposes is that the works rules may be unilaterally varied by the employer at its discretion, depending upon changed circumstances. Indeed, it may be that the employer never intends its employees to carry out tasks that are detailed in the works rules, and which may simply be there for other reasons, such as liability and insurance. It is for this reason that a 'work to rule' as a form of industrial action (whereby employees undertake to perform their tasks as laid down in the works rules to the letter) can be so annoying and disruptive to employers and often effective for trade unions.

Works rules thus seem to go quite contrary to the idea of the contractual regulation of the employment relationship. A classic contractual relationship is simply based upon the idea of giving effect to the agreement between the parties and eschews the idea that one party can place obligations upon the other, or can vary them, unilaterally. However, far from the courts viewing this as a contradiction of the contractual analysis of employment, they have skilfully used contractual ideas to give it further contractual credence. The courts have given employers an 'umbrella-right' under the contract itself to a degree of managerial prerogative. To make the contract work both parties agree that it is necessary for the employer to have the power to manage in a manner that involves some unilateral privilege. This may be expressly provided for in the contract. If that is the case (and it is rarely, if ever, so) then the position would seem to be unproblematic. It would be a case of the employer merely exercising powers to which the employee has readily assented. It is not so free of difficulty where the employee has not expressly so agreed, because the courts will need to find an implied term in the contract that gives the employer that right. That is not difficult to do, for the very reason that it may be thought necessary in order for the employment contract to have business efficacy – one of the standard methods by which terms can be implied into any employment contract. The courts have, in addition, used another implied term to the same effect. It is implied into every contract of employment that the employee is required to co-operate with their employer, although only within the confines of the law. To rigidly abide by the employer's own works rules might, on the face of it, appear to be co-operation *par excellence*. What more could the employer require of a dutiful employee? However, the courts have interpreted that, in some circumstances, nevertheless to amount to a breach of contract, by way of a breach of the implied term to co-operate. Where the employer does not really require of its employees that they do something that it has told them in the works rules is required of them, and the employees know this, to stick by those duties is to fail to co-operate. Alternatively, it may simply be seen as a situation where an employer is exercising the unilateral right to vary the obligations that are contained in the works rules. In this way, a work to rule as a form of industrial action can be seen to be unlawful, entitling the employer to an interim injunction to break the action.[110]

Implied terms

The content of works rules appear different to contractual terms, are contained in another document, and operate differently to contractual terms in that, as we have seen, they openly allow the employer to be given unilateral entitlement to which the employee is subjected. This is very indicative of a status relationship. However, the courts have also placed incidences of status on the employment relationship, again through the technique of implied terms but in a rather different way. It goes to the root of the nature of implied terms.

There is no need for a contract that provides for something expressly also to contain an implied term. The purpose of implied terms is to supplement express terms where the latter are silent on a particular point. That does not mean, of course, that they necessarily are in opposition to express terms. It might be that they are required to supplement implied terms for the reasons I mentioned above, namely that the operational costs on the employer to reduce everything to express terms might be too great, or that to require of the employer that degree of prescience is both unfair and unrealistic. Implied terms can be related to the intentions of the parties through giving effect to the intentions of the parties had they taken the opportunity to put them into express form. The so-called 'officious bystander' test has this as its aim.[111] If the parties would have responded to any query from a third party as to

---

[110] See *Secretary of State for Employment v ASLEF (No.2)* [1972] 2 QB 455; [1972] ICR 19.
[111] *Shirlaw v Southern Foundries (1926) Ltd* [1939] 2 KB 206.

whether they had intended to have included something in their contract, if they would have replied to the effect that it would have gone without saying, the courts give effect to it by way of an implied term. Similarly, they might be supposed to agree to any term that is necessary to make the contract work – they can hardly be supposed to have based their agreement on a footing that was unworkable. The so-called 'business efficacy' test[112] can therefore be linked to the intention of the parties.[113] Alternatively, it might be thought that the intention of the parties as to particular rules are irrelevant, but that their overriding objective for the contract as a whole to be effective should trump any other contrary intention and should be given effect to. These types of implied terms are therefore much like default rules, and is the more modern approach.[114]

When one moves away from the primary intention of the parties it is more difficult to see the connection between the relationship and the volitional agreement of the parties. This is indeed so by definition. In other words, the implied terms of the contract come to appear less like a mechanism to give effect to what the parties intended but failed to state expressly, either intentionally or for pragmatic reasons, and be more like terms regulating their relationship that are imposed on the parties from outside by the courts. Indeed, there is a concept in contract law of the imposed term that can be distinguished from implied terms. Sometimes, if they are distinguished, imposed terms are characterized as types of implied terms, but sometimes no distinction is made at all. I would argue that they should be seen as very different types of term. If implied terms have at least some sort of root in the intention or the desires of the parties, imposed terms (even if they are coincidental with those intentions and desires) operate even when contradictory to them. An imposed term cannot be trumped by the intention of the parties – indeed, they cannot even be overridden by express terms of the contract. So, if imposed terms are a species of implied term, they operate in a way very different from the manner in which implied terms have traditionally operated in contracts of all types, namely as subservient to them.

Take, for example, the law on equality of pay between the sexes to be found in the Equality Act 2010 (EA) and originally in the Equal Pay Act 1970. By virtue of EA 2010, ss. 64–66, a 'sex equality clause' is *implied* into the contract of every person (A) who is employed on 'like work'; 'work rated as equivalent' or 'work of equal value' with a person of the opposite sex (B). This means that if any aspect of A's conditions is or becomes less favourable to A than a term of a

---

[112] *Reigate v Union Manufacturing Co. Ltd* [1918] 1 KB 892.

[113] See the view of Bowen LJ in *The Moorcock* (1889) 14 PD 64 who added reason to intention.

[114] See e.g. the decision of the House of Lords, particularly the speech of Lord Steyn, in *Malik v Bank of Credit and Commerce International* [1997] IRLR 462.

similar kind in B's contract, the term is modified so as to be as favourable. B's contract is not to be read as modified to bring it into line with the less favourable term in A's contract – s. 66(2)(a). If there is no corresponding term, the contract is deemed to include one – s. 66(2)(b). Thus, if men have a right to four weeks' holiday and women to three, and the women are found to be engaged on equal work, their entitlement must be increased to four. If women have no right to holidays at all, a term to that effect must be inserted. However, it is necessary to be able to compare oneself with a person of the opposite sex in order to found a claim. Where this is not possible equal pay cannot be claimed. It is clear that the Act does not entail that an equality clause is 'implied' into contracts of employment in any traditional sense. It operates quite independently of the intention and wishes of the parties, and may not be signed away. It may appear strange that such a claim, which was created in statute and was capable of being brought in industrial tribunals (as they then were) at a time when breach of contract claims could not be brought in a tribunal but had to be pursued through the ordinary courts, was nevertheless designed as a claim in contract. It would have been quite possible for the government of the day to have based an equal pay claim on a purely statutory footing, and to be recognized as a purely statutory animal as are claims in unfair dismissal, redundancy, other discrimination claims, health and safety and many others, but they chose not to do so. The claim is a claim in contract law, even if the remedies are not ones recognized by the law of contract – a breach of contract does not, under classical contract doctrine, result in the alteration of a term of a contract in order to bring it into line with the contract of another, and neither does it involve the incorporation of a term into the contract where it does not expressly exist.

It is therefore clear that the law here is imposing rights and obligations on the parties, not in consequence of their will (even if it is in accordance with it) and which they may not contract out of. It is also to be noted that it is dependent upon their employment relationship that the law imposes these terms on their contracts. This is paradigmatic of a status relationship – it is not for nothing that the term 'employment status' is one used in this area of law, and raises no eyebrows.

Statute

I will end this chapter by briefly looking at another reason why it has been argued that the employment relationship is better viewed as a status relationship, rather than as contractual. This is the idea that the volume of statute law governing the relationship far outweighs the contractual element.

There can be little doubt that there is far more legislation now than there has ever been regarding the world of work. Much of it, of course, is driven by membership of the European Union, particularly with regards to individual employment protection rights in general, and discrimination law in particular. In addition, however, there is much that is the product of predominantly domestic generation. The law of unfair dismissal and redundancy payments was in part, it is true, introduced against a background of international obligations in virtue of membership of the United Nations through its arm, the International Labour Organization (ILO). But it was not driven in the same way that much legislation has been the product of EU membership. Indeed, the whole period of the Labour Government between 1964 and 1970 was one where there existed ILO measures to introduce domestic protection for employees against unfair dismissal.[115] Surprisingly now, perhaps, it took the Conservative government under Edward Heath in 1971 to introduce this in the then infamous, but now rather tame-looking, Industrial Relations Act of that year.

In addition though, of course, there is much else besides, from legislation on health and safety, to pensions provision and record-keeping, to name a few. In that much of this imposes rights and obligations on the parties, on each other, to others, or to the state, it cannot be denied that the importance of contractual terms of employment must necessarily be concomitantly downgraded. But it is a separate question whether this entails the idea that employment is moving away from contract to status. If it were the case, then there are many more, otherwise archetypal, contractual relationships that would deserve to have the appellation 'status' attached to them. Most particularly, commercial and property contracts in relation to which there has been equally as much legislative overlay would have to be denied contractual quality. (I hesitate to employ the word 'status' here). It would be difficult to assess what could be characterized as a contractual relationship. Of course, this is not to deny that we may be moving in law generally away from contract back towards status, in contradiction to Sir Henry Maine's famous phrase,[116] but it *would* be to deny that there is something peculiar happening in the land of employment in that regard.

Further Reading

N. Contouris and R. Horton, 'The Temporary Agency Work Directive: Another Broken Promise?' [2009] *Industrial Law Journal* 329.

S. Deakin, 'The Evolution of the Contract of Employment 1900–1950: the Influence of the Welfare State' in N. Whiteside and R. Salais (eds), *Governance, Industry and Market Relations in Britain and France* (Routledge, 1989).

---

[115] ILO Recommendation No.119, 1964.
[116] As referred to by Maine, *Ancient Law*, see n. 106.

R. Fentiman, 'Frustration of Contract of Employment' (1986) 15 *Industrial Law Journal* 54.

M. Freedland, *The Personal Employment Contract* (Oxford University Press, 2003).

S. Honeyball, 'Employment Law and the Primacy of Contract' (1988) 17 *Industrial Law Journal* 97.

S. Honeyball and D. Pearce, 'Contract, Employment and the Contract of Employment' [2006] *Industrial Law Journal* 30.

J. McMullen, 'An Analysis of the Transfer of Undertakings Regulations (Protection of Employment) Regulations 2006' (2006) 35 *Industrial Law Journal* 113.

A. Merritt, 'The Historical Role of the Law in the Regulation of Employment – Abstentionist or Interventionist?' *Australian Journal of Law and Society* 1.

M. Pilgerstorfer and S. Forshaw, 'A Dog's Dinner? Reconsidering Contractual Illegality in the Employment Sphere' (2008) 37 *Industrial Law Journal* 279.

3

THE EMPLOYMENT CONTRACT AND PRACTICE

INTRODUCTION

In the previous chapter I examined some debates concerning theoretical aspects of the employment relationship, but concentrated on the question whether employment can best (most accurately) be described as a contractual relationship. However, it is one question whether, from an analytical point of view, employment *is* contractual. It is another, quite separate, prescriptive or normative question if that is the most *beneficial* theoretical foundation employment could have. The latter is the main focus of the present chapter.

Debate 1

Is the employment contract fit for purpose?

THE EMPLOYER'S INTEREST IN THE QUESTION

In asking the question whether the employment contract is fit for purpose it is important to remember that several parties have a beneficial interest in its answer. The natural tendency for much of the time is to concentrate on the needs of employees because the context of the law is usually whether they have claims, or should have claims, against their employers. But, of course, employers have a viewpoint too, and need some protection against the costs, in financial and other terms, of employees being given legal rights against them. Government also has a keen interest for a variety of reasons. If employees have a great deal of job protection, for example, that might have a negative impact on the labour market and the profitability of businesses.[1]

---

[1] This is the argument the Coalition Government advanced in early 2011 to justify extending the qualifying period of employment to bring an unfair dismissal claim from one year to two years.

There is also the social function of government to protect its citizens from unfairness and injustice and to provide a legal mechanism which is affordable, speedy and readily accessible for the resolution of disputes. Governments also have international obligations to fulfil, with consequences if they fail to do so. Then, of course, there is the consumer who has an interest in value for money, and the goods and services that they purchase not having a price that is inflated because of employment costs that could be passed on to them. So much is obvious and trite in one sense, but important nonetheless.

THE INCIDENCE OF STATUTORY INTERVENTION

That the contract of employment does not fulfil the demands made of it in the modern world of work is an easy case to make out in some ways. The very existence of a huge array of statutory remedies in employment is indicative of the failure of the common law to have filled the shoes legislation has been required to intervene to secure. That this is generally so is undoubted, almost axiomatic, but it not universally true. For example, obligations placed upon all member states of the European Union by way of a Council Directive require each government to introduce legislation in their own countries to comply. It is of no avail that the common law might already have covered the area in question. Nevertheless, most domestic employment legislation has been introduced where the common law has feared or failed to tread. It is obvious that legislation on unfair dismissal, redundancy, discrimination, health and safety, pensions, working time, whistleblowing, the minimum wage and so on, has been introduced where there has been no or insufficient case-law in the area.

That this is an obvious point does not, however, entail that it is necessarily so. To some extent the nature of the contract of employment has meant that it has not stepped into the legislative shoes I mentioned above. Take, for example, the law on unfair dismissal. The necessity for this (from a social policy point of view if not a historical imperative) was occasioned by the law of contract being rooted in *laissez-faire* ideas, concerned not with content so much as with form. As I mentioned in the last chapter, this means that contract law simply gives remedies where a party to a contract has not fulfilled their part of the bargain. On the whole, the common law is not concerned with what that agreement was about (considerations of illegality and the like apart) but with the issue of whether the contractual obligations have been fulfilled. Thus, the doctrine of consideration requires that consideration must pass from both parties to a contract, but it is not concerned with whether the consideration that passes constitutes a good bargain. That is purely a matter for the parties themselves. When this is applied in the employment context it is easy to see how it does not satisfy the moral and social requirements of a modern world where parties are in a relationship often on unequal terms. The common law of contract is not concerned with the content of the terms of a contract, only with whether the obligations under them have been performed, and so it necessarily follows that it is not concerned with whether those terms are fair. Still less is it concerned with the idea that the performance of the contract within its terms is fair. Thus, so long as an employer abides by the contract and gives its employees sufficient notice in accordance with the contract, the common law is unconcerned with whether the employer does so justly. It is therefore necessary for legislation to intervene to provide a remedy.

IS LEGISLATIVE INTERVENTION NECESSARY?

The necessity for legislative intervention just mentioned is, however, in a way contingent. What I mean by this (seemingly contradictory idea) is that it does not have to be necessary – it is only necessary because of the constraints the common law has placed upon itself. Let me give some examples.

Fairness

There is nothing inherent in the idea of contract that prevents it from addressing the issue of fairness.[2] It could do so in at least two ways. The first way would be for the law of contract itself to develop ideas of fairness as a condition of its lawful performance. It might do that, for example, by way of an implied term. It would not be too difficult for this to be achieved through a number of the well-established methods by which implied terms are incorporated into any contract, including contracts of employment. It would be a strange agreement between normal people entering into an employment relationship that was not predicated upon the unspoken assumption that they would perform the contract reasonably and fairly, and that this was so obvious that reasonable and fair terms would be ones that went without saying they would agree to being implied into their contract. Likewise, if a business were to be run on the basis that contracts of employment (or indeed any other) could consist in, and be performed using, unreasonable and unjust practices, that would be detrimental to a smooth and efficacious economy. Furthermore, if the parties have hitherto behaved themselves in a reasonable, fair and just way to each other, and to others, would it not be reasonable to allow that to be a required basis for their future dealings? All of these ideas are not

---

[2] Mark Freedland has written: 'Until the mid-1960s, while it was quite apparent that the common law of the contract of employment provided no protection of fairness ... there was reasonable confidence in the collectivized system of industrial relations to do so. The breakdown of confidence in that capacity produced a demand for a new kind of legislative intervention, the main response to which was the introduction of unfair dismissal legislation in 1971'. See M. Freedland, 'Constructing Fairness in Employment Contracts' (2007) 36 *Industrial Law Journal* 136.

unreasonable or illogical, and they reflect the bases on which implied terms are normally incorporated into any contract. There would not seem to be an insuperable bar, then, for the common law of contract to view employment relationships on this basis. Of course, as the mechanism used would be the implied term that has the disadvantage that it comes up against the well-established rule of contract law that implied terms are subservient to express terms. But it would at least have the merit of requiring a party who wishes to behave unreasonably or unfairly in an employment relationship to rely upon an express term of the contract that allows them to do so.

A second way by which the fairness could be introduced into contracts of employment is by the parties themselves making the idea explicit in their agreement. More specifically, there could be express terms that provide for a remedy in the event of unfairness, and to the degree and extent that the statutory remedies do the same thing.

Contractual restrictions

Keith Ewing argued in 1989 (but it seems without the idea having taken firm root in practice) that there could be a variety of ways in which the employer's power to dismiss could be restricted.[3] For example, he argued, there could be a clause that provides a guarantee of no compulsory redundancies. Although there might be some public bodies that would be acting beyond their powers were they to enter into such agreements, no such difficulty would present itself for employers in the private sector. A second suggestion is that there could be an express clause to the effect that employees could be dismissed only for specific reasons and in a specified manner. More simply, and most effectively, however, there could be an express clause to the effect that employees have the right not to be unfairly dismissed.[4] This is an interesting idea. The right to dismiss might not be inherent in contracts of employment, but dependent on an express provision detailing the extent to which the employer has that right. This would require a fundamental alteration in the way that contracts of employment are viewed. However, less radical would be the view that the employer has an inherent right to dismiss at common law for any reason, and however unfairly, so long as it does so in accordance with the terms of the contract, and therefore subject to an express clause that sets out the circumstances in which that right exists.

There are number of difficulties with this idea, attractive as it might be to employees. The first is that it is dependent upon employers agreeing to such terms. In a climate where employees have very little bargaining power, on the

---

[3] K.D. Ewing, 'Job Security and the Contract of Employment' (1989) 18 *Industrial Law Journal* 217.

[4] Ewing points out this was a feature of Australian labour law – see Ewing, 'Job Security and the Contract of Employment', ibid, pp. 218–19.

whole, to effect such an outcome would be dependent upon such terms being incorporated by way of collective agreements. There is no evidence that trade unions have considered this idea in collective bargaining, at least on any scale.

Another difficulty is that the remedies for breach of contract by the employer do not normally permit anything that amounts to job protection. The remedies are normally for damages, and injunctive relief is rarely awarded. The usual measure is the wages the employee would have earned, and pension rights that would have accrued[5] if due notice had been given[6] for that is the only period when the employee is entitled by contract to continue in employment. If the employee's contract can be determined by six weeks' notice they cannot claim loss over the next few years even if out of work for that length of time, because within that period at any time the employee might have been dismissed with six weeks' notice.

Given that the principle seems to be that the employee is entitled to actual loss during the notice period not received, it might seem surprising that an increase in wages that would have occurred during that period will not be taken into account,[7] unless there is capriciousness or bad faith on behalf of the employer.[8] However, it is in line with the traditional approach which prevents a windfall payment to the employee. So, the effective date of termination for unfair dismissal is extended only so far as the statutory, not the contractual, minimum according to the Court of Appeal in *Harper v Virgin Net Ltd*[9] and so damages for loss of protection caused by not being given the full contractual entitlement are not recoverable. This approach tends to suggest that the courts would not be sympathetic to the idea that the contract of employment could be used to provide a contractual remedy that reflects what would be available in statute if that were greater. In other words, the courts' approach seems not to be rooted in the contract-statute divide, but in not providing a remedy in one that might be greater than that in another area of law. Therefore, Ewing's suggestion that the contractual damages could be equivalent to that of compensation had the employee been eligible to bring a claim for unfair dismissal would not seem likely to find favour with the judiciary.

The difficulty that the courts do not seem predisposed to provide employees with contractual remedies that reflect those provided by statute is quite apart from the further argument that damages would be difficult to assess if the employer were found to have no power to dismiss simply on reasonable notice but only for a specified cause. This is because the contract of employment

[5] *Silvey v Pendragon plc* [2001] IRLR 685.
[6] See e.g. *Radford v De Froberville* [1977] 1 WLR 1262; *FOCSA Services (UK) Ltd v Birkett* [1996] IRLR 325.
[7] *Lavarack v Woods of Colchester Ltd* [1966] 3 All ER 683; [1967] 1 QB 278.
[8] *Clark v BET plc* [1997] IRLR 348.
[9] *Harper v Virgin Net Ltd* [2004] IRLR 390; [2005] ICR 921.

would then become an open-ended one, not determinable except for events that may never occur, but which might. However, the counter-argument to that might be that contracts of employment are almost always determined on one event, namely retirement, and may be terminated earlier by events other than cause, such as death or winding up of the employer company.[10]

Certainly the courts on occasion have allowed the idea that contracts of employment might not be terminated other than for reasons specified by the contract. So, in *McClelland v Northern Ireland General Health Services Board*[11] the House of Lords, although by a bare majority, held that the inherent idea in contracts of employment that they could be terminated by notice was subject to express provisions in the contract to the contrary. In this case, the contract specified that notice by the employer could be given, but only in specified circumstances. Redundancy was not one of them, and therefore the employee could not be made redundant. As such, as Mark Freedland rightly says,[12] the issue in that case is not best seen as a an esoteric or marginal one concerned with employment contracts that are described as 'permanent' as this is very rare, particularly in the modern economic climate. It is better viewed as about the much more frequent case where there is express provision as to the grounds on which the contract may be terminated by the employer and whether that excludes the default rule that notice may be given on any ground. The House of Lords' decision is that it does.

Into this mix, however, must be thrown the point that, even if contract fails to give the employee full job protection by seeking to emulate the unfair dismissal remedy in contractual terms, it is doing no less than the law of unfair dismissal itself. This is for the simple reason that the latter does not achieve meaningful employment protection either. Although on a finding of unfair dismissal the remedies of reinstatement (back to the employee's old position)[13] and re-engagement (back to another position with the same employer)[14] remain as remedies, and indeed were originally intended, from the inception of the legislation in 1971 with the Industrial Relations Act of that year, to be the primary remedies, that is not the case in practice. One assumption is that applicants do not generally want re-employment (the reinstatement and re-engagement remedies taken together) for the reasons that by the time of the hearing they will have another job, or because understandably they have no desire to return to work for an employer who has already dismissed them and against whom they have successfully pursued a

[10] See Ewing, n. 3, p. 221.
[11] *McClelland v Northern Ireland General Health Services Board* [1957] 2 All ER 129.
[12] M. Freedland, *The Personal Employment Contract* (Oxford University Press, 2003) p. 331.
[13] Employment Rights Act 1996, s. 114.
[14] Ibid, s. 115.

claim in an employment tribunal. A survey carried out by Evans, Goodman, and Hargreaves found that, while trade union officials tried to ensure that claimants stipulated their desire for re-employment in their applications, this was essentially a tactical move to enhance their bargaining position for compensation.[15] Hugh Collins has argued that the lack of reinstatement as a viable remedy should not be considered as a serious criticism of the law. He feels that the aims of the legislation are achievable through appropriate levels of compensation. It is important that the remedy is sufficient to deter employers from acting unfairly, and this can be achieved better by compensation than by reinstatement and re-engagement, he argues.[16] It would appear, however, that the relative deterrent effect is dependent upon variables relating to each employer on which it is difficult to generalize. For whatever reason, however, the default remedy of compensation is that normally awarded on a finding of unfair dismissal. It is thus the case that a contractual remedy that is commuted to a payment of damages in the absence of injunctive relief is not to put the employee in any worse position in terms of type of remedy.

However, to what extent is it the case that injunctive relief will not be awarded on a contract of employment? As we have seen in the previous chapter the courts have always been reluctant to grant specific performance or injunctions where they have the effect of forcing the parties of an employment contract to work together.[17] Perhaps the main reason is that the performance of employment contracts would be very difficult for the court to supervise, although not impossible particularly with regard to short fixed term contracts or contracts for a particular purpose, and that in any event in most circumstances damages are an adequate remedy. However, the traditional reason given is that to order specific performance and similar injunctive relief against the employee would be tantamount to forced labour.[18] A further, more convincing, modern analysis is that it would undermine the trust and confidence which must exist between employer and employee. It would also offend against the doctrine of mutuality since, if the remedy were not available against the employee, to force an employer to reinstate would be unjust. Nevertheless, the courts have held that these rules do not prevent them from

---

[15] See S. Evans, J. Goodman and L. Hargreaves, 'Unfair Dismissal Law and Changes in the Role of Trade Unions and Employers' Associations' (1985) 14 *Industrial Law Journal* 91.

[16] H. Collins, 'The Meaning of Job Security' (1991) 20 *Industrial Law Journal* 227.

[17] Section 236, Trade Union and Labour Relations (Consolidation) Act 1992 enacts part of this long-established common law principle, providing that 'no court shall issue an order compelling an employee to do any work or attend at any place for the doing of any work' (see D. Brodie, 'Specific Performance and Employment Contracts' (1998) 27 *Industrial Law Journal* 37, where the author argues that specific performance should be available).

[18] See *De Francesco v Barnum* (1890) 43 ChD 165; 59 LJ Ch 151.

enforcing an agreement by way of restrictive covenants not to compete with the employer whether during or after employment, even where this may have the indirect effect of putting pressure on the employee to carry on working in that employment.[19] The courts will not, however, enforce a provision not to take any employment at all for a period after termination of the contract of service for this would constitute a thinly disguised form of compelling service.[20] The Court of Appeal in *Hill v C.A. Parsons and Co. Ltd*[21] in 1972 went considerably further in granting an injunction which had the effect of specific performance although only in very particular circumstances. The majority of the Court of Appeal thought that the normal arguments against enforcement did not apply, since there was continued confidence between employer and employee as it was the employee's union and not the company who sought to remove him and damages would not be an adequate remedy.[22]

However, sometimes the award of injunctive relief does not equate to job security, and neither is it intended to. The employee may seek an injunction, not to remain in their job, but to treat the original dismissal as void in order to recover pay until the proper procedures are gone through. In this event the retention of trust and confidence is not so material. As Ewing pointed has out, it is not clear why the employer's lack of confidence should operate as an impediment to employees seeking relief for repudiatory conduct. It is an impediment which is unnecessary, for if there is genuinely no confidence in the employee, the employer may dismiss without fear from either common law or statute, as long as the proper procedures are followed.[23]

Despite the possibilities considered in this section, the possibility that progress can be made in using contract as a mechanism for employees to secure statutory-like aims is doubtful. That the courts continue to be unsympathetic is indicated by the leading case of *Johnson v Unysis*.[24] There the House of Lords held that the implied term of mutual trust and confidence does not apply to the manner of the dismissal. Therefore an employee cannot rely on this if they are denied a fair disciplinary or appeal hearing. The difficulty is not that the implied term of trust and confidence derives from the contract as such, but that it is an implied term, and an implied term cannot contradict an express term at common law which allows the employer to dismiss with due

---

19 See *Warner Bros Pictures Inc. v Nelson* [1937] 1 KB 209; [1936] 3 All ER 160.
20 *Page One Records Ltd v Britton* [1967] 3 All ER 822; [1968] 1 WLR 157.
21 *Hill v C.A. Parsons and Co. Ltd* [1972] 1 Ch 305; [1971] 3 All ER 1345.
22 See too *Powell v London Borough of Brent* [1987] IRLR 466; [1988] ICR 176; *Wishart v National Association of Citizens Advice Bureaux Ltd* [1990] IRLR 393; and *Alexander v Standard Telephones and Cables plc* [1990] ICR 291.
23 K.D. Ewing, 'The New Labour Injunction' [1989] *Cambridge Law Journal* 28.
24 *Johnson v Unysis Ltd* [2001] ICR 480; [2001] IRLR 279; [2001] 2 All ER 811.

notice. Also, the term is concerned with the relationship during its existence, and therefore does not apply where that is being terminated.[25] This seems insurmountable.[26] However, the House of Lords also held that the term could not operate on dismissal because Parliament had put a cap on unfair dismissal compensation, and therefore to have a contractual remedy without limit would run counter to that. It would also be unnecessary given the existence of the statutory remedy. This reasoning seems less logical, particularly given the fact that not every employee is eligible to bring an unfair dismissal claim. Perhaps a ray of hope for those wishing to run the argument that contractual quasi-statutory remedies are viable can take comfort from the fact that their Lordships were nevertheless prepared to allow that contractual remedies were recoverable at least up to the point of the unfair dismissal ceiling. Also, of course, if the claim is not based on fairness of the manner of dismissal but actual loss, there is no cap under the ordinary rules of contract.

THE LOGICAL BASIS OF STATUTORY PROTECTION

As I stated above, the inadequacy of contract is borne out by the necessity for a large number of statutory provisions giving protection to employees. If the contract of employment were to contain an implied term of reasonableness this might not be the case, although a formalized system of protection is probably an improvement on case-by-case consideration of entitlements. However, it is striking that there does not appear to be an underlying theoretical thread running through these provisions, but rather a piecemeal approach has been adopted depending on the claims in issue.

Most obviously, perhaps, the unfair dismissal provisions in the Employment Rights Act 1996 are concerned with notions of reasonableness, although these are based on the fair actions of the employer rather than any injustice done to the employee. This is curious in that one might imagine that the framers of the legislation would have been concerned primarily with fairness to employees rather than punishing unfairness to employers, but that is not the case. Naturally, where there has been unfairness by the employer that will normally be reflected in injustice done to the employee.

---

[25] *Johnson* was followed by the decision of the House of Lords in *Eastwood v Magnox Electric plc* [2004] IRLR 733; [2005] ICR 1064 to the effect that this is so at least in relation to the employer's acts forming part of the dismissal process. See C. Barnard, 'Cherries: One Bite or Two' [2006] *Cambridge Law Journal* 27.

[26] The courts, however, are sometimes prepared to allow implied terms in contracts of employment to 'trump' express terms. So, in *Johnstone v Bloomsbury Health Authority* [1991] ICR 269, Stuart-Smith LJ was prepared to accept the argument that an express term concerning the hours of work of a hospital doctor was to be read subject to the implied term of care and safety in contracts of employment.

However there are occasions when the two do not coincide. For example, if an employer is found by the employment tribunal to have acted reasonably on evidence it had before it in dismissing an employee, even if it also finds that that evidence were false (for example, that the employee did not act dishonestly, as the employer had determined) no claim for unfair dismissal will lie. This works both ways, however. If, for example, an employer holds out that the reason for dismissing an employee is (say) capability but in reality is misconduct, although it might have been objectively fair to dismiss the employee for that reason the dismissal will be unfair. The employer has not acted fairly.[27]

Compare this with the approach taken in other legislation. It might be thought that the overriding impetus behind employee protection provisions was that, without them, unfairness would be done to employees and so, like the unfair dismissal legislation, the emphasis would be on reasonableness and fairness. But this is not the case. Take, for example, the Equality Act 2010 which is perhaps closest in this regard to the law on unfair dismissal. Indeed, on some occasions (such as where an employee is dismissed for a protected characteristic under the Act, such as age, sex, race, disability or sexual orientation) the concepts of fairness and reasonableness do not appear on the face of it at all. There are concepts such as proportionality, legitimacy, justification and so on, but the focus is not on overt ideas of fairness as such. Similarly, take the National Minimum Wage Act 1998. This does not entitle employees to a fair reward for a fair day's work, but rather applies a floor of entitlement, applied across the board, regardless of worth. Again, take the Working Time Regulations 1998[28] which operate in the same way, quite devoid of notions of what is or is not reasonable. Other examples would include protection for fixed term workers,[29] part-time workers,[30] rights against unlawful deductions of wages,[31] rights to time off work,[32] protection for whistleblowers,[33] and so on. The list is extensive. Each has its own basis which considerations of space do not allow me to explore here.

---

[27] *Polkey v Dayton Sevices* [1988] AC 344; [1988] ICR 142; [1987] IRLR 503. See by way of example *Hotson v Wisbech Conservative Club* [1984] IRLR 422; [1984] ICR 859.

[28] SI 1998 No. 1833.

[29] Fixed Term Employees (Prevention of Less Favourable Treatment) Regulations 2002 (SI 2002 No. 2034).

[30] Part-Time Workers (Prevention of Less Favourable Treatment) Regulations 2002 (SI 2000 No. 1551).

[31] Employment Rights Act 1996, ss. 13–27.

[32] Ibid, ss. 50–63.

[33] Public Interest Disclosure Act 1998.

Debate 2

Do employers have too much power in determining the basis of the relationship?

Whatever the contractual basis of the employment relationship is in terms of theory, and however pliable contract is in terms of the possibilities it could afford to employees in the abstract, there can be little doubt that in practice the employer seems to hold most of the cards. In many ways that is inherent in the relationship because it is contractual. Whoever offers a contract is inevitably the party who is setting the terms, at least in a broad and general sense, for the other party to consider accepting. But that is not restricted to, or determined by, the contractual nature of the employment relationship. It is a feature of human relations. Whether the employment relationship is contractual or not, it is the fact that the employer generally makes the offer that renders it the dominant party with regard to the terms on which the employment is founded. Even in non-contractual human relations the person offering something is steering the course and the nature of the dealings between them. To take a simple example, if I invite you to dinner in my home next Saturday evening, this is clearly not intended to be a contractual relationship, or indeed any type of legal relationship, between us. But by the very fact that it is I who makes the offer I put myself in a position, if not of dominance, of being the person who determines the nature of our relationship for that particular event. So, the employer is inevitably put on the front foot as far as the basis of the relationship between it and the employee is concerned, at least at the beginning of the relationship. This raises the further practical question as to whether the employer, in terms of policy, is given too much power and whether, if so, it is possible for the law to use techniques to rein that in to a degree.

I will consider here two contexts in which the issue of the practical power of the employer in determining the basis of the employment relationship might be thought too great. The first is in determining the terms of the employment contract, and the second is in the capacity to lay down rules in relation to which an employee cannot legally withdraw agreement – namely works rules.

DETERMINING THE TERMS OF THE CONTRACT

The creation of the contract

The primary deceit of contract law with regards to the employment relationship may be seen to lie in the idea that its creation, at least, is paradigmatically contractual in nature. It has all the hallmarks in practice (as well as in theory) of a contract being formed. After all, an employer makes an offer to the employee, which they are free to accept or reject, with consideration moving between them in the form of the payment of a salary or wages (and perhaps some other types of consideration), together with the tacit agreement that, if the relationship should break down, the parties may air their grievances and seek redress in the courts, or at least an employment tribunal.

This might be thought to be a deceit because this is not what happens in practice. It is rare for the parties to agree more than the barest necessary terms for their relationship, perhaps going no further than an agreement on an outline of the task to be performed, on what grade, with what job title, in return for what pay, during which hours, with what holiday and on what probation. This may seem a good deal, but if the agreement between them were left at that the relationship would be pregnant with the possibilities of confusion, ambiguity and disagreement. It makes sense therefore, as I have discussed above, for one party, particularly the employer, to be given the task of putting the agreement down on paper by way of the written statement. But the law requires more than that. It requires the employer to put flesh on the bare bones of the agreement even though by doing so it, by definition, goes further than the agreement actually reached between the parties. This is the nature of the deceit, for the employer is required (not just able) to provide information and detail that may not have been agreed by it and the employee. Consider the Employment Rights Act 1996, s. 1 of which lays down this obligation. It states that the statement must be given to an employee (who has at least a month's continuous employment) within two months after they start work and must contain the identity of the parties, specify the date on which employment began and when the employee's period of continuous employment began, as there may have been a period of employment with a previous employer which may count in such a calculation. There must also be details, correct as at one week before giving the statement, of remuneration, the intervals at which it will be paid, sick pay, pensions, notice, and a brief description of the work for which the employee is employed. Also, if there are any terms and conditions on hours of work and holidays, these must be stated. The terms must be sufficient to enable the employee's entitlement, including any entitlement to accrued holiday pay, on the termination of employment to be precisely calculated. The statement must also include, in the case of non-permanent employment, the period for which it is expected to continue – either the place of work or, where the employee is required or permitted to work at various places, an indication of that fact and the address of the employer; any collective agreements which directly affect the terms and conditions of the employment including, where the employer is not a party, the persons by whom they were made; in the case of an employee required to work outside the UK for a period of more than one month, the period of such work, the currency of remuneration, any additional remuneration or benefit by reason of the requirement to work outside the UK and any terms and conditions relating to his return to the UK. Matters relating to sickness and most pension schemes may be contained in some other document which the employee has reasonable opportunities of reading in the course of their employment or is made reasonably accessible to them in some other way. For the length of the period of the employee's notice, they may be referred to the law on the case of minimum periods of notice or to the provisions of any collective agreement which directly affects the terms and conditions of the employment. The statement must also contain a note specifying any disciplinary rules applicable to the employee or refer them to a reasonably accessible document setting them down. The employee must be notified of a person to whom they can apply if he is dissatisfied with any disciplinary decision, and how such application should be made. Any further steps are to be specified, and the employer should include as much detail as possible as a protection against unfair dismissal claims.

It is clear that the obligations on the employer in constructing the written statement go far beyond that which is required to evidence the agreement that the parties have already entered into. However, that is the how the courts have frequently stated that they view the position.[34] They have maintained the pretence even when stating that the written statement is the sole evidence permissible of the terms of the contract.[35] It is difficult to see how, under those conditions, the written statement does not become the contract of employment, and furthermore does so on the terms laid down by the employer. In this event, in so far as the written statement is different from the original agreement, the best logical way to retain a contractual analysis of this is that the written statement is a proposed variation of the original contract, which the employee is free to reject under the ordinary rules of variation of contracts. However, even if this is satisfactory in terms of the legal analysis of what has occurred, it looks decidedly odd in practical terms. It may well be, for example, that the employer provides the written statement to the employee when they turn up for work on the first day. This would be the case with many larger employers. It may even be the case that the employer has sent the employee a copy of the written statement before they start work. It looks peculiar to enter into an agreement to begin work on a particular date but, before that date arrives, for one of the parties to propose a variation, as a matter of course, in the terms of that contract before the employee begins work. It looks more than odd, but questionable in policy terms to allow this to

---

[34] See e.g. *Turriff Construction Ltd v Bryant* [1967] ITR 292; *System Floors (UK) Ltd v Daniel* [1982] IRLR 475; [1982] ICR 54.
[35] *Gascol Conversions Ltd v Mercer* [1974] IRLR 155; [1974] ICR 420.

happen when an employee is in a particularly vulnerable position in legal terms, having in the normal circumstance no protection against unfair dismissal should they refuse to accept the proposed variation. But, of course, the employee is very often not in a position to object for practical reasons, having invested a great deal in terms of perhaps moving house from one end of the country to the other and all the expense that entails, a spouse or partner giving up a job and finding work in a different place (also giving up employment protection in their previous employment), disrupting children who need to move to different schools, leaving friends behind and so on. There can perhaps be no better example of how the law is at odds in giving real and practical protection to employees whilst at the same time maintaining the requirements of legal form.

Variation of terms

On the face of it, the normal contractual rules relating to variation of contractual terms apply to contracts of employment. These require any variation to have the assent of both parties, supported by consideration, and so it would seem that there is no imbalance of power between them in this respect. However, this is not always the case. In *Lee v GEC Plessey Telecommunications*[36] it was held that where a contract expressly incorporates the terms of collective agreements there is no need for fresh consideration with regard to each variation of the contract of employment. Nevertheless, employers could not rely on other external documents incorporated into the contract of employment to unilaterally vary those contracts unless there were a right to vary terms clearly specified in the contract itself. If the employer unilaterally enforces a variation, this amounts to a repudiation of the contract of employment and the employee is put to their election whether to accept the fundamental breach, and resign, or to carry on working and seek damages.[37] But many contracts contain such wide flexibility clauses to the effect that a change of actual duties performed (even a radical variation) may lie within the contractual job description. An example is where there is a term that the employee will perform such duties as are from time to time assigned to them by their line manager.

A practical problem with regard to variation of terms can be thrown up by a theoretical one. This is the question as to whether, where a contract of employment has become extensively varied, it in reality amounts to a new contract. This can be important. For example, a unilateral deduction of an employee's pay may amount to a fundamental breach of contract and its termination dependent on the election of the employee, while the replacement

---

[36] *Lee v GEC Plessey Telecommunications* [1993] IRLR 383.
[37] *Burdett-Coutts v Hertfordshire County Council* [1984] IRLR 91.

of one contract by another with agreement would not have this effect. In *Marriott v Oxford and District Co-operative Society Ltd (No.2)*[38] the appellant had been employed by the respondents for two years when they found that there was insufficient work for him. They were prepared to offer him another post for lower pay and the employee reluctantly accepted it, worked for a short while in the new post but then terminated his contract by notice. In defence to his claim for a redundancy payment, the respondents claimed that they had not terminated the agreement by insisting on his taking the new job (which was necessary for him to claim his statutory rights), but had merely varied it. However, the Court of Appeal took the view that by their insistence, the employees had terminated the contract. What this shows is the courts' reluctance to find that there has been real agreement by the employee where their employment is at stake due to a variation of the contract.[39]

Employers frequently seek to vary terms unilaterally by giving the employee the notice to which they are entitled under their contract. In this event the employer must make it clear that it is terminating one contract and offering another. So, in *Burdett-Coutts v Hertfordshire County Council*[40] the employers sought to change the hours of the employees by means of a circular letter. The plaintiffs, who were entitled to twelve weeks' notice of termination, sought a declaration that the purported variation was invalid and a repudiatory breach, to which the defendants responded that the letter should be read as a termination of the employment coupled with an offer of new terms. The court found that the employees had elected not to accept the repudiation and could claim the total wages to which they were entitled under the contract. However, employers can simply avoid this consequence by using a different form of words.[41]

At first sight it might be thought that the Employment Rights Act 1996, s. 4 reflects an extensive power in the employer to unilaterally vary contracts of employment. This is because it states that there is a duty to give notice to an employee of changes in terms at the earliest opportunity, and in any event no later than one month after the change or, where the change results in the employee being required to work outside the United Kingdom for a period of more than one month, the time when they leave the United Kingdom in order to begin so to work, if that is earlier. The notion of one party to a contract informing the other of a variation in terms rather than seeking assent to it

---

[38] *Marriott v Oxford and District Co-operative Society Ltd (No.2)* [1970] 1 QB 186.

[39] *Shields Furniture Ltd v Goff* [1973] ICR 187; [1973] 2 All ER 653; *Sheet Metal Components Ltd v Plumridge* [1974] ICR 373; [1974] ITR 238; *Norwest Holst Group Administration Ltd v Harrison* [1985] IRLR 240; [1985] ICR 668.

[40] *Burdett-Coutts v Hertfordshire County Council*, n 37.

[41] See further, S. Fredman, 'Contract of Employment' (1984) 13 *Industrial Law Journal* 177 and *Aparau v Iceland Frozen Foods plc* [1996] IRLR 119.

seems contrary to classical contract theory. However, it is not so drastic as that. For example, some of the terms relate to matters of mere fact, rather than substantive agreement, such as the name and address of the employer. Should those change, there is no real variation in what has been agreed between the parties. Furthermore, the courts have been quite insistent that any substantive changes to the written statement must, reflecting the analysis that it merely amounts to evidence of the contract reached between the parties, have root in an already agreed variation.

Where employers have sought to have a power of unilateral variation of substantive terms by retaining contractual authority for the idea, the courts have been very reluctant to allow this. If the rights of employees would be affected by a variation, that is unlikely to succeed. However, if it relates to a term with which the employer has an obligation to comply which would not affect employees' rights, that might be allowable.[42]

As a matter of contract then it might appear that an attempted unilateral variation will not succeed, and that this denies to the employer what would otherwise in practice be a quite powerful tool in the regulation of relations between the company and its employees. However, when it comes to statutory employment protection the courts seem to take a rather different view. A perceived need for the employer to bring about a change in terms and conditions has amounted to a dismissal for 'some other substantial reason' under the Employment Rights Act 1996, s. 98(1)(b) justifying the dismissal. So in R.S. Components Ltd v Irwin[43] the company required their employees to agree to new restrictive covenants to arrest a decline in profits. When some refused, the National Industrial Relations Court (the predecessor to the Employment Appeal Tribunal) held their consequent dismissal fair on the ground that it was a reasonable request. Several other cases have reached a similar conclusion.[44] This illustrates the point that one important way in which the law of unfair dismissal differs from contract is that it focuses on the reasonableness of the employer's order. So, in Farrant v The Woodroffe School,[45] the Employment Appeal Tribunal held that, even where an order was unlawful in that it was in breach of contract, this did not render the consequent dismissal necessarily unfair. Breaches of contract are not, therefore, necessarily unfair. This leads to the quite extraordinary idea that in practice (levels of compensation levels apart)

---

[42] See Wandsworth London Borough Council v D'Silva [1998] IRLR 193 but compare Airlie v City of Edinburgh District Council [1996] IRLR 516 where a variation was allowed without an express term.

[43] R.S. Components Ltd v Irwin [1973] IRLR 239; [1973] ICR 535; [1974] 1 All ER 41.

[44] See e.g. Robinson v Flitwick Frames Ltd [1975] IRLR 261; Farr v Hoveringham Gravels Ltd [1972] IRLR 104; Industrial Rubber Products Ltd v Gillon [1977] IRLR 389; [1978] ITR 100 and Martin v Automobile Proprietary Ltd [1979] IRLR 64.

[45] Farrant v The Woodroffe School [1998] ICR 184.

employees may have less protection against an unfair dismissal under statute than they do at common law in contract.

Works rules

Another route by which employers can inject a degree of unilateralism into relations with employees is through works rules. These appear to give employers autonomy to vary the contractual obligations of employees unilaterally, and are widely used. However, the situation is not quite as it appears.[46]

Works rules contain matters such as dress codes, machinery operating procedures, managerial and disciplinary procedures as well as rules relating to sickness, safety provisions, employee sports facilities and holidays. The employer is free to alter these rules as and when it thinks fit. However, it is important to distinguish works rules from contractual terms. They need to have contractual authority but they may not form part of the contract of employment as such. They might be given contractual effect by way of express or implied incorporation, but another way of seeing it is that the rules themselves are separate from the contract, but have contractual authority in that they are made by the employer who is empowered by the contract to make, and vary, them. So, as rules independent of the contract in that sense they need to be communicated perhaps by being placed on a notice board, in a dedicated handbook, electronically, or even by word of mouth. A typical format is where the employee signs a declaration that they accept the conditions of employment as set out in the works rules, and such acceptance may be implied if the employee has reasonable notice of them.

The employer may be given authority to make and vary works rules expressly in the contract of employment itself, or impliedly on the basis that it is usual for the employer to have the managerial prerogative to do so, and that it is necessary for business efficacy. In the leading case, *Secretary of State for Employment v ASLEF (No.2)*,[47] the Court of Appeal had to determine whether the respondent union's 'work to rule' was in breach of contract. The union claimed that it was merely following the employer's rule book to the letter and was therefore not in breach. The court held, however, that the rules of the employer were not all contractually binding as some were clearly out of date and others were trivial. Although each employee signed a form saying that they would abide by the rules, this did not mean that they became terms of the contract. They were only instructions as to how the work should be done made under the umbrella authority provided by the contract. The employer was thus

---

[46] I have already considered the position of works rules in the context of the theory of contract and status in Chapter 2.

[47] *Secretary of State for Employment v ASLEF (No.2)* [1972] ICR 19; [1972] 2 QB 455; [1972] 2 All ER 949.

empowered to alter the rules at will. In this way, a work to rule is a breach of contract, not because the rules themselves are contractual terms but because the employer makes rules under contractual authority, and no longer requires a particular set of rules to be followed when the work to rule occurs. A work to rule is thus something of a misnomer, because the rules being followed are no longer the employer's operating works rules. It is, furthermore, a further breach of contract by way of a breach of the implied term of co-operation not to be disruptive to the employer's business.

The consequences for the employee of a work to rule may be very serious. They may be lawfully locked out at common law[48] and (depending on all the circumstances) probably fairly dismissed under statute because of the implied term of the employment contract that the employee must obey lawful and reasonable orders.

Sometimes, however, the notion that works rules operate as a form of delegated authority under the contract of employment as part of the managerial prerogative inherent in it, or expressly provided for, is not the basis on which the courts decide cases in this area. They sometimes state that works rules do have contractual effect. So, those sections of rule books which deal with particulars required in the statutory statement of terms are generally considered to be part of the contract. Otherwise the test is what the parties intend to be contractual terms. This has an odd effect in that, if such rules are contractual terms themselves, then their creation and variation should be subject to the normal contractual principles relating to mutual agreement. But this is not always the case. So, in *Petrie v MacFisheries Ltd*[49] a notice about sick pay posted on the factory notice board was held to have contractual effect, even though the employees had never had their attention specifically drawn to it. This authority of this decision, dating from 1939, of course now has to be read in the light of the notification requirements under Employment Rights Act 1996, s. 1 considered above, but it is still instructive I suggest in the context of examining the approach of the courts regarding the power they are prepared to give employers by way of contract.

The power in practice that is obtainable through the ability to make and vary works rules is a considerable one because of their dual characteristics. First, they usually have contractual authority by way of an umbrella provision so that not to obey them is to be in breach of contract, by way of both the failure to abide by the contractual sub-terms that the employer has contractual authority to make and vary, as well as a separate breach of the implied term of co-operation. Secondly, despite their contractual basis, in one

---

[48] *Ticehurst v British Telecommunications plc* [1992] IRLR 219; [1992] ICR 383.
[49] *Petrie v MacFisheries Ltd* [1939] 4 All ER 281; [1940] 1 KB 258.

way or another, the works rules are not rooted in agreement but mandatory direction and subservience. This represents the best of all worlds for the employer, and a very powerful tool in regulating the employment relationship.

The relationship between express and implied terms

It is not only in respect of the grant of greater power to employers through the process of what I have termed above 'unilateralism' that the issue of a diminished role of agreement in determining the terms of the contract of employment becomes relevant. Sometimes agreement between the parties can be ignored in practice to the benefit of the employee.

There might be an argument that implied terms in contracts of employment (or indeed other types of contract) cut across the purpose of the common law. The common law, on the whole, is not interested in the terms on which a contract is made. This most obviously manifests itself in the notion that consideration need not be adequate, but merely sufficient. Rather, the common law is concerned only with what the parties have agreed to abide by, whatever that may be. As a statement of the basis of the common law of contract it thus may seem curious that it accords an important role to implied terms for the very nature of implied terms is that they are not, by definition, those to which the parties have agreed.

This might be so at first sight, but in fact the common law redeems the notion that it is interested in giving effect only to actual agreements between the parties by implying terms only on bases that can be linked to agreement. So, implied terms are terms that the parties would have agreed upon expressly if they had not thought it unnecessary to do so; or in order to give efficacy to their agreement because they cannot be supposed to have intended their contract not to be workable; or because the terms are so well-known to be implied into other contracts that the parties would certainly have expressly agreed for them to be excluded from their own if that is what they had intended. And so on.

Nevertheless it is curious that the courts have from time to time given rein to the notion that implied terms are so important that they can trump express terms. Take, for example, the decision of the Court of Appeal in *Johnstone v Bloomsbury Health Authority*.[50] A hospital doctor was under an obligation to work a certain number of hours and possibly some more hours if called upon by the hospital so to do. In consequence, the doctor became ill. Stuart-Smith LJ said that the express obligation to work the additional hours was subject to the implied term that the employer had an obligation to take care of its employees.

---

[50] *Johnstone v Bloomsbury Health Authority* [1991] ICR 269.

This was because such an implied term was necessary in order to give efficacy to the contract. Sir Nicolas Browne-Wilkinson V-C thought instead that the implied term took effect as to the additional hours because there was no absolute obligation to work the overtime. Therefore there was no conflict between the express and the implied term.[51] In both judgements, however, there was an acceptance that the implied term could trump the express term which is quite contrary, of course, to classical contract doctrine. It is particularly curious that the court felt able to countenance this idea when there was a perfectly simple and straightforward way the same result could have been achieved whilst complying with accepted contract theory. It need simply have been a matter of interpretation of the express term that it was intended by the parties to apply only to the point that it did not affect the health of the employees concerned. However, it is not clear whether this option occurred to them or if the court felt that the route they took was equally as natural.[52]

There is one sense, however, in which implied terms have come in recent years to have a lesser role in regulating the employment relationship, and to an extent that has perhaps not been as widely recognized as it should have been. Instead of implied terms operating as a kind of source of default rules for the contract, whereby the parties need not be engaged in specifying what the regulatory terms of their relationship consists in, this function has become increasingly overtaken by the standard form employment contract. Standard form contracts have many advantages for the parties, and particularly the employer, in being able to grant complete specificity together with incorporated documents and techniques that enable the employer to restrict all the obligations under the contract to those that are expressly stated in the written contract. As Hugh Collins has pointed out: 'Implied terms must be largely irrelevant in such contexts'.[53]

---

[51] The reasoning here is curious. It was not that there was no absolute obligation to work, for whether the doctor did so or not was at the hospital's option and therefore when it required him to work he had an absolute obligation to do so. It was, however, not *absolutely* clear that the hospital would call upon him to work the extra hours. It is hard to see how that fact can be linked to the precedence of the implied term over the express.

[52] A further striking feature of this case is that junior hospital doctors today are now arguing that legislative restrictions on working time result in a prejudicial curtailment of the training to which they feel they should be exposed. See the General Medical Council's *National Training Surveys* 2010.

[53] H. Collins, 'Legal Responses to the Standard Form Contract of Employment' [2007] 36 *Industrial Law Journal* 2, at p. 6.

Debate 3

Should contract be abandoned?

In the light of the discussion in the preceding Debates in this chapter, it might be thought that there is a strong case, in providing a practical and workable basis for the parties in their employment relationship, to abandon the contractual nature of it altogether. There can be no doubt that it is exceedingly difficult to provide the parties, and particularly employees, with the protection they need in the modern world through the contract of employment alone. Even if there were methods, insufficiently explored as we have just seen, by which the contract of employment could be better utilized to this end, these have not been taken up. There would appear to be two possible alternatives for those seeking to do something about this situation. One is to campaign for greater statutory provisions to regulate the relationship, and it can hardly not be conceded that employment law in the past few decades has had more than its fair share of the parliamentary time and the resultant pages of the Statute Book. However, the second alternative is the most drastic, if possibly the most attractive. This is to abandon the employment contract as the route to further protection and to seek a further foundation for employment rights.

The most notable suggestion along these lines in relatively recent years came from Bob Hepple in the 1980s. Hepple, in a seminal article,[54] argued particularly for the greater use of legislative promotion of collective bargaining to secure workers' rights, arguing that the development of labour law in several European countries was based on the realization that the employment relationship had to be freed from the law of contracts (sic) and of property.

Hepple makes the telling observation that the shortcomings of the contract of employment in providing adequate protection to employees are not evidenced by the types of cases coming before the courts. It is not as if the nature of employment has changed so much that the contractual analysis has struggled to keep up with it. Rather, the types of cases exercising the courts when he was writing concerned those which were familiar to the Victorians. The casual worker and the homeworker were not atypical types of employees in the nineteenth century and they are not today. Indeed, the contractual analysis was causing difficulties for the courts in the nineteenth century. As he pointed out, there never was a time (or 'golden age' as he termed it) when the contractual concept of employment matched the needs of industrial society. By way of example from the modern era Hepple points out that the protection granted by statute to anti-union dismissals was within unfair dismissal legislation[55] which

[54] B.A. Hepple, 'Restructuring Employment Rights' [1986] 15 *Industrial Law Journal* 69.
[55] See now Trade Union and Labour Relations (Consolidation) Act 1992, s. 152(1).

protect employees rather than the wider category of 'worker' by which a trade union is defined.[56]

The solution proffered by Hepple was for there to be a broad definition of an 'employment relationship' involving a contract (because it would be based on voluntary agreement) but of a new kind covering short-term intermittent relationships as well as continuous contracts. This would involve a uniform definition with exceptions from time to time as required. It would also go behind the corporate veil to establish the true identity of the employer, or that person or body that has control of the undertaking, based on the European model of the enterprise. This would all need to be supported by legally-strengthened collective bargaining.

Nothing has as yet come of this. One has to wonder how successful it would be to have a single, common, definition covering varieties of employment rights. Certainly, there is a plethora of definitions at the moment, even if they are of the same concept, be it 'contract of service' or 'contract of employment'.[57] If the courts were to take a more purposive and policy-oriented approach,[58] it is not inconceivable that over time a variety of judge-made distinctions would begin to appear in a common definition of employment, depending upon context. In that event, we would be no, or little, further than we are now.

It seems very unlikely that the extent to which the contractual basis of employment hinders the operation and development of employment relationships in practice will in the short or even medium-term result in its demise. As Mark Freedland has argued, his seminal work was written 'in the conviction that English employment law is deeply, perhaps irrevocably, committed to a contractual analysis of the individual employment relationship'.[59] Indeed, there is every indication that, with the ever-growing increase in statutory provisions relating to employment, contract is becoming

---

56 Ibid, s. 1 which defines a trade union as: 'an organization (whether temporary or permanent) –

(a) which consists wholly or mainly of workers of one or more descriptions and whose principal purposes include the regulation of relations between workers of that description or those descriptions and employers or employers' associations; or
(b) which consists wholly or mainly of –
(i) constituent or affiliated organizations which fulfil the conditions in paragraph (a) (or themselves consist wholly or mainly of constituent or affiliated organizations which fulfil those conditions), or (ii) representatives of such constituent or affiliated organizations, and whose principal purposes include the regulation of relations between workers and employers or between workers and employers' associations, or the regulation of relations between its constituent or affiliated organizations'.

57 See S. Honeyball, 'The Conceptual Integrity of Employment' [2005] Cambrian Law Review 1.

58 Hepple berates the courts for adopting a 'common sense' approach which: 'fails to focus on the purpose of the particular statute in question' – Hepple, 'Restructuring Employment Rights', n 54, p. 73.

59 Freedland, The Personal Employment Contract, n 12, p. 6.

ever more embedded. Take, for example, the provisions in the Equality Act 2010[60] on equality of terms, originally to be found in the Equal Pay Act 1970. Prior to the 1970 Act there was no equivalent at common law. Employers were free to pay men and women different rates of pay, and treat them differently with regard to all of the terms of the contract of employment, with impunity. The introduction of a claim on this basis in the Act was clearly then a novel statutory provision, not a codification of prior precedent. And yet the claim was contractual, not statutory. Every contract that did not have an equality clause in it was deemed to have one, and differential treatment between men and women with regard to terms resulted in a contractual, not statutory, claim. And yet it would have been a very simple matter for the claim to be statutory, pursuable in industrial tribunals. Freedland gives the example of unlawful deductions from wages under Part II of the ERA 1996.[61] This leads him to say that we 'should understand that we are now talking about not so much the common law of employment contracts, as the *common law based* law of employment contracts'.[62]

Freedland, however, is not affiliated to the idea of work relationships being rooted to contracts of employment. On the contrary, his argument is that the category should be extended to cover personal employment contracts in the sense of work contracts where the worker undertakes to perform work personally for another which is wider than at least some definitions of employment contracts in that it covers work contracts which lack the continuity of obligation that is thought necessary to amount to contracts of employment. What he refers to as 'the legal relevance of the law of the contracts of employment'[63] in fact only serves to heighten concern about the obsolescence of contract in employment that had been felt in the middle part of the twentieth century. In a telling phrase, he writes that:

> 'even if that ideology was undergoing changes, it might be difficult for those changes to filter through a discourse derived from the nineteenth – or early twentieth-century law of master and servant, still drawing some of its case law, and quite a lot of its idiom, from issues and disputes concerning valets, cooks and chambermaids, gardeners and agricultural labourers, millworkers, and black-coated clerks'.[64]

What this discussion shows is that, despite the chapter arrangements at the beginning of this book, there is after all no fine dividing line between the

---

[60] Equality Act 2010, ss. 64–80.
[61] Curiously Freedland in fact refers to the Wages Act 1986 which contained the original law in this area before being superseded by the 1996 Act. See Freedland *The Personal Employment Contract*, n 12, p. 4.
[62] Freedland, ibid, p. 4. (The italics are in the original).
[63] Freedland, ibid, p. 4.
[64] Freedland, ibid, pp. 4–5.

theoretical analysis of the contract of employment and the operation of the contract of employment in practice. They can be distinguished, but they cannot live apart in worlds of their own. Theory impacts upon practice in a very marked way, and the extent to which the policy requirements of employment practice do, or should, relate to theory are matters of real and pressing import.

Further Reading

C. Barnard, 'Cherries: One Bite or Two' [2006] *Cambridge Law Journal* 27.

D. Brodie, 'Specific Performance and Employment Contracts' (1998) 27 *Industrial Law Journal* 37.

H. Collins, 'The Meaning of Job Security' (1991) 20 *Industrial Law Journal* 227.

H. Collins, 'Legal Responses to the Standard Form Contract of Employment' [2007] 36 *Industrial Law Journal* 2.

S. Evans, J. Goodman and L. Hargreaves, 'Unfair Dismissal Law and Changes in the Role of Trade Unions and Employers' Associations' (1985) 14 *Industrial Law Journal* 91.

K.D. Ewing, 'Job Security and the Contract of Employment' (1989) 18 *Industrial Law Journal* 217.

K.D. Ewing, 'The New Labour Injunction' [1989] *Cambridge Law Journal* 28.

S. Fredman, 'Contract of Employment' (1984) 13 *Industrial Law Journal* 177.

M. Freedland, *The Personal Employment Contract* (Oxford University Press, 2003).

M. Freedland, 'Constructing Fairness in Employment Contracts' (2007) 36 *Industrial Law Journal* 136.

B.A. Hepple, 'Restructuring Employment Rights' [1986] 15 *Industrial Law Journal* 69.

4

DISCRIMINATION AT WORK

INTRODUCTION

It is clear that the introduction and development of discrimination legislation has been a major feature of employment law (and of course many other areas of law) over the past forty and more years. It has been thrown into sharp relief because the common law previously provided very little protection indeed for employees, or would-be employees, who were discriminated against. And it still fails to do so. For example, discriminatory conduct is, almost by definition, unreasonable, and so it might be thought that this would provide a basis for a contractual remedy. A non-lawyer in particular might feel that a contract of employment would contain, if not an express term to this effect, an implied term that the employer will be deemed to be acting unreasonably if it acts in a discriminatory manner. However, the employment contract does not contain an implied term that the parties will act reasonably towards each other, even though the parties, if asked whether they would consider reasonable behaviour to be part of their relationship, presumably would almost invariably answer that this went without saying. In other words, reasonableness is something that would seem easily to pass the 'officious bystander' test for the implication of terms into contracts, but the courts have never adopted this approach with regard to employment contracts. Even if they had, and this were a method of protecting employees against discrimination at common law, it would in any event exclude an ambit where much employment discrimination takes place, namely failure to offer work to someone for a discriminatory reason. Implied terms in a contract that these employees would have had but do not have because of a discriminatory reason would clearly be of no avail here.

There is some history of the involvement of law in discrimination matters before 1970 when the Equal Pay Act was passed.[1] However, it is very limited.

---

[1] However, the Equal Pay Act 1970 did not come into force until December 1975, along with the Sex Discrimination Act of that year.

The Sex Disqualification (Removal) Act 1919 removed any disqualification by way of sex or marriage for those who wished to exercise a public function, hold a civil or judicial office or post, enter any civil profession or vocation or be admitted to any incorporated society. It had little practical effect. What other impetus for legislative change there might have been did not produce results. Even those few events that might have led to a social movement for change were not always driven by moral considerations or high principle. For example, there was an initiative by the Trades Union Congress in 1888 to secure equal pay between the sexes. This seems laudable but in fact appears to have been motivated more by a desire to prevent women from undercutting men rather than by any great desire to right a moral wrong. Indeed, this was a feature of the Equal Pay Act 1970 itself. Although there had been a significant drive for equality between the sexes at work, driven particularly by Barbara Castle, an Employment Secretary in Harold Wilson's government of the 1960s, it appears that the 1970 Act was also thought necessary to placate the French who had repeatedly blocked the United Kingdom's entry into the Common Market. Without equality legislation the argument was that this gave the UK an unfair economic advantage.

It is possible to see the anti-slavery legislation in the nineteenth century as a form of anti-discrimination policy in the context of employment, but it is at the extreme end of the scale. There was no legislation preventing, outside slavery, anyone from an ethnic minority from being denied a job, or losing it, because of their race. It is noteworthy, though, that the earliest piece of discrimination legislation addressed race rather than sex even though, in the 1960s, there were proportionately far fewer members of ethnic minorities in the workforce than women. The first of these, the Race Relations Act 1965, did not address employment issues, but the Race Relations Act 1968 did give some protection to employees and would-be employees, although only by way of a highly complex and practically difficult procedural mechanism. Further, the legislation itself was part of a package of ideas that involved the imposition of curbs on immigration, and its regulation.

It should not be thought, however, that there was no moral impetus for legislative change in discrimination. Clearly there was, even in the nineteenth century, when the calls for legislative protection extending into the workplace arose in wider contexts, such as electoral reform. Some of these came from international sources, and after the Second World War the United Kingdom accumulated a variety of international obligations to introduce anti-discrimination legislation, most notably under the International Labour Organization Conventions No. 100 in 1951 and No. 111 in 1958, the United Nations International Convention on Social and Cultural Rights, and the European

Convention for the Protection of Human Rights and Fundamental Freedoms – generally known as the European Convention on Human Rights. Neither should it be thought that the resistance was rooted entirely in the absence of moral principle. It has to be remembered that the idea of the legal basis of employment until well into the middle of the twentieth century was rooted in another principle, namely freedom of contract. This point is often made, particularly in the context of Lord Davey's speech in *Allen v Flood*[2] in 1898.[3] But it must also be remembered that this did not involve a denial that discrimination was wrong – indeed, Lord Davey's speech in that case made it very clear, in that he stated that there was no redress in law against 'the most mistaken, capricious, malicious or morally reprehensible motives that can be conceived'. The argument was thus about the superiority of the freedom of contract doctrine. This was no mere contractual or even legal doctrine and it was, at least in part, a moral idea about freedoms that people should enjoy without undue interference from the State.

It also needs to be borne in mind that the move towards discrimination law in any context is inevitably closely linked to the incidence of discrimination. In a society where few women are working outside the home, or where few ethnic minorities are present, discrimination law to protect them seems less urgent or pressing. Of course, to the individuals involved there may be no lesser sense of grievance if discrimination should occur, but numbers clearly are a factor in the move towards legislative protection. So, naturally, with increased immigration came the drive towards race discrimination legislation. Likewise, when after the Second World War women had been used to occupying skilled and responsible jobs, and continued to be needed due to a depleted male workforce, came the drive towards sex discrimination legislation.

In this chapter I will consider a number of Debates on discrimination in employment. However, all that I can do here is to alight on a few of the most interesting and controversial questions that have arisen in the area. I cannot hope to cover the ground even lightly, or perhaps even to give a representative flavour of what has proved to be a highly debated area of employment law. In the first Debate I consider whether it is possible to have a unified approach to discrimination law. In other words, are the instances of discrimination recognized in legal examples of a single idea, or closely-related but separate instances of discrimination. Then I go on to examine the role of equality in discrimination and in particular whether it is the quality discrimination law should be seeking to secure. The third Debate will be concerned with the highly important question

---

[2] *Allen v Flood* [1898] AC 1 at 172.
[3] See e.g. S. Deakin and G. Morris, *Labour Law* (Hart Publishing, 5th edn, 2009) p. 158.

as to whether discrimination rights should be personal in the sense that it might be justified to have legal claims for discrimination in the context of protected characteristics one does not oneself have. The fourth Debate considers tests for the causation of discrimination. What is the best test for determining if disadvantage has been brought about by a discriminatory act? Lastly, I briefly consider whether a distinction that is fundamental to discrimination law – between direct and indirect discrimination – is as coherent as it first appears.

Debate 1

Is it possible to have a unified approach to discrimination?

In posing this question I refer to the idea that it might be possible to have a piece of legislation that covers unjustified discrimination in whatever form and that the hitherto piecemeal approach of the law has merely reflected different contexts in which discrimination has become so serious that it needs addressing. There is one argument that all discrimination is wrong in that it connotes the idea that irrelevant factors are taken into account in the treatment by one person of another. To discriminate against someone is to be unjust towards them and this justifies the law's intervention to give protection. This is a difficult argument to sustain, for a number of reasons. One reason is that it is not true, it would seem, that it is necessarily unjust to discriminate between people. It is right that an employer should treat pregnant employees more favourably with regard to their pregnancy than others. The reply to that, of course, is that discrimination occurs only where like cases are not treated alike. Where cases are unalike it is right to treat them differently. But that does not follow, of course, because it might be right to treat them alike too, because the differences are irrelevant. And this highlights one very difficult problem in this area. If discrimination is dependent on identifying which cases are alike it is important to do so not only on the basis of similarity of facts but similarity in principle. One has to identify difference in principle between different cases in order to establish that the difference in issue is one that is relevant for the purposes of establishing that their cases are not alike. Two women, Alison and Belinda, may be treated differently, and rightly so. But Belinda may be given more favourable treatment than Alison, not because she's called Belinda but because she is pregnant and Alison is not. In other words, it may be essential to treat like cases alike to avoid discrimination, but what constitutes like cases being alike is dependent on establishing that the differences between them are unjustified in principle. So, the business of treating their cases alike comes after, not before, identifying what is and is not discriminatory in their cases. Furthermore, it does not necessarily follow that it is necessary to treat unlike cases differently unless one has identified that, due to principle, the cases are unlike in a way that makes it necessary for them to be treated differently.[4]

This point takes us into issues of equality and its relationship to discrimination law, which I will deal with later. But the point for present purposes is that it is possible to argue that the justification for discrimination law is that discrimination of itself, having been found to be rooted in a difference in treatment between like cases, those cases being identified as being different because they are different in moral principle, is the basis of legal interference. It follows that different contexts of discrimination found in law – sex, race, disability and so on – are merely examples of the outworking of a single discrimination idea. It is wrong to discriminate on any ground, the argument might go, but the law has identified particular areas of coverage in response to pressing and urgent social or other requirements.

The history of discrimination law would certainly seem to bear this argument out to some extent. As I have shown already discrimination law began with the race legislation in the 1960s followed by the Equal Pay Act 1970 and the Sex Discrimination Act 1975. In 1995 it was followed by the Disability Discrimination Act and subsequently further subordinate legislation covering sexual orientation, religious and other beliefs, gender reassignment, pregnancy and maternity and then age. These were all drafted in similar but different ways. Then the Equality Act 2010 was passed. This reflected a growing perception that the earlier provisions were instances of an overarching discrimination principle – namely that it is wrong to discriminate against people without justification and that this is so regardless of context.

This has a number of consequences. One is that it makes sense to approach the law in these areas in as uniform a way as possible. The second is that the context of discrimination is irrelevant. It is always wrong. These ideas would seem to involve the notion that the law should not be contextually constrained. There should not be particular provisions relating only to the protected characteristics as defined in the legislation. It is as wrong to discriminate against an employee (or anyone else) because they have red hair, are short, or have little taste in modern art as it is if they were female, black or disabled. One might expect, then, that the Equality Act 2010 would reflect this approach. But it does not. It is clear that it was passed in order to give effect to

---

[4] Aristotle's principle of formal equality – that like cases should be treated alike – cannot, according to one view, involve the argument that the fact that people are alike entails that they should be alike because that commits the 'naturalistic fallacy' and breaches Hume's Law that an ought-statement cannot be derived from an is-statement (see P. Westen, 'The Empty Idea of Equality' (1982) 95 *Harvard Law Review* 537, at p. 542f). It also seems circular as, to identify who like people are, one has to establish who should be treated alike by identifying what is relevant in the comparison – see Westen, p. 547.

the idea that there is justification in a uniform approach to discrimination legislation, but it goes only a very short way in promoting that idea. First, the contexts the Act covers are those that existed in the previous law. The 'protected characteristics' that lead to legislative protection are still age; disability; gender reassignment; marriage and civil partnership; pregnancy and maternity; race; religion or belief; sex; and sexual orientation.[5] The red-headed, the short and the artistically-challenged remain as unprotected by the legislation as before, even if for example the loss of a job to them remains as devastating as it would be to anyone discriminated against because of a recognized protected characteristic.

However, it needs to be asked, to what extent would a uniform approach be justified? It is not at all clear that the different contexts of discrimination as identified in the legislation (let alone outside it) are not different in principle but merely are instances of examples of an overarching discrimination idea that should themselves be treated alike. For example, a clear difference is that someone who is discriminated against because they are disabled is treated differently than someone discriminated against because they are a woman. It is not merely that the contexts are simply different. The contexts are different in principle. Not everyone has a disability, but everyone has a sex. To be discriminated against for the latter is because of the particular sex that one has, not because one has a sex at all. It is doubtful that anyone has been discriminated against because of that particular characteristic. But to be discriminated against because of disability is exactly that. It may not be, although it often is of course, that someone is discriminated against because of the particular disability that they have, but it usually is simply because they are disabled. Should this make a difference to the way these cases are respectively handled? It may well be that it should, but that would take me beyond my present point that the protected characteristics themselves, let alone others that have not made it into the list, may not be mere instances or examples of a general discrimination idea.

Debate 2

Is equality the goal of discrimination legislation?

EQUALITY AND VALUE

The history of discrimination as rooted in moral ideas is, of course, very old indeed. The concept of justice clearly entails the idea that like cases should be treated alike. This can be traced to Aristotle's *Nicomachean Ethics*.[6] Most

---

[5] Equality Act 2010, s. 4.
[6] Aristotle, *Ethica Nicomachea* Book V.3.1131a–1131b (ed. W. Ross, Oxford University Press, 1925).

people would easily recognize the close connection between this idea and discrimination, not least because it connotes equality and inequality is seen as the essence of discrimination. And most people see equality as a moral value.[7]

It is therefore a good starting point for debate that equality should be seen as the aim of discrimination legislation, or that it should be. Clearly, many people closely associated with discrimination law place great emphasis on equality. Indeed, Trevor Phillips as its first Chair, quickly re-named the Commission for Equality and Human Rights the Equality and Human Rights Commission in order to make clear the emphasis that he thought should be placed on the idea of equality.[8] The legislation originally providing protection for non-discriminatory pay between the sexes was the Equal Pay Act 1970. It, and other discrimination legislation, has been replaced by the Equality Act 2010.

The language of equality is not mere rhetoric. Equality is what much (but not all) of the legislation seeks to achieve. So, for example, if a woman were to seek to bring an equal pay claim under the 2010 Act she would have to show that she was not receiving equal pay (or some other contractual entitlement) when compared with that of a man doing work, or if not the same, of equal value to hers. And here the equality she needs to seek is not necessarily to be seen in identical treatment, but in the idea of equal value. Although she and her comparator need not be doing the same job, but are doing work of equal value as determined by particular principles, the outcome she will be entitled to will only extend to an identical level of (if not the same) treatment. In crude terms, the 2010 Act seeks to treat people who are the same, or who are equivalent, identically or equally.

This has an important consequence. If the employee wishes to claim that she is not valued as much as her comparator, she will not necessarily succeed. There is no protection in the Equality Act 2010 for what might be termed 'justified proportionate inequality'. So, if she is not doing the same or equivalent work to that of her desired comparator but is, say, several grades higher than he is, but paid only marginally more than he is she will not have a claim. Even if she could show that, had she been a man, she would have been paid significantly more than her comparator, no claim will lie. The 2010 Act does not seek to ensure that employees are paid what they are worth

---

[7] However, it seems that William Gladstone, the nineteenth century Prime Minister, argued that there was no political idea that had entered into the political system less than equality – see D. Thomson, *Equality* (Cambridge University Press, 1949) p. 1. Some have argued that inequality is the source of everything that is good – see R. Dahrendorf, 'On the Origin of Social Inequality' in P. Laslett and W.G. Runciman (eds), *Philosophy, Politics and Society* (Basil Blackwell, 1964) ch.5.

[8] See Equality Act 2006, s. 1. The legislation has not re-named the Commission's official title.

irrespective of their sex, but merely that they are paid the same as other employees who are of equal value to them.[9]

This would seem to highlight a serious flaw in the legislation. It is quite debatable that a great deal of discrimination, particularly perhaps in the employment context, is of the 'justified proportionate inequality' type. Discrimination can occur where people are not valued in the proportion that they should be entitled to where the differences in their worth compared with other people is not reflected in the treatment afforded to them, and this is because of a reason which should be irrelevant – a protected reason.

The counter-argument to this might be that this is not the purpose of the legislation. It is not about making sure that people are paid what they are worth. That is a matter of individual agreement, market forces and so on. What the discrimination legislation is concerned with is ensuring that employees are treated on an equal footing. Men and women are inherently of equal worth and it is this principle that the legislation is seeking to uphold. There are other laudable aims for legislation, such as ensuring that people are paid what they are worth, but this should not be the subject of discrimination legislation, but rather of other provisions, such as minimum wage legislation.[10] It may well be that the reason why people are not paid what they are worth, rather than merely differently from other people, is because of a protected characteristic, but to include that would be to muddy the waters. It would also be more difficult, perhaps, to establish such claims and might require hypothetical comparisons which has never been part of the equal pay claim structure. In other words, the counter-argument is rooted more in practical considerations than in high principle.

It is interesting that it has been a feature of feminist legal theory since the sex discrimination legislation first came into being that equality with men may not be what women should be striving for. Some feminist writers argue that the differences between women and men should be the focus of special treatment rather than seeking equality. Others believe that the focus should be on equality. But it is also worthy of note that a recognition of justified special treatment for women has been grafted, occasionally somewhat uncomfortably, onto legislation that is designed primarily to eradicate discrimination and to do so on the basis of achieving identical treatment rather than reflecting justified differential treatment based upon different personal value. So, for example, it is considered justified to give women advantageous treatment that is not afforded to men because of a woman's pregnancy or childbirth. It is more than justified discrimination – it is discrimination that is obligatory.

---

[9] See *Pointon v University of Sussex* [1979] IRLR 199 and *Benveniste v University of Southampton* [1989] IRLR 122.
[10] See National Minimum Wage Act 1998.

This obligatory, rather than justified, aspect of such differential treatment might go some way to meeting the objections of some writers to provisions aimed at women that are specific to them. For example, Sandra Fredman has four objections to the idea of such positive rights.[11] First, although these rights exist without making reference to a male comparator, a male norm lurks beneath the surface. Secondly, positive rights occupy a lower place than the perceived dictates of the market, employers' needs and government economic policies. Thirdly, positive rights are inaccessible because they must be enforced by individuals in the absence of class actions and finally, by giving rights to women the differences between men and women are reinforced, particularly the assumption that women are responsible for childcare.

There is a further argument that part of the relationship between discrimination and equality seems to be particularly significant in law because the law necessarily operates through rules. There is a notion that anyone whose case falls under a legal rule is entitled to be treated equally with anyone else whose case also falls under the rule. It is a procedural rather than a substantive idea, often encapsulated in the idea that 'justice according to law' is a virtue in itself. In other words, equality at least in part is seen as a necessary moral foundation to cases decided according to rules, and arises independently from the content of those rules. On the other hand, it is difficult to see how far this argument can be taken, as it is an idea inherent in all law and not special to discrimination. It would certainly appear, at the very least, to be an argument that could explain the importance of equality to discrimination to the extent that the debate is about procedural justice, because it is clear that the emphasis on equality has been primarily concerned with notions of substantive justice.

EQUAL PAY

There has been a long-running debate about equal pay in this country. Since the late 1960s the issue of the extent to which women's pay does not match that of men's has been a constant feature of political and legal debate. Various figures are frequently published to illustrate that, on the whole, women are paid about eighty per cent of the salary that men are paid and, furthermore, that this figure has not increased for many years. The latest statistics at the time of writing show that the median weekly pay for female employees working full-time was £426 and for male employees working full-time, £531. The rate of increase in women's pay is faster than that of men at 3.5 per cent per annum compared with 1.8 per cent for men.[12] This is seen as a failure of the equal pay legislation.

---

[11] S. Fredman, *Women and the Law* (Clarendon Press, 1997) p. 192f.
[12] 2009 Annual Survey of Hours and Earnings (Office for National Statistics).

There is an argument, however, that equality in one sense is an unachievable goal in this area, and something that in fact should not be considered to be the aim of the legislation. As I have mentioned before, the equality of terms provisions of the 2010 Act do not seek to reflect justified proportionate equality between the sexes whereby differences that should exist in treatment of employees of different sexes (because, for example, they are on different grades) are protected. Rather the Act gives protection only for those employees who, because of their sex, are not paid the same as employees of the other sex when they are doing a job which, if not identical, is of equal value. It is therefore entailed in the legislative scheme, it might be thought, that it is inevitable that women will be paid, on the whole, less than men. This is because there are several reasons why men and women are paid differently that, although related to the sex differences between employees, cannot be attributed to sex discrimination.

What are these non-sex reasons? First, it is still the case that women take career breaks far more frequently than men, and it is inevitable that employees who take career breaks are likely to be paid less than those who do not, for several reasons. They may not return to the same job, for example, and therefore start a new career. They may not think any longer in terms of a career but more in terms of financial provision for the family and family-friendly aspects of work available to them, such as more flexible hours. Or they look more for a job that allows shorter hours, of itself resulting in a lower income. And these types of jobs are more likely to be of a lower status than those which are more career-orientated and therefore are lower paid.

The counter-argument to this, however, is that it is true that, at least to a degree, the reasons why women take more career breaks than men can be attributed to societal pressure on women to be the primary partner in a mixed-sex couple to look after children, at least in their early years. It may not be something that women desire more than men but they would feel more obligated than men to fulfil. In other words, this is a form of sex discrimination in that women take career breaks for child-rearing because of a stereotypical assumption that society makes about them that is not inevitable. Of course, in the early stages, when there may be breastfeeding, physical recovery and other issues to consider, certain sex-related factors have an inevitable role, but after that time, there is no reason why men should not play an equal part in the child-rearing responsibilities which could involve them in taking career breaks at least as much as their partners. They do not do so, the argument runs, because of societal assumptions and traditions which themselves display a form of sex discrimination in that the result is that women are adversely treated. The difficulty with this argument, for the purposes of legal protection of women against sex discrimination, is that it does not amount to discrimination by an employer but by society at large. It is hardly feasible to construct legislation that gives a claim to women which they can exercise against society at large. To some extent the positive rights that are afforded to women with regard to pregnancy and childbirth reflect this, but it is only to a very limited degree and of a rather different nature to protection against discrimination.

It also needs to be remembered that women who take career breaks for the purposes of child-rearing may not only lose the time that they have taken off work and the lack of progression in seniority that this entails compared with their previous male counterparts who have continued to climb the tree, but that frequently women will return to a different occupation, or if they remain in the same field of work possibly to a different employer. It is inevitable that such a move will entail lower pay on average.

The second reason why women may be paid less on the whole than men that cannot be put down to discrimination, at least by their employer, is that the work that men and women do are quite different when considered generally. Twice as many men as women are self-employed. Of these, a greater proportion of men work full-time and women part-time. This is a discrepancy which is likely to grow as more and more people become self-employed. It does not necessarily follow that the self-employed are paid more than those who are employed, but it might follow that there is a greater incentive to work longer hours more profitably if workers do so for themselves rather than for another. But there are other work sectors where we can see a disparity between the sexes. For example, women tend to work more in the so-called 'caring professions' than men. This of itself does not lead to lower pay, except that nurses, teachers, social workers and so on are predominantly in the public sector of the economy and for that reason will traditionally have been paid less on average. It may also be – but this should not be overstated – that those who choose to work in the caring professions may do so because they are less likely to be career minded, or at least not so much driven by the financial rewards that their job affords them.

It is also true that women traditionally have worked in those sectors of the economy that are more fragmented, with a few employees scattered here and there. These types of workers are less likely to belong to a trade union than those who work in labour-intensive situations such as a factory or national firms. Hairdressing, hotels, catering and so on, with a dispersed workforce, have lower density union membership. Trade unions find these types of workers particularly difficult to recruit, if only for simple practical reasons.

Another factor is that the proportion of women in part-time work is clearly an important factor in lower pay rates compared with men. About half of all married women in work are in part-time work, and perhaps surprisingly, a quarter of all non-married women. Only about four per cent of men with dependent children, and nine per cent without, work part-time.[13] Not only does part-time work result in less pay, at lower rates (which is indirectly discriminatory) but clearly can result in slower occupational advancement.

Such are the arguments in favour of the idea that, perhaps, the figures on the relative pay of men and women reflect a non-discriminatory profile of differences between male and female working. There are certainly differences between the sexes in pay, but these are to be expected given the differences in working patterns between them which are not caused by discrimination (at least by employers) but by individual and couple choices, and by societal attitudes towards the differing roles that men and women play in child-rearing. However, it is important to bear in mind that the arguments here do operate on different levels. It may not be that there are many examples of where women are paid less than men although they are doing the same job, as efficiently, with the same experience, with the same number of hours and so on. But, the counter-argument might go, the fact that women on the whole are paid less than men is itself discriminatory, whatever the cause. It may not be that there are identifiable perpetrators of discrimination against whom individual women should be able to claim legal protection, but society as a whole has arranged itself in such a way that women nevertheless are the victims of adverse treatment when it comes to pay and conditions at work. It may be that some of this is self-inflicted as it is due to decisions made of free choice, but the considerations weighed up by women in the exercise of these choices may reflect more deep-seated social influences that have the effect that women come out disadvantaged. It is nonetheless discrimination for all that.

The fundamental problem is, however, what can the law do about this? What should it do about it? What is legitimate to do about it? What should it not do about it? These questions take us into very difficult and fascinating philosophical issues, not least the question as to the extent to which it is legitimate for the State to use the law as a tool of moral enforcement.[14] Although I cannot enter into these issues here, they remain entirely relevant.

Debate 3

Should discrimination rights be personal?

In this Debate I consider the idea that discrimination rights are not personal in the sense that one does not need to have the protected characteristic

---

[13] 2009 Labour Force Survey (Office for National Statistics).

[14] This is the issue raised by the famous jurisprudential debate between Lord Devlin and H.L.A. Hart – see P. Devlin, *The Enforcement of Morals* (Clarendon, 1965); H.L.A. Hart, *Law, Liberty and Morality* (Clarendon, 1963).

oneself in order to be protected from discrimination because of it.[15] It is an issue that I consider to be of fundamental importance to discrimination law. The difference between discrimination remedies being available, on the one hand, to those who have a characteristic identified by the law as worthy of protection and, on the other hand, to those affected by being close, or sometimes not so close, to people with such characteristics, will prove to be of enormous significance. My view is that the repercussions of recent developments of the law in this area will take some time to be fully digested and realized. This Debate justifies close analysis.

A relevant scenario would be this. A discriminates against B (treats B less favourably than they treat, or would treat, C) but where the prohibited ground pertains to D. So, if A discriminates against B because B is associated with (for example, is married to) D, then discrimination against B may be said to occur because of D's (not B's) characteristics. The reason for the discrimination against B is that D has certain particular characteristics. This is known as associative discrimination, or discrimination by association. It has also been referred to as transferred discrimination which is perhaps the better term.

Not all discrimination, as described above, is associative in any normal recognized sense. The bouncer at the entrance to a club whose employer gives instructions that they are to refuse to allow entry to ethnic minorities or female women has no association as such with those people. Rather, the discrimination that is intended to be directed towards the people refused entry has an additional discriminatory effect on another person – the bouncer. In this sense, the discrimination is 'transferred' from one party to another, although the discrimination to the other party may well remain.

It is clear that this form of discrimination could apply in all the protected characteristics identified in the Equality Act 2010. Not all of these types of discrimination are peripheral or incidental to the purposes of the legislation, but some lie at its core. So, if A discriminates against B because B's spouse is black; because B's children are girls; because B is a carer for a disabled dependant relative; because B's friend is a Muslim; because B provides services to homosexuals or transsexuals; because B's friend is married or pregnant; or because B's spouse is of a particular age, then discrimination by association has occurred.

The issue became particularly obvious with the differences between the original legislation on sex and race discrimination. The Race Relations Act 1976, section 1(1) covered less favourable treatment 'on racial grounds' whereas the Sex Discrimination Act 1975, section 1(1) covered less favourable

---

[15] In this Debate I draw extensively on my 'Discrimination by Association' [2007] *Web Journal of Current Legal Issues*. http://webjcl.ncl.ac.ukk/2007.issue4/honeyball4.html.

treatment 'on the grounds of [the claimant's] sex'. This was despite the fact that, in the vast majority of other respects, the two Acts were very similar. The issue particularly came to the fore with *Coleman v Attridge Law*,[16] a case of disability discrimination. This case is unusual in that it was a reference to the European Court of Justice made directly from an employment tribunal. The claimant, who was herself not disabled, argued that her employers had treated her unfavourably due to her need to care for her disabled son. She based this on the fact that Article 2.1 of the Equal Treatment Framework Directive[17] states that the principle of equal treatment means that there shall be no direct or indirect discrimination whatsoever 'on any of the grounds' referred to in Article 1. These are, namely, religion or belief, disability, age and sexual orientation regarding 'employment and occupation'. There is no restriction of these grounds to those relating to the claimant only but, in addition, the wording reflects that in other Council Directives, namely the Equal Pay Directive,[18] the Equal Treatment Directive[19] and the Race Directive.[20] She succeeded.

THE LAW

It was curious that, prior to the Equality Act 2010, different discrimination provisions contained different approaches to this issue. Associative discrimination was not specifically identified in any legislation[21] as a head of claim. Indeed, the term 'discrimination by association' had no statutory or, it seems, even judicial uniform basis. Whether it was covered in any given instance was a matter of construction of the relevant provision only. This was particularly curious given that there had been various amendments to these provisions since they were first introduced and yet the opportunity had not been taken to iron out the inconsistencies between them. The distinction had, after all, been one that has been noticed for some time in the jurisprudence of the courts, even if the reasons for it had not been explored. That this has not happened suggests that it is thought that there is a rational basis for it.

However, it is not at all clear what justification there could have been for treating sex and race differently in relation to this. Nevertheless, the government in its Green Paper on harmonization of discrimination law prior to the 2010 Act

---

[16] *Coleman v Attridge Law* [2008] ICR 1128. See M. Pilgerstorfer and S. Forshaw, 'Transferred Discrimination in European Law' (2008) 37 *Industrial Law Journal* 384.

[17] Council Directive No.2000/78/EC.

[18] Council Directive No.75/117, Art.1.

[19] Council Directive No.76/207, Art.2.

[20] Council Directive No.2000/43, Art.2.

[21] Namely the Sex Discrimination Act 1975, the Race Relations Act 1976, the Disability Discrimination Act 1995, the Employment Equality (Religion or Belief) Regulations 2003, the Employment Equality (Sexual Orientation) Regulations 2007 and the Employment Equality (Age) Regulations 2006.

indicated that it did not see the need for harmonization in this regard. It merely stated that, although discrimination by association on the grounds of race (along with other grounds) was rightly covered in existing legislation, the law of sex discrimination was aimed at protecting people in relation to their actual sex, not their perceived sex or because they associate with someone of a particular sex. They saw no 'practical benefit' in extending the law.[22] This suggested that the government did not envisage situations where discrimination by association with regard to sex was of significance, rather than because it saw any powerful arguments in principle for treating it differently to race discrimination. Indeed, apart from the possibly of gender reassignment (which clearly has no racial equivalent) and possibly a different degree of social impact (which would be highly questionable) there seems to be no difference between the two that could justify different treatment based on principle. The barman who is dismissed for refusing to obey instructions not to serve women should surely have the same protection as if he had been instructed not to serve blacks. Or the man who is discriminated against because his offer of a job is withdrawn because he is called Lesley, the employer having the mistaken belief that he is a woman, should surely have the same protection as if a woman called Lesley had been refused for the same reason. This would seem to be axiomatic.

As I have said, there were, however, divergent approaches in later discrimination legislation and there may have been good reasons for this. The Disability Discrimination Act 1995 required the discrimination to be for a reason which related to the disabled person's disability.[23] It had been thought that this excluded the possibility of discrimination by association, although on the wording that would not seem to be an inevitable conclusion. It does not appear that, in expanding the 1995 Act in the Disability Discrimination Act 2005, the Government considered including the possibility of discrimination by association in considering the definition of discrimination.[24] However, the issue was raised by the Disability Law Association with the Disability Rights Commission when it was consulting on the definition of disability prior to the 2005 Act and the DRC remained unconvinced that to do so would be 'proportionate'.[25] However, under Reg. 3 of the Employment Equality (Religion or Belief) Regulations[26] as in their original form, a person (A) discriminated against B if A treated B less favourably 'on the grounds of religion or belief'.

[22] 'A Framework for Fairness' (Department for Communities and Local Government, 2007) pp. 35–36.
[23] Section 3A, as inserted by the Disability Discrimination Act 1995 (Amendment) Regulations 2003 (SI 2003 No. 1673).
[24] See the Memorandum from the Department for Work and Pensions (DDB 96) to the Joint Committee on the Draft Disability Discrimination Bill at para.4 – http://www.parliament.the-stationery-office.com/pa/jt200304/jtselect/jtdisab/82/4033108.htm.
[25] 'A Framework for Fairness', n 22, p. 35.
[26] 2003 SI 2003 No. 1660.

This suggests that discrimination by association was covered by the provision. However, section 77(2) of the Equality Act 2006 changed this to treatment of A by B 'on the grounds of the religion or belief of B or any other person except A (whether or not it is also A's religion or belief)'. It is interesting that this seems to make quite explicit that discrimination by association was still caught by the definition, but explicitly excluded the discriminator only. It is not clear why it was thought necessary to change this aspect of the definition, except for the obvious fact that it was to bring it into line with the definition in section 44 which extended protection against discrimination on grounds of religion or belief to the provision of goods, facilities, services, education, premises and the exercise of public functions.

The Employment Equality (Sexual Orientation) Regulations 2003,[27] generally considered to be the sibling of the Religion or Belief Regulations, likewise stated only that discrimination occurred when it was 'on grounds of sexual orientation'.[28] Although this seemed to include the possibility of discrimination by association, it did not do so explicitly in the way that the Religion or Belief Regulations did. It was certainly the government's explicit intention that discrimination by association should be covered in new Regulations covering the provision of goods and services.[29] It was also the government's understanding that the 2003 sexual orientation regulations already covered discrimination by association.[30] The Equality Act (Sexual Orientation) Regulations 2007[31] therefore explicitly did so using similar wording in Reg. 3(1).

I will give one more example. The Employment Equality (Age) Regulations 2006[32] seemed to exclude entirely the possibility of discrimination by association on grounds of age by requiring that discrimination by A must be 'on grounds of B's age'.[33] The government did not intend to alter this, the reason being, in effect, that too many categories of persons were affected by discrimination by association on this ground, namely 'parents, carers, teachers, dependants and many others, taking the legislation far beyond its intended scope'.[34] This was a most curious argument, and the mirror version of that for not extending coverage to cases of sex discrimination considered earlier. It seems that the government was not persuaded by views that there

---

[27] SI 2003 No. 1661.

[28] Reg. 3(1)(a).

[29] See the Department of Trade and Industry's *Getting Equal: Proposals to Outlaw Sexual Orientation Discrimination in the Provision of Goods and Services* at http://www.stonewall.org.uk/documents/getting_equal_march_2006.pdf.

[30] 'A Framework for Fairness', n 22, p. 36.

[31] SI 2007 No. 1263.

[32] SI 2006 No. 1031.

[33] Reg. 3(1)(a).

[34] 'A Framework for Fairness', n 22, p. 36.

was a great need for such an extension in the law and neither by the argument that its effect would be minimal.

The position under the Equality Act, s. 13 now is that A discriminates B if, *because of a protected characteristic,* A treats B less favourably than A treats or would treat others. So, associative discrimination would appear to be covered for any protected characteristic. However, should this be the case? There are several arguments why it should.

THE ARGUMENTS IN FAVOUR

The first argument is one of social policy. This turns on the idea that all discrimination legislation exists to effect social change. Its aims are to protect those in society from detrimental treatment on grounds that are unjustified in moral principle. It is also functional in the sense that it seeks to bring about change in social attitudes by making such grounds recognized by the public at large as being morally unacceptable as grounds of action or decision. This being the case, it does not matter (the argument might run) in what manner or by what route anyone is detrimentally treated on such grounds. If they are, that is enough to make such treatment unlawful.

There is clearly much force in this argument in that it reflects the public perception of discrimination legislation. It would also seem to have much weight in morality, and appears to be almost self-evidently justifiable. A difficulty with the argument, however, as a tool for the construction of existing legislation, is that the historical basis for much discrimination legislation does not lie in moral considerations, but in economic and political ones, as I have already explained. Furthermore, the law itself does not fully support such a view of its foundation as is shown, for example, by the inability to bring class actions.

The second argument is that there is virtue in principle for legislation, the justification of which exists in the pursuit of a single principled aim, to achieve that with the maximum amount of consistency. For different pieces of discrimination legislation to have unnecessary differences clearly tends against that. This is not only undesirable but also is irrational, and it is undoubtedly a fundamental feature of good law that it does not display irrationality. However, it is also arguable that the protected characteristics in the Equality Act 2010 do not belong to any identifiable genus, other than that they concern areas of social life where discrimination has been such a problem that it has been deemed necessary for the law to intervene.

Closely linked to this argument is the practical one that the EU Framework Directive provides an overarching justification for all discrimination legislation. As we have seen, it clearly provides for the inclusion of discrimination by association within its definition of discrimination. Article 2.1

states that the principle of equal treatment shall mean that there shall be no direct or indirect discrimination whatsoever 'on any of the grounds' referred to in Article 1, namely religion or belief, disability, age or sexual orientation regarding 'employment and occupation'. It is therefore arguable that any failure to include discrimination by association within domestic legislation will involve a breach of the Directive. A further practical consideration is that not to include discrimination by association within the definition of discrimination would leave open the door to forms of direct discrimination failing to be covered by the legislation. In other words, some unlawful discrimination could be avoided by diverting or directing the discriminatory act to a person who is not within a designated protected category. This form would appear to include unintentional as well as intentional discrimination. Even if this were to have an indirect detrimental impact on the person within that category, that is not something that comes under the statutory definitions of indirect discrimination. This is because such discrimination requires, for example, a provision, criterion or practice to be applied to the person with the protected characteristic. By definition, this is not the case with discrimination by association.

A final argument is that discrimination by association is a two-way concept. If one thinks of it as transferred discrimination, this idea is a little clearer. If A treats B less favourably than they treat, or would treat, C on a ground that pertains not to B but to D, then it can be seen that, whilst A (in principle if not in law) discriminates against B, they may also be discriminating against D. This is, of course, contingent rather than necessary in practical terms, but in psychological, social and moral terms it may be seen to be much stronger than that. There is something that is (perhaps necessarily) diminishing to D if, because of a feature or characteristic that pertains to him or her that is a protected ground if applied to D directly, B thereby suffers a detriment. D has become the instrument of detrimental treatment to B for reasons that, in other circumstances, are considered sufficient grounds for legal protection.

THE ARGUMENTS AGAINST

There are, however, some arguments for excluding discrimination by association from the definition of discrimination. One argument is that, far from advancing the moral purpose of anti-discrimination legislation, to include discrimination by association in the 2010 Act allows discrimination of the very type the legislation seeks to forbid. One only needs to consider the case of *Redfearn v Serco Ltd*[35] to understand the possibilities here. The employee, who

---

[35] *Redfearn v Serco Ltd* [2006] IRLR 623.

was white, was unable to bring an unfair dismissal claim against his employers because of insufficient continuity of employment. He thus brought a claim under the Race Relations Act 1976 that he had been dismissed 'on racial grounds'. The grounds were his membership of the British National Party, restricted to whites, and which espoused right wing views on racial matters. He claimed that he was dismissed on the grounds of the ethnic origin (primarily Asian) of the members of the public with whom he closely worked. The employers claimed that they dismissed him on grounds of health and safety, fearing violence from fellow employees and Asian members of the public if they were to discover his political (indeed racial) opinions. The employers also feared annoyance and anger would be directed towards them for continuing to employ someone with his views, even though these had never been aired at work. Unsurprisingly, perhaps, Mr Redfearn lost his case in the employment tribunal, but unexpectedly won in the Employment Appeal Tribunal. Even more startlingly, the appeal tribunal refused to grant leave to appeal, which he sought and obtained from the Court of Appeal, but which eventually decided against him. It is a dangerous strategy to rely on the courts to give effect to the policy of the legislation when the wording of the text seems to go against it. The difficulty here is that it is problematic to arrive at a definition of discrimination that includes discrimination by association that does not allow people like Mr Redfearn to succeed. It should include a restriction on the field of application of the definition determined by particular policy considerations.

A second policy consideration is that to include discrimination by association does not necessarily protect the intended group or category. It is not immediately obvious why someone who does not belong to such a category protected by legislation should be protected as if they were members of it. Whilst initially attractive, this argument does seem to fall to two replies. The first is that, insofar as the legislation is at all created in order to eradicate discrimination driven by certain attitudes and beliefs, the mechanism required to give effect to that is irrelevant. It is a consideration quite distinct from directly protecting members of those particular groups. The second is that discrimination often occurs in situations where a person is being used merely as the agency by which discrimination against someone in a protected group is sought to be brought about. This is most obvious in those cases involving instructions to discriminate. Whilst it might be possible for those in the protected categories to bring claims in such circumstances, this is an additional means of protection.

Debate 4

What is the best causation test for discrimination?

If someone wishes to bring a claim under the Equality Act 2010 it is necessary to show that there is a link between their protected characteristic and the alleged discriminatory act. Without this there cannot, of course, be any liability. Where this is direct discrimination the test is that the discrimination has occurred 'because of' a protected characteristic.[36] The way that this has been shown to occur in legislation is by way of a comparison between the claimant and others. So, under the 2010 Act it is necessary to show that, because of a protected characteristic, A (the defendant) has treated B less favourably than A treats or would treat others.

Such an approach would seem to be necessary in order to establish discrimination in that it appears inherent in the idea of discrimination that there is a comparison between treatments of two people, or sets of people. It is not confined to direct discrimination where (in broad terms) it is necessary to show that A has been treated less favourably than somebody of the opposite sex (B) or would have been so treated if there is in fact no-one of the opposite sex with which to compare oneself. It also applies to indirect discrimination which occurs when A discriminates against B if A applies a 'provision, criterion or practice' which is discriminatory in relation to a relevant protected characteristic of B's. It is discriminatory if A applies, or would apply, the provision, criterion or practice to persons with whom B does not share the characteristic; it puts, or would put, persons with whom B shares the characteristic at a particular disadvantage when compared with persons with whom B does not share it; it puts, or would put, B at this disadvantage; and A cannot show it to be a proportionate means of achieving a legitimate aim. There is, as might be assumed, a great deal of case-law on each of these elements. I will not go into this case-law now, because I am simply making the point here that, be the discrimination direct or indirect, a comparative element is required by the legislation.

However, it is not at all clear that a comparative element is required by this principle. Indeed, there has long been recognition that some types of discrimination do not require this sort of comparison. It is no longer necessary to show that pregnancy discrimination is sex discrimination in that 'pregnancy and maternity' is a distinct head of protected characteristics, independently of sex, in the Equality Act 2010. However, when it was necessary to bring pregnancy cases under the sex discrimination legislation it was held that it was not necessary for the woman to be compared with a comparator,

---

[36] Section 13.

real or hypothetical. This is understandable. In that pregnancy is peculiar to women, at least in the present state of medical science, it would appear to be a very arguable view that it is impossible to compare pregnant women to men.

The European Court of Justice in *Dekker*[37] (a case brought under the Equal Treatment Directive) held that a comparison was not necessary between the treatment of women and either a real or hypothetical man, or vice versa. The reasoning was very simple. The Court stated that this was because only women could be refused employment on the ground of pregnancy. It followed that such a refusal therefore constituted direct discrimination on the ground of sex. This is, of course, not strictly true. A man can be discriminated against on the grounds of pregnancy, for example because he has made a woman pregnant and refuses to marry her. What cannot occur (at least at present) is that he is discriminated against on the grounds of his own pregnancy. With the expansion of associative discrimination considered in the previous Debate, this would seem to open up several further possibilities. However, the European Court of Justice also held that the reason for the refusal was also very important. If that reason were to be found in the fact that the person concerned were pregnant, that was sufficient. This is because at the time, it will be remembered, it was necessary to show that the discrimination amounted to sex discrimination, there being no separate head for pregnancy, and only women could become pregnant. Thus the Court seemed to conflate the two issues as to whether there can be sex discrimination when it is on the grounds of pregnancy and whether a comparator was required in such circumstances. The Court seemed to take it as self-evident.

It would also seem possible, in principle, for a comparison in pregnancy cases to be drawn between pregnant women and others, be they male or female, who have a medical condition or some other characteristic that entails them having circumstances that lead employers to discriminate against pregnant women. So, for example, if it is because women need time off work, or cause other organizational disruption because of their pregnancy, they could be compared with others with characteristics that lead to the same requirements. This was attempted in a few cases, but the argument against it was that this somehow denigrated women and pregnancy.[38] It is difficult to see how this argument has much strength in that it is predicated on the idea that those who are ill have somehow been denigrated themselves, or have been otherwise denigrated, by their illness, which would be very difficult to maintain.

Robert Wintemute has argued that comparison is always required in a

---

[37] *Dekker v Stichting Vormingscentrum voor Jonge Volwassenen-Plus* [1991] IRLR 27.
[38] See *Boyle v Equal Opportunities Commission* [1998] IRLR 717.

discrimination claim, be it direct or indirect, because equality is a comparative concept. He has written:

> 'When an individual claims direct discrimination, they compare their treatment with that (actually or hypothetically) received by another person and argue that the difference in treatment would not have occurred "but for" a particular difference between them and the other person which is a prohibited ground (e.g. sex). The treatment of one person can only be "less favourable" when compared with that of another person. When a person claims indirect discrimination, they argue that neutral treatment applied to them and to other persons has a disproportionate impact on their group (defined by one manifestation of the prohibited ground) when compared with the impact the treatment has on other groups (defined by manifestations of the prohibited ground). Comparison is thus essential to show either that the prohibited ground is the cause of or reason for the different (less favourable) treatment, or to demonstrate the disproportionate impact of neutral treatment. Claims of discrimination without comparison are impossible'.[39]

However, it is not altogether clear that this is the case. What has to be established in principle is that someone has been discriminated against because of a protected characteristic. Let me take associative discrimination out of the picture for this purpose and assume that the protected characteristic is one possessed by the claimant. With regard to showing adverse treatment of the claimant because of a protected characteristic, it would appear that the way to establish that would be to keep as many of the features of the scenario as intact as possible between the two sides of the comparison and remove merely the discriminatory feature to establish if there is, or would have been, a difference. In other words, in a case of race discrimination for example, what would need to be involved is the removal of the racial features, but all other variables would remain. This takes out the possibility that it is one of the other, non-racial, features that is the reason for the discrimination. If that is accepted, it would appear to be desirable, and even necessary, that a comparator is not involved, because that comparator would bring with them a host of other features that could form the reason for the discrimination. If only racial features in my example were to be removed that would entail that the comparison would need to be between the claimant with her racial characteristic and the claimant again without her racial characteristic. So, although a comparison would still be required, it would be self-comparison, not comparison with a comparator. The purity, if it can be called that, of the comparison process requires this methodology.

---

[39] R. Wintemute, 'When is Pregnancy Discrimination Indirect Discrimination?' (1998) 27 *Industrial Law Journal* 23.

There is a powerful counter-argument to this idea, however. The courts have attempted an approach to comparison that does not require a comparator, and this is the so-called 'but-for' test. This derives from the House of Lords' decision in *James v Eastleigh Borough Council*.[40] This is the idea that direct discrimination occurs when a person is treated in a particular way if they would not have been *but for* some fact about them. Thus a woman is discriminated against because of her sex when she is treated in a particular way which would not have occurred but for the fact that she was a woman. Hence no comparison is required. However, it would not seem to be a test that defines or delineates direct discrimination at all. It can be applied equally well to indirect discrimination cases in that it is possible to say that, but for the victim's sex, she would not have had a provision, criterion or practice applied to her which women are less able to fulfil than men, or at least, but for her sex, the woman would not have failed to satisfy the requirement or condition which is applied to both sexes.

It would seem, in any event, that the 'but-for' idea is flawed as a useful causal test of discrimination. Consider, for example, a case of race discrimination.[41] Imagine an argument that a claimant has been discriminated against because they are white in that they have been discriminated against because they have red hair. There are four relevant categories, it seems to me, in such an analysis – (1) all white people; (2) naturally red-headed people; (3) white people with other-coloured hair; and (4) all non-white people. The composition of, and the relationship between, these groups is crucial to understanding whether discrimination has occurred. Category (1) consists entirely of categories (2) and (3). Categories (2) and (3) belong only to category (1) and never to (4). Those in category (4) cannot belong to any of categories (1), (2) or (3). The argument that to discriminate against a redhead is necessarily to discriminate against them on the grounds of their race is to say this: discrimination based on membership of (2) is discrimination on grounds of sex because (2) is in (1) (a feature shared by (3)) and never in (4) which is a distinction based on race. The illogicality is, I presume, clear. Is there discrimination against redheads because they are white people because only white people are natural redheads? Of course not, because category (3) is relevant – it may be that redheads are discriminated against only as against natural blondes, who also do not belong to category (4) but do belong to (1), along with those in (2). They may never be discriminated against as against non-whites. There would not have been discrimination but for the fact that the redheads were white, but that is not the reason for the discrimination. It can hardly be labelled race discrimination. The treatment is not in favour of non-whites. That category, (4), (though relevant to note in that it completes the possible categories) is not active in either. And yet it is quite true of course that,

40 *James v Eastleigh Borough Council* [1990] IRLR 288.
41 See my 'Pregnancy and Sex Discrimination' (2000) 29 *Industrial Law Journal* 43.

but for being white, the redheads would not have been discriminated against. But that does not mean it was because of their whiteness that they were discriminated against, for the reasons I have given.

Debate 5

Is there a difference between direct and indirect discrimination?

The Equality Act 2010 makes a distinction between direct and indirect sex discrimination. This is something that has had a place in the legislation since the earliest days of discrimination. So, as I have already shown, but it is worth repeating for ease here, indirect discrimination occurs when A discriminates against B if A applies a 'provision, criterion or practice' which is discriminatory in relation to a relevant protected characteristic of B's. It is discriminatory if A applies, or would apply, the provision, criterion or practice to persons with whom B does not share the characteristic; it puts, or would put, persons with whom B shares the characteristic at a particular disadvantage when compared with persons with whom B does not share it; it puts, or would put, B at this disadvantage; and A cannot show it to be a proportionate means of achieving a legitimate aim. It is thought necessary to include indirect discrimination because, without it, a person could easily avoid the Act by stating that some characteristic, other than one of the protected characteristics, was necessary or desirable in the employee it was looking for, even though this had a detrimental effect particularly on one group having a protected characteristic. So, to take commonly-cited examples, if a building firm were to state that it required applicants for a 'brickie' to work shirtless, or a pub owner were to say that it required its bar staff to wear short skirts, this would amount to indirect discrimination.

It might seem obvious that it is a necessity if the Act is to be effective to include both direct and indirect forms of discrimination. However, I will here put forward a different view. This is that it is necessary only if one begins with the idea of direct discrimination. However, if the legislation were merely to include indirect discrimination it is not at all clear that the legislation would not be just as effective. This is partly for a contingent, purely factual, reason. Of course direct discrimination occurs – people are discriminated against because they have a protected characteristic. However, it may not happen so much as it might appear. If a woman is discriminated against, is it frequently simply because she is a woman? In the employment sphere is it common that women fail to be offered a job or be promoted because of simple misogyny? This, I would suggest, is very debatable. It is far more likely that she will be discriminated against because of something that is associated with her being a woman, such as that she will be more likely to want time off for family reasons, that she will be less ruthlessly efficient than a man, or that she will be less logical and more emotional in her decision-making than a man. Indeed, it may even be that she should not be an assistant referee at a football match because, it is thought, women do not understand the offside rule. Of course, I am not seeking to defend discrimination in these circumstances because in each case to make such assumptions about someone because of their sex is simply wrong. However, the point is that the discrimination occurs because of something that is associated with the woman's sex, or perceived to be. In other words, even though the language of the discrimination may be in terms of it being direct – she is discriminated against because she is a woman – it is also possible to view it entirely as being indirect in that it arises because of something that is associated with her being a woman.

It is easy, of course, to make the same point with regard to the other protected characteristics. Disability discrimination at work occurs because some employers do not feel they can or want to take the necessary steps to make a disabled worker as efficient as other employees, or see that the disabled worker is in fact as capable of doing the job as well as any employee who is not disabled without any adjustments needing to be made. Again, I would doubt that few employers discriminate against disabled workers irrespective of their ability to do the job and simply because they have that protected characteristic.

It does not follow from what I am putting forward here that the legislation should abandon the notion of protecting people from direct discrimination. If that were to be the case then the out-and-out misogynist or racist would escape the legislation. But it would give a different focus to the legislation, not least because there are important differences between direct and indirect discrimination not simply as methods by which the fact of discrimination can be established. One is that there is no justification defence for most cases of direct discrimination but there is for indirect discrimination in that if the employer can show that the provision, criterion or practice is a proportionate means of achieving a legitimate aim, no claim is made out.[42] It has been argued, however, that there should be no difference in this regard, but it remains a matter of debate.[43] So, if what initially appears to be a case of direct discrimination can also be interpreted as indirect discrimination, it would

---

[42] This is invariably referred to as a defence, but technically it is not in that it is part of the definition of indirect discrimination. In other words, if the alleged discriminatory act is a proportionate means of achieving a legitimate aim there is no indirect discrimination at all, and therefore there is no form of discrimination that requires a defence.

[43] See J. Bowers and E. Moran, 'Justification in Direct Sex Discrimination Law: Breaking the Taboo' (2002) 31 *Industrial Law Journal* 307; cf T. Gill and K. Monaghan, 'Justification in Direct Sex Discrimination Law: Taboo Upheld' (2003) 32 *Industrial Law Journal* 115. However, see too the counter-reply by J. Bowers, E. Moran and S. Honeyball, 'Justification in Direct Sex Discrimination: a Reply' (2003) *Industrial Law Journal* 185.

seem to follow that the defence to the indirect discrimination claim could be made out.

Further Reading

Aristotle, *Ethica Nicomachea*, Book V (ed. W. Ross, Oxford University Press, 1925).

J. Bowers and E. Moran, 'Justification in Direct Sex Discrimination Law: Breaking the Taboo' (2002) 31 *Industrial Law Journal* 307.

J. Bowers, E. Moran and S. Honeyball, 'Justification in Direct Sex Discrimination: a Reply' (2003) *Industrial Law Journal* 185.

R. Dahrendorf, 'On the Origin of Social Inequality' in P. Laslett and W.G. Runciman (eds), *Philosophy, Politics and Society* (Basil Blackwell, 1964) ch.5.

S. Fredman, *Women and the Law* (Clarendon Press, 1997).

T. Gill and K. Monaghan, 'Justification in Direct Sex Discrimination Law: Taboo Upheld' (2003) 32 *Industrial Law Journal* 115.

D. Hellman, *When Is Discrimination Wrong?* (Harvard University Press, 2008).

S. Honeyball, 'Pregnancy and Sex Discrimination' (2000) 29 *Industrial Law Journal* 43.

S. Honeyball, 'Discrimination by Association' [2007] *Web Journal of Current Legal Issues* http://webjcl.ncl.ac.ukk/2007.issue4/honeyball4.html.

T. Macklem, *Beyond Comparison* (Cambridge University Press, 2003).

M. Pilgerstorfer and S. Forshaw, 'Transferred Discrimination in European Law' (2008) 37 *Industrial Law Journal* 384.

D. Thomson, *Equality* (Cambridge University Press, 1949).

P. Westen, 'The Empty Idea of Equality' (1982) 95 *Harvard Law Review* 537.

R. Wintemute, 'When is Pregnancy Discrimination Indirect Discrimination?' (1998) 27 *Industrial Law Journal* 23.

5

TERMINATION OF EMPLOYMENT

INTRODUCTION

For most people, having employment is one of the most important features of their lives, and probably the most important outside their family. Whilst obtaining a job can be a very disruptive and life-changing event, losing it can be even more so. In this chapter I will consider a number of issues arising out of the termination of employment. I will begin by considering whether it can be justified for legal remedies to be dependent upon the employee having acquired a period of employment with an employer. I will then examine if the concept of dismissal in law is coherent and then consider issues concerning the idea of termination by agreement of the parties. I will conclude by assessing whether or not the law provides adequate protection to employees when they are dismissed, and how far the law of unfair dismissal is really concerned with fairness.

Debate 1

Are the eligibility requirements for statutory employment protection justified?

In order to claim for statutory employment protection remedies it is essential that the claimant fulfils the eligibility requirements. These are well-established, but it is not altogether clear that there is justification for all of them. I will consider two of them in particular here, namely the requirement of employment status and the requirement for a period of continuous employment.

EMPLOYMENT

Workers wishing to claim for statutory employment protection remedies must be employees. Who amounts to an employee varies from Act to Act. For example, for the purposes of unfair dismissal and redundancy amongst other matters this is determined by the definition of employment in the Employment Rights Act 1996[1] which states, none too helpfully, that employment means employment under a contract of employment. A contract of employment in turn is defined as a contract of service or apprenticeship, whether express or implied, and (if it is express) whether it is oral or in writing.[2] An employee is likewise defined as an individual who has entered into or works under (or, where employment has ceased, worked under) a contract of employment.[3] On the other hand, under the discrimination legislation 'employment' is defined more widely as:

a) employment under a contract of employment, a contract of apprenticeship or a contract personally to do work;
b) Crown employment;
c) employment as a relevant member of the House of Commons staff; or
d) employment as a relevant member of the House of Lords staff.[4]

In one sense it is entirely logical that the statutory remedies should be available to employees only. I considered in a previous chapter the idea that it is not the case that the remedies are extended only to employees, but that those types of workers who are considered, as a matter of policy, should be entitled to protection are defined as employees. In other words, as I put it there, the term 'employee' is merely a form of shorthand for whoever is determined as a matter of policy to be entitled. It is therefore to put the position wrongly to state that only employees should be entitled to claim for the statutory remedies, because it is rather that those who are entitled to claim are called employees, however defined. When addressing the issue of whether the statutory protection remedies should be available only to employees the focus must therefore be on the extent of the definition rather than any abstract notion of who is an employee.

It is not clear why the definition of employee in the Employment Rights Act 1996 is defined so narrowly, for several reasons. First, the dividing line between employment and other forms of work relationships do not seem to relate closely to the purposes of the relevant Act. For example, it is not clear why someone who requires to be paid for their services may have protection against unfair dismissal, but someone who works on an entirely voluntary basis can be unfairly dismissed without redress. But that is the inevitable consequence of defining an employee as someone who works under a contract of employment, because where there is no consideration moving from the

---

[1] Employment Rights Act 1996 (hereafter ERA), s. 230(5).
[2] s. 230(2).
[3] s. 230(1).
[4] Equality Act 2010, s. 83.

employer there can be no contract at all. But it might be no less important for the volunteer to have protection in their position. Neither is it at all obvious why someone who, under the terms of their work contract, may delegate their obligations to someone else, but who never does, should be denied an employment protection remedy.[5] It might be clear why they should not be termed an employee in the ordinary everyday sense but less clear why the provider of their work should be entitled to terminate their relationship unfairly. Even if, in this case, it might be thought that a necessary degree of dependence is lacking,[6] it would seem to be a logical leap from there to argue that dependence on someone is a necessary condition of being treated fairly by them.

Likewise, it is difficult to see why the discrimination legislation is open to a wider category of workers to those entitled to unfair dismissal and redundancy protection. If I hire a gardener to come to my home twice a week, and he does so for many years, I am able to terminate our relationship without fear of legal redress if I do so because I dislike the way he combs his hair, as he is unlikely to be my employee under the 1996 Act. But I cannot dismiss him without legal redress because he is bald, because that is a condition that affects men far more than women. To my gardener, the fact of the unfair treatment is what matters, more than the underlying basis of it. My argument here is not that there should be one definition of employment to cover various types of claim. Rather, my point is that the dividing line between what amounts to employment and what is not, however defined, is not always clearly correlated to the policy of the legislation.

CONTINUOUS EMPLOYMENT

In addition to being an employee, the worker who wishes to claim for unfair dismissal or redundancy must, in the main,[7] also have a period of continuous employment dating from the termination of their employment backwards. For unfair dismissal claims this must be one year,[8] and two years for redundancy.[9]

In one sense, the requirement of continuity works in favour of the employee

---

[5] See *Express and Echo Publications Ltd v Tanton* [1999] IRLR 367.

[6] It is difficult to see how the power under a contract that a worker has to delegate tasks to someone else necessarily makes that worker any less dependent on the party who provides them with that work.

[7] If the dismissal is connected with trade union membership or activities, pregnancy or maternity, health and safety, the assertion of a statutory right, a public interest disclosure or the refusal of a retail or betting worker to work on a Sunday, there is no qualifying period required at all – ERA 1996, s. 108(3). Where the dismissal follows a refusal by the employer to pay an employee who is suspended from work on medical grounds, there is a four-week qualification period.

[8] Unfair Dismissal (Variation of Qualifying Period) Order 1999 No. 1436. The coalition government has announced, however, that this will increase to two years.

[9] ERA 1996, s. 155.

in that one of its purposes is to overcome the common law rule that every fundamental change of terms constitutes a new contract. This doctrine would artificially restrict employee rights if statutory protection were limited to contracts of employment rather than employment itself. The statutory concept of continuity thus means there can be continuity of employment even though that employment consists of a number of different contracts. Given that there is deemed to be a requirement of some form of accumulated period of employment in order to be entitled to make certain claims, the concept of continuity prevents employers from constantly firing and re-hiring employees to prevent them from being able to claim unfair dismissal or redundancy when it finally decides not to re-hire.

On the other hand, the requirement of continuity means that many employees do not have statutory employment protection, regardless of the unfairness that may result. It is difficult to see why employees need to accumulate periods of employment at all to protect them from the actions of an unfair employer. One argument for the requirement of continuity is that it gives the parties an opportunity for a trial period. If it does not work out, their relationship can be terminated by the employer without fear of legal redress. That may be true, but there is nothing in the law of unfair dismissal that prevents an employer from dismissing employees because the relationship has not worked out because the employee does not fit in. The law gives redress only where the employer has fired the employee unfairly. It is an odd argument to the effect that it is fair to allow an employer to dismiss its employees unfairly.

Another argument in favour of requiring continuity is that an employee who loses their job after a short time in work has not really suffered very much. This is palpably not true in many cases. As I have mentioned before, an employee who leaves a secure job far away, moves house and family, and maybe leaves friends and extended family behind, has lost a great deal, on top of the financial cost of moving home, stamp duty and removal expenses. In any event, even one year's employment is hardly a short time. To be vulnerable during that period to a whim of an employer who does not care for your haircut is difficult to justify.

A closely-related, but different, argument is this. If the employee has a right to unfair dismissal protection in the initial period of their employment, and successfully brings a claim, their compensation will likely be very small, and does not justify troubling an employment tribunal. This argument ignores several points. First, it is hardly a justification for the law to fail to provide a remedy at all because the alternative would be to provide a very poor one. But, furthermore, it is the fact of having suffered an injustice that makes it right for the law to provide a remedy. It is rarely a small matter for someone to lose a job, and even more rarely that they have lost it unfairly. In addition, there is the fact that it can be an important consideration for an employee for it to be established that they were dismissed unfairly and not for a justifiable reason. Although no employer likes the idea that an employee it is taking on has previously been prepared to take another employer to law for a remedy, this has to be weighed against the detriment to an employee who does not have a finding that they were not at fault in losing their previous employment. Finally, there is the point that, in any event, compensation is not the only remedy open to the employment tribunal. Although it is the remedy most often awarded, and to a large extent very often because of the employee's own position and wishes, there are also the remedies of reinstatement to the job from which they were unfairly dismissed, or re-engagement to an equivalent position with the same employer. Indeed, when unfair dismissal protection was introduced in the early 1970s, it was envisaged that these would be the primary remedies.

One of the arguments in favour of having a requirement of continuity is that the employee to a degree should earn the right to employment protection by showing a degree of loyalty to the employer's business. This is less obviously the case with unfair dismissal protection, but could be made out for redundancy. The purpose of redundancy payments in part, it could be argued, is to reward previous service. Because of this, the payment is owed to the employee even if they have immediately taken on another, perhaps better-paid, job and have suffered no financial loss in having been dismissed.[10] But if this is true, it is not clear that continuous employment is the obvious mechanism for it. Why should not accumulated service, consisting of aggregated periods each less than the two years of continuous service required but amounting to much more than that in total, be a better basis for such a reward for loyalty? When the courts have been confronted with this problem they have sometimes strained to find a way of converting the requirement of continuity into, in effect, an aggregate test.[11] At other times they have allowed

---

[10] There have been various attempts at explaining the justification for the redundancy legislative scheme, not all particularly convincing. Some have described it as establishing a 'proprietary interest in the job'. Thus, the President of Industrial Tribunals in *Wynes v Southrepps Hall Broiler Farm Ltd* [1968] 3 ITR 407 said that a long-term employee is considered to have a right of property in his job. Some have seen redundancy protection as having a role to play in assisting training and resettlement, and thus stimulating mobility of labour. However, as P. Elias, B. Napier, and P. Wallington pointed out (*Labour Law: Cases and Materials* (Butterworth, 1981) p. 646) this is difficult to sustain as a primary function, since the way in which payments are assessed means that the most money goes to the older, longer-serving workers who are the least likely, as a group, to be prepared to leave their homes and families in search of new work. Others have seen the payment less idealistically as a 'bribe' to employees to go quietly. Grunfeld described the scheme more pragmatically. He saw the original purpose of redundancy protection legislation as an attempt to mitigate the resistance of individual employees and their unions to the extensive changes demanded by British industry, commerce and finance to the 'searching demands of world trade and competition' (C. Grunfeld, *Law of Redundancy* (Sweet & Maxwell, 3rd edn, 1989) p. 2).

[11] See *Ford v Warwickshire County Council* [1983] IRLR 126.

employers to take advantage of their power to dismiss before sufficient continuity has been built up, in effect deliberately removing statutory protection from employees.[12]

If it is thought legitimate for claims under the Employment Rights Act 1996 to require a period of continuous employment, it might be thought that employment claims under other legislation would have the same requirement. However, this is not the case. For example, for discrimination claims under the Equality Act 2010 it is not necessary to have built up continuity. It is difficult to see what can found the distinction here. One argument might be that this would not be possible without contravening European Union law. In *R v Secretary of State ex parte Seymour-Smith and Perez*[13] the House of Lords had to consider the impact of the (then) two-year qualifying period for unfair dismissal on EU provisions on equal treatment. It held that the period had an adverse impact on women and thus was indirectly discriminatory, but that it could be justified as within the broad discretion that governments have in this field to encourage employers to recruit. There would seem to be no reason why this reasoning could not apply to the discrimination legislation itself.

Perhaps, therefore, the reason is that unfair dismissal legislation is more concerned with righting wrongs in individual cases, whereas the discrimination legislation is more concerned with social policy. However, as a matter of historical fact this is not so. The Equal Pay Act 1970 (the legislative first ancestor of the Equality Act 2010) was passed with more of an eye on creating a level economic playing field to ease the agreement of the French to the United Kingdom's accession to the Common Market, as it then was. Also, the omission, for example, of the possibility of bringing class actions in discrimination cases rather undercuts the idea that it was legislation brought about for policy ends.

Debate 2

Is the concept of dismissal coherent?

THE MEANING OF 'DISMISSAL'

If the employer terminates the employee's contract of employment, that amounts to a dismissal at common law. If the employer commits a sufficiently serious breach of contract (for example by giving insufficient notice) in the process of terminating the contract, that amounts to wrongful dismissal. The claim of wrongful dismissal therefore looks to form, and asks

---

[12] See *Booth v United States of America* [1999] IRLR 16.

[13] *R v Secretary of State for Employment ex parte Seymour-Smith and Perez (No.2)* [2000] IRLR 263.

the question as to whether there has been a breach of the terms of the contract of employment. It does not examine the fairness of the dismissal or the reasonableness of the terms being broken. The common law is not interested in such matters, only in giving remedies should the parties not abide by the terms of their agreement. It is thus left to statute, by way of the Employment Rights Act 1996, to provide substantive remedies for employment protection in the way of unfair dismissal and redundancy payments. For these purposes there is a rather different definition of dismissal than that which operates at common law. So the first complication is encountered, namely that the concept of dismissal applies in both a common law and statutory context but also that the concept is different in each case.

I will examine the importance of the differences between these definitions shortly, but first the point needs to be made that, although the concept of dismissal has its origins in the common law, it is one which does not apply generally in the field where people undertake to do work for others under a variety of contractual forms, but only to those situations where the parties have a contract of employment.[14]

It is also worth pointing out that dismissal does not cover all of the situations in which an employment contract comes to an end without the consent of the employee. Where it is terminated by operation of law, such as by way of frustration, death of either party or the winding up of a company or a partnership, there is no consent. Of course, one might be able to imply consent in such cases because it would surely normally go without saying that the parties would have readily agreed that there would be automatic termination in such circumstances, but there has nevertheless been no express consent.

It would seem to be because of the historical contractual basis of the concept of dismissal that it is not, even under statute, a concept applied to the termination of employment as such, but to the termination of contracts of employment. Although employment will cease on the termination of a contract of employment, it is not always the case that the termination of an employment contract will result in the termination of employment for the reason that one period of employment may consist in a series of different contracts of employment such as, for example, where the employee is promoted. As Sir Patrick Elias has pointed out, this has consequences which appear curious, for it permits the possibility that an employee might take unfair dismissal proceedings against an employer who has terminated their

---

[14] It therefore does not appear to apply to the whole of Mark Freedland's suggested wider concept of 'personal work or employment contracts' which I considered elsewhere in this book – see M. Freedland, *The Personal Employment Contract* (Oxford University Press, 2003) particularly ch.6.

contract, even though the employment relationship itself is maintained under a fresh service contract.[15] It is even more curious, perhaps, that the employee could also or alternatively make a claim for redundancy arising out of the same dismissal.

Employer termination

What amounts to dismissal under the Employment Rights Act 1996 for unfair dismissal and redundancy purposes is wider than at common law. However, the first limb of the definition is that which pertains at common law – namely when the contract under which the employee is employed is terminated by the employer, whether with or without notice.[16] This definition is not as straightforward as it would initially appear. For example, there is no definition in the Act as to what amounts to termination. This has caused the courts significant difficulties in a number of respects. For example, there is a wide range of tests that can be applied to this. The courts have tried to make matters as clear as possible by requiring that words of dismissal must be clear and unequivocal.[17] But that could mean a number of things. Is it what appeared to this employer to be clear; or what should have been clear to this employer; or what would have been understood by a reasonable employer in this employer's position; or what was clear to the employee; what should have been clear to this employee; or what a reasonable bystander would have understood by the words used? There are of course several other similar tests that could be applied, but the risk of tedium in setting out them all serves to illustrate how wide the range of possibilities is.

There are also technical difficulties that get in the way of identifying what might amount to a dismissal by the employer terminating the employment contract. Most people would understand, I imagine, that if they were told that they would be fired at some time over the next few weeks, depending upon when the employing company is wound up, that this would itself amount to a dismissal in law. But it does not,[18] and cannot. This is because it is essential for a number of purposes, as I have already examined, to establish a precise date on which employment is terminated. For example, it is necessary for making precise calculations of continuity of employment periods and when the employee has become available for work in order to be eligible for benefits.

---

15 P. Elias, 'Unravelling the Concept of Dismissal – I' [1978] *Industrial Law Journal* 16.

16 ERA 1996, ss. 95(1)(a), 136(1)(a). There is also a dismissal when the employer has given notice to the employee, but during that period the employee gives shorter counter-notice – ss. 95(2), 136(3). This is to deal with the situation where an employee, who may not have otherwise left their employment, on being dismissed seeks another job which they need or want to begin before their employer's notice expires. In such circumstances the reason for the dismissal remains that for the employer's notice as if there had there been no counter-notice.

17 See e.g. *Tanner v D.T. Kean Ltd* [1978] IRLR 110.

18 See e.g. *Doble v Firestone Tyre and Rubber Co. Ltd* [1981] IRLR 300.

There are occasions when the distinction between an employer termination and other ideas not amounting to dismissal is difficult to establish. For example, as I have mentioned above, the doctrine of frustration does not result in employment contracts terminating by way of dismissal, and that is one of the reasons the courts are reluctant to apply the doctrine to employment contracts in that the termination can then not be tested for fairness. Termination by reason of frustration is termination by operation of law. Similarly, it might be thought, if a contract were to terminate automatically because the law deems this to have happened when either party commits a repudiatory breach of contract, when the employer is the guilty party there can be no dismissal. Again, the termination would be by operation of law, the argument might go, and not by the employer. If this were to be the case it would mean, of course, that the employer would be able to avoid the consequences of the unfairness of its repudiatory breach.[19]

However, the normal contractual doctrine is against the 'automatic termination' theory in that 'an unaccepted repudiation is a thing writ in water', and this was restated by the House of Lords in *Photo Production Ltd v Securicor Transport Ltd*.[20] The courts sometimes took the view that a repudiation operated automatically to determine the contract of employment. Megarry V-C reviewed an extensive array of cases in what is still a very persuasive judgement in *Thomas Marshall (Exports) Ltd v Guinlé*[21] and rejected the automatic termination theory for convincing reasons. The first was concerned with policy – why should a person who makes a contract of service have the right at any moment to put an end to their contractual obligations? Secondly, he felt that any other decision would be difficult to reconcile with authority. Finally, he thought that the courts must be astute to prevent a wrongdoer from profiting too greatly from their wrong and this was supported by the discussion of the House of Lords on the general law of contract in *Photo Production*. The issue arose again in *London Transport Executive v Clarke*.[22] Dunn and Templeman LJJ referred to the automatic theory as contrary to principle, unsupported by authority and undesirable in practice. It was manifestly unjust to allow a wrongdoer to terminate a contract if the innocent party wished to affirm the contract for good reason. Lord Denning MR dissented, arguing that this weighted the scales too heavily against the employer. For him a fundamental breach or breach going to the root of the contract led to the

---

[19] It is important to remember that, although the employee may have a remedy here for the breach of contract itself, the common law does not give a remedy on the basis of any unfairness the breach might entail.

[20] *Photo Production Ltd v Securicor Transport Ltd* [1980] AC 827; [1980] 1 All ER 556.

[21] *Thomas Marshall (Exports) Ltd v Guinlé* [1974] IRLR 236.

[22] *London Transport Executive v Clarke* [1981] IRLR 166.

discharge of the contract without any need for acceptance. This happens when the misconduct of the employee is such that it is completely inconsistent with the continuance of the contract so that the ordinary member of the employment tribunal would say of the employee 'he sacked himself'. The House of Lords in *Rigby v Ferodo*[23] stated the now generally-accepted position. Although declining to consider whether or not as a general principle acceptance was always required to bring a contract which was the subject of a repudiatory breach to an end, it held that the circumstances in which it would not be necessary were limited to extreme cases where there was an outright wrongful dismissal by the employer or a walk-out by the employee. In *Boyo v Lambeth LBC*[24] the Court of Appeal therefore accepted that it was bound to hold that an unlawful repudiation was of no effect until accepted. The majority of the court stated however that, free from authority, they would have reached the opposite conclusion. It therefore remains a matter of lack of unanimity if not live debate.

There is, in my view, a further strong argument why the automatic termination theory is incorrect, if the conceptual integrity of the law in this area is to be maintained. Sections 237 and 238 of the Trade Union and Labour Relations (Consolidation) Act 1992 contain provisions concerning the dismissal of employees who are taking part in industrial action. Section 237 relates to those taking part in unofficial industrial action and s. 238 relates to other industrial action. It lays down the circumstances in which dismissals in those circumstances will or may be fair or unfair. The details for present purposes need not concern us. What is important is that industrial action certainly amounts to repudiatory breaches of contract. If the automatic theory were correct, there would be no conceptual room in which ss. 237 and 238 could work – there could be no dismissals of employees whose industrial action has already terminated their contracts of employment as their contracts would already have been terminated.[25]

If, however, the automatic theory were correct, all would not be lost for the employee. It could be that the dismissal could be viewed as a termination, if not by the employer, by the employee, which would open up the possibility that it could be considered to be a constructive dismissal. However, a difficulty arises where the employee does nothing by way of resigning but is taken to have waived the right to affirm the contract, because then there is no effective date of termination which is essential to employment contracts, as we have seen. Deakin and Morris argue that there should be a distinction drawn here between the statutory remedy and common law claims, because an effective

---

[23] *Rigby v Ferodo* [1988] ICR 29; [1987] IRLR 516.
[24] *Boyo v Lambeth London Borough Council* [1994] ICR 727.
[25] See *London Transport Executive v Clarke,* n 22.

date of termination is not required for the latter.[26] There is a limit to that response, however, because the employee needs to identify a date when they are unemployed for reasons other than bringing an unfair dismissal claim, as we have seen. But it can also be relevant to a breach of contract claim, for example in establishing when the period of limitation starts to run.

Non-renewal of a limited term contract

The second type of dismissal under statute is not to be found at common law. This is where a limited term contract comes to an end and is not renewed under the same contract.[27] On the face of it this does not appear to be a dismissal at all but termination by agreement or performance[28] in that the parties have agreed to such a termination at the outset. The contract ends automatically and the employer need take no steps to terminate it. Of course, this form of termination is known to common law, and was very common in the guise of annual hiring, particularly in agriculture, but disappeared to be replaced by employment contracts of indefinite duration terminable by either side on notice.

It would thus appear to be illogical for the expiry of a limited term contract to amount to a dismissal. And indeed it is, in terms of theory. But it is necessary, an argument runs, for practical reasons. If such terminations could not amount to dismissals all employers would need to do to avoid the effect of the employment protection legislation would be to hire all their employees on short limited term contracts. Then all they would need to do if they wanted to dismiss employees, is wait for the period to expire. However, even that is unnecessary on the argument that limited contracts may be terminable by notice. It would be reasonable to assume that a limited term contract was just that, and not terminable at an earlier time. This was the view reached in *Wiltshire CC v NATFHE and Guy*.[29] However, even assuming a limited term contract may be terminated at common law before the term expires, there is a dismissal under the subsection only where it expires without being renewed under the same contract, and not when it is prematurely terminated or renewed.[30] This leaves open the conclusion that earlier notice by the employer amounts to an employer termination, and a dismissal by that route.

There is an argument, however, that the statutory fiction that there is a dismissal when a limited term contract expires, when it would clearly seem to

---

[26] S. Deakin and G. Morris, *Labour Law* (Oxford University Press, 5th edn, 2009) p. 380.

[27] ERA 1996, ss. 95(1)(b), 136(1)(b).

[28] A contract is for a fixed term if the duration is fixed by time, but a limited term contract also includes employment for a particular task, terminated by performance.

[29] *Wiltshire County Council v National Association of Teachers in Further and Higher Education and Guy* [1980] IRLR 198; [1980] ICR 455.

[30] ERA 1996, s. 235 states that renewal includes extension.

be by agreement or performance, is misconceived, and amounts to an employer termination in any event. This is that this head of dismissal requires the non-renewal of the original contract, at least on the same terms. All the Act requires is the fact of non-renewal to amount to a dismissal. If the contract is not renewed because the employee does not wish it to be, on the face of it the legislation nevertheless deems that to be a dismissal. This seems nonsensical. However, it would not be nonsensical to say that it is where the employer is the only party who does not wish to renew that there is a dismissal. It is the employer's decision that the contract should no longer continue. That being the case, albeit by omission, expiry of a limited term contract without renewal would also appear to be an employer termination.

Constructive dismissal
The third type of statutory dismissal is known as constructive dismissal. This occurs where the employee resigns from the contract, with or without notice, in circumstances in which they are entitled to do so by reason of the employer's conduct.[31] Again, as with the expiry of a limited term contract without renewal, it seems counter-intuitive that a resignation could amount to a dismissal, but the reasons for it are likewise practical. If it were not so, all that the employer would need to do to avoid an unfair dismissal claim would be to make the working life of its employee so unpleasant that they are forced to resign. So, although it is not actually a dismissal (in the ordinary everyday sense) it is construed as a dismissal.

This would seem to make eminent sense, but it has thrown up several difficulties over the years since its creation in the Industrial Relations Act 1971. I have already referred in Chapter 1 to *Western Excavating (ECC) Ltd v Sharp*.[32] The employee needs, for their resignation to amount to a dismissal, to be 'entitled to resign'. This was originally thought to occur where the employer had acted unreasonably to a sufficient degree, which would seem to be a natural test in the context of unfair dismissal. However, the Court of Appeal held that the correct test to apply was whether the employer had committed a repudiatory breach of contract. I explained earlier why it is in fact a better, and more logical, test. Not least, to introduce the concept of unreasonableness when considering whether the employer's actions amounted to a dismissal would render the idea otiose when it comes to testing the dismissal for fairness.

I suggested above that the expiry of a limited term contract could be interpreted as termination by the employer. I would suggest that the same could be said of constructive dismissal. Indeed, the word 'constructive'

---

[31] ERA 1996, ss. 95(1)(c), 136(1)(c).
[32] *Western Excavating (ECC) Ltd v Sharp* [1978] IRLR 27; [1978] ICR 221.

suggests that it is something that appears not to be, but could be construed as a dismissal. If the employer commits a repudiatory breach of contract which automatically terminates the contract of employment, that can quite easily be seen as an employer termination.[33] The employee has had to do nothing to bring the contract to an end. It is the repudiation that does so. Were it not for the repudiation the contract would continue. However, what of the situation under the elective theory? If the employee does not accept the repudiation, but nevertheless continues to work (under new terms, the imposition of which perhaps constituted the breach) the employee could be seen to be in the position of remaining in the same employment but under a new contract. The distinction between termination of a contract of employment and employment itself is therefore important here as it must be remembered that dismissal refers to the termination of the former, not the latter. In that case, it would not seem to be that it is the employee who is bringing the contract to an end, but that the employer has done so with the employee continuing to work under a new contract. This does not prevent there having been a dismissal by way of a repudiatory termination of the previous contract even though the employment has continued. It may be that it is for the employee to decide whether the employment is to continue (by deciding whether to accept the new contract or not) but that is a different matter. What the employee does not have any choice about is to continue to work under the old contract, and should continue working under the new terms and seek damages. They should not attempt to continue working under the old contract.[34] Indeed, any attempt to do so will itself amount to a breach of contract.[35]

Some counter-arguments to the argument that there has been a termination by the employer of the original contract are these. That the employee cannot keep the original terms alive in effect gives the power to the employer to impose a unilateral variation of the terms of the original contract, subject to a monetary remedy of damages for the breach in so doing, without the need to see the original contract being replaced by a different contract. In that case, the imposed variation does not of itself constitute termination by the employer as there has been no termination at all, but simply a breach in imposing the variation subject to remedy of damages without a right of continuation of the old terms of the contract. Alternatively, if the analysis is that the original contract has been replaced by a new contract, that does not entail that the termination of the original contract involved a dismissal at all,

---

[33] Indeed, several early cases treated constructive dismissals as employer terminations, although it would not appear that it was the intention behind the legislation as originally framed – see Elias, 'Unravelling the Concept of Dismissal – I', n 15, p. 21f.

[34] *Burdett-Coutts v Hertfordshire County Council* [1984] IRLR 91.

[35] *Robinson v Tescom Corporation* [2008] IRLR 408.

whether by way of termination by the employer or resignation of the employee. It could, if there is nothing contrary from the employee, be analysed as a termination by agreement.

Dismissal, facts and minds

A judge famously said once that the state of a man's mind was as much a fact as the state of his digestion.[36] That is true, but the distinction between facts and minds can nevertheless be a useful one to draw. It may be particularly useful in determining what amounts to a dismissal in law because it seems to have been the cause of a significant amount of confusion.

Sometimes the courts have struggled with the issue as to whether a contract of employment has been terminated by dismissal by the employer or whether it was by agreement between the parties, resignation of the employee, frustration and the whole host of concepts that are relevant on the termination of employment. For example, this has occurred where the employee has been granted leave of absence on the understanding in some shape or form that they will return to work by a designated date, and they fail to do so. That could be viewed as an automatic dismissal in that the conditions laid down by the employer as to what will amount to termination have occurred. On the other hand, if it is in the employee's power to return but they have chosen not to do so, that could be interpreted as a resignation in that it was the employee's act that brings about the termination. Or it could be viewed as an agreement to terminate on a due date should a certain event not occur, which has done so. Or, if the employee is prevented from returning for reasons outside their control, this might be seen as termination by frustration, which is to say, by operation of law.

In these cases, much can turn on the form of words used. In *British Leyland UK Ltd v Ashraf*[37] the employee signed a form stating: 'You have agreed to return to work on 21/2/77. If you fail to do this, your contract of employment will terminate on that date'. The Employment Appeal Tribunal interpreted this as an agreed termination in the light of the employee's full knowledge of its terms and acceptance of them. However, it also said that the result would have been the same if the plane had been hijacked or diverted because of fog. However, in *Midland Electric Manufacturing Co. Ltd v Kanji*[38] the employee's leave of absence was conditional on the 'warning that if you fail to return ... for whatever reason the company will consider that you have terminated your employment'. Illness prevented her return but the appeal tribunal found the letter was a mere statement of intention by the employer as to what would

---

[36] See *Edgington v Fitzmaurice* (1885) 29 ChD 459 per Bowen LJ.
[37] *British Leyland UK Ltd v Ashraf* [1979] ICR 979.
[38] *Midland Electric Manufacturing Co. Ltd v Kanji* [1980] IRLR 185.

happen in the event of failure to return, which is to say that she would be dismissed. The EAT was conscious that the employer should not be given the possibility of manipulating the employee into signing away their employment protection rights, which would be void.[39] Nevertheless, a return to the *Ashraf* approach was taken by the EAT in *Igbo v Johnson Matthey Chemicals Ltd*.[40] The letter granting leave of absence stated that, if the employee failed to return by the due date: 'your contract of employment will automatically terminate on that date'. She sent a medical certificate explaining her failure to return to work. The EAT thought that this was an agreed termination. However, the Court of Appeal disagreed, holding that this purported to limit the operation of the employment protection legislation and was void. This is a policy decision and is not the point in issue here. What is of interest is the basis of the confusion as to what type of termination was in issue. It is clearly of importance because the understanding underlying all of these cases is that a consensual termination bars the employee from bringing an unfair dismissal claim.

But should it? Were false distinctions being drawn in these cases between the different methods of termination? Are they mutually exclusive or do they overlap? In other words, it might be that, for example, a consensual termination does not preclude a termination by the employer, and vice versa.

The statutory concept of dismissal is dependent upon a state of affairs rather than states of mind. A dismissal occurs in the Employment Rights Act 1996, as we have seen, when the employer terminates the contract with or without notice, or where a limited term contract is not renewed under the same contract, or where the employee terminates by reason of the employer's repudiatory breach. Notice in each of these cases that they concern what happens in the process of termination. They are to do with what brings about the termination. They are not concerned with the intention or other state of mind of the terminating party. Even more so are these not provisions about the state of mind of the other party. Therefore, it would seem to follow, if the issue is whether there has been a termination by the employer, the employee's views on the matter should be irrelevant. It is of no import whether the employee opposes the termination and acceptance of the circumstances of termination should not negate the dismissal. This is because acceptance here connotes acquiescence. On the other hand, where termination by agreement occurs this is because one party (normally the employer) makes an offer to the other which the latter accepts. This is a different form of acceptance, and one without which there would be no termination. It would thus seem quite

---

[39] See now ERA 1996, s. 203.
[40] *Igbo v Johnson Matthey Chemicals Ltd* [1986] IRLR 215.

possible to have a concept of consensual dismissal, in the sense that the employee acquiesces in the state of affairs. This should not blur the distinction between dismissal and mutual termination, as the Court of Appeal claimed in *Burton, Allton and Johnson Ltd v Peck*,[41] because consensus where there is a dismissal connotes acceptance in the form of acquiescence, not acceptance in the sense of converting an offer into an agreement. If there is no acceptance of an offer there is no agreement. But acceptance in the sense of acquiescence should not, I suggest, be an element where the employer terminates the contract by dismissing the employee. It is an irrelevance.

The confusion between facts and states of mind seems also to be at the root of the claim that is sometimes made that there is a concept of legal relevance known as 'self-dismissal'. It is not an idea that is to be found in statute but has been used by the courts on occasion. For example, Lord Denning said in *London Transport Executive v Clarke*[42] that, where there is an act of misconduct on the part of the employee with the intention that it terminates the contract: 'In these cases it is the employee himself who terminates the contract. His misconduct itself is such as to evince an intention himself to bring the contract to an end … The man dismisses himself'. The idea is to be found in other cases too.[43] This is, of course, an idea to be distinguished from the notion that a repudiatory breach needs to be wilful and deliberate. An employee who fails to fulfil a condition of the contract through no fault of their own will not have committed a fundamental breach. Self-dismissal involves the idea that the employee must not only intend to commit the breach but must also intend that it is sufficient to terminate the contract.

I am not concerned here with whether this is an accurate statement of the law, which I have covered earlier. What I am interested in is why the notion of self-dismissal is one that the judges have thought worthwhile using. Why use a term that suggests an employee has been dismissed, at first sight a gateway to granting an employee a remedy for unfair dismissal rather than use another (such as resignation) that makes it clear that the employee has terminated their employment contract by their own actions without having been dismissed? One view might be that the courts wish to avoid the notion of resignation (even 'constructive resignation' whereby the employee's actions are to be taken as evidencing an intention to terminate without an act explicitly doing so) because this could be negated on the facts by showing a lack of any such intention, or indeed by showing that the employee had the contrary intention. This would often be the case in industrial action cases,

---

[41] *Burton, Allton and Johnson Ltd v Peck* [1975] IRLR 87.

[42] *London Transport Executive v Clarke* [1981] ICR 355 at 363.

[43] See *Gannon v J.C. Firth Ltd* [1976] IRLR 415; *Kallinos v London Electric Wire Ltd* [1980] IRLR 11. See too S. Deakin and G. Morris, *Labour Law*, n 26, pp. 414–19.

because there the employee often clearly wishes the relationship to continue. Thus, Deakin and Morris have written:

> 'Such conduct may be regarded, in effect, as a form of resignation; but the conditions for drawing such an inference are strict. In principle, it should not be appropriate to do so, for example, in the context of industrial action, since it is very rarely the intention of striking employees to give up the employment in question and seek another; by definition, they are normally seeking improvement to the terms and conditions contained in their *existing* contracts of employment'.[44]

It is a moot point whether striking employees wish their existing contracts to be continued in varied form or replaced by improved contracts. But they do not intend their existing contracts as they presently exist to continue. What they wish to continue and not to terminate is their employment. The intention to terminate the contracts as they presently stand remains, although the intention to terminate the employment relationship does not. However, whatever the intention, what would seem to be at the root of the idea of resignation is that there is an intention to terminate something. It is the presence of intention that is key. I have argued however that, unlike resignation, the concept of dismissal should not be dependent on intention. That is why self-dismissal is a concept (quite independent of the issue of elective or automatic termination) that has no place in the law on termination of employment contracts.

Debate 3

What is the theoretical basis of termination by agreement?

It is often crucial for an employee that there is a finding that they have been dismissed by their employer. Without a dismissal there can, for example, be no finding of unfair dismissal or redundancy. It is therefore in the employer's interest in those cases to show that the termination of the employee's contract has been brought about by some other method.

There are several ways by which employment may be terminated. A preliminary distinction, however, needs to be made between the methods of termination at common law and those under statute. At common law a termination may be, most obviously, by the employer (a dismissal), by the employee (a resignation) or by consensus (termination by agreement). In addition, however, there may also be other types of termination. First, there is

---

[44] Deakin and Morris, *Labour Law,* ibid, at p. 415.

termination by operation of law, sometimes referred to as automatic termination. The death of either of the parties brings this about, including the putative 'death' of a company by way of a winding up in certain circumstances. Another example of termination by operation of law is where there is frustration. This occurs when, through no fault of either party, the contract is deemed incapable of performance. If someone is employed to paint a house which, unknown to either party, has been destroyed by a fire caused by an electrical fault, the contract is deemed to be at an end. Frustration has to be contrasted with the situation where a volitional act of one of the parties brings about an event, but which is deemed by law to amount to a termination. This occurs, for example, where the employer consists of a partnership (which is by law necessarily an unincorporated body consisting of two or more persons) and whose membership changes. This is usually referred to as termination on the happening of an event, as in the situation where the contract is terminated on the happening of an event not brought about by either of the parties. An example would be where finance for a project is withdrawn, making further employment impossible. Finally, employment may be terminated by performance, where the purpose of the contract has been completed. So, where someone has been employed to paint a house, and has done so, that contact is deemed to be at an end. This is not at all common compared with other forms of termination, but is useful where time is not of the essence of the contract.

The position with regard to statutory provisions is slightly different. Unlike at common law, where the termination of a contract alone is in issue, under statute there is the further distinction to be drawn between termination of contracts of employment and termination of employment itself. Employment refers to the relationship between the employer and the employee, and this may consist of several contracts.[45] Some law is concerned with the termination of employment, in contrast to contracts of employment. For example, there are rules (largely, but not exclusively, drawn from European Union law) preserving continuity of employment which are concerned with establishing a relationship between various contracts of employment as well as gaps in working within a single contract. However, when it comes to establishing termination for employment protection entitlements, statute law nevertheless is concerned with the ways by which a *contract* of employment has been terminated. In other words, for a statutory dismissal to be brought about, the law looks not to the fact of employment coming to an end, but to see if a contract of employment has terminated. Nevertheless, having said this,

---

[45] This would occur, for example, when an employee is promoted, or changes jobs within an organization.

a statutory dismissal is wider than a dismissal at common law. For example, a dismissal for the purposes of an unfair dismissal or redundancy payment claim may be established on the expiry of a limited term contract without renewal under the same contract, or where the employee has resigned in circumstances entitling him or her to do so by reason of the employer's conduct.[46] Neither of these amounts to dismissal at common law.

The theoretical basis for acknowledging termination by agreement as a legitimate form of termination is rooted at common law in the *laissez faire* ideas underlying the doctrine of freedom of contract.[47] The parties who are able to enter into a contract quite freely, and on what terms they wish, should as easily be able to agree to terminate that contract. This much is uncontroversial.

There would seem to be no theoretical objection to such an analysis which sees agreement as an alternative to, and distinct from, other forms of termination, such as dismissal. If the parties have brought about an end to their contract by consensual and mutual action, that would not seem to fit the model of other types of termination. On the other hand there would seem in principle to be no objection to the concept of an agreed, or consensual, dismissal where the contract has been terminated by the employer. In other words, agreement and dismissal, although distinct, would not appear to be mutually exclusive concepts. This is because the concept of dismissal is defined by reason of the manner, or method, of the termination. It is not part of that idea, I would suggest, that the parties must disagree with there being a dismissal, as I have already discussed. The fact of a dismissal and the views of the parties about it are, it might be thought, in quite different conceptual territory. However, the courts have had great difficulty in accepting this idea. In one case[48] the Court of Appeal said that 'a "consensual dismissal" is not a concept which is acknowledged or understood in law'. But occasionally the idea does appear to retain credence in the eyes of the judiciary. The Court of Appeal said in a case[49] in 2004 that the reality of a voluntary redundancy is that it is a consensual dismissal.

With regard to the statutory concept of dismissal outlined above, there does not seem to be as much difficulty in entertaining the idea of consensual dismissal. It is not necessary for there to be a lack of agreement for there to be a statutory dismissal. For example, if the parties agree to a limited term for the

---

[46] ERA 1996, s. 95.

[47] *Birch and Humber v University of Liverpool* [1985] IRLR 165; [1985] ICR 470.

[48] *Scott v Coalite Fuels and Chemicals Ltd* [1988] ICR 355 at 363. See too *Burton, Allton & Johnson Ltd v Peck* [1975] IRLR 87; [1975] ICR 193 and the decision of the EAT in *Birch and Humber v University of Liverpool* [1984] IRLR 54 at 57. The case was finally decided by the Court of Appeal – see [1985] IRLR 165.

[49] *AGCO v Massey Ferguson Ltd* [2004] ICR 13 at 37.

duration of the contract and it expires, that amounts (under statute[50] but not at common law) to a dismissal where it is not renewed under the same contract. Nevertheless, it has clearly expired by virtue of an agreement between the parties. Furthermore, it has not expired by virtue of an agreement that post-dates entry into the contract but one that was prior to it. It forms part of the original agreement as to what the terms are.

OBJECTIONS TO AGREEMENT AMOUNTING TO DISMISSAL

A major difficulty with termination by agreement not amounting to dismissal is not theoretical, of course, but practical. An employer might attempt to obtain a termination by agreement in order to avoid the possibility of the employee pursuing employment protection rights. If the agreement to terminate amounts to coercion then the courts will not be slow to interfere.[51] This should not be seen as an assault on the idea of the freedom of contract basis for allowing agreement as a method of termination because interference is based upon the fact that there is in fact no agreement, but merely the appearance of one.

PARTICULAR INSTANCES OF TERMINATION BY AGREEMENT

The competing considerations of theory, policy and pragmatism mean that it is difficult to uncover any uniform and consistent approach to the issue of termination by agreement. It is useful, therefore, to examine the most common particular instances in which it might be thought to occur to see how the courts have responded in each instance.

A scenario at common law where there is genuine agreement to terminate, but which nevertheless would seem to deprive the employee of a legitimate remedy, is where there has been a termination by the employer with notice, but before expiry of the notice the employee finds another job and wishes to leave before any sufficient counter-notice of his own would expire. The employee thus obtains the agreement of the employer to leave early. In one case[52] it was stated that it would be 'very rare' for such an agreement to override the original dismissal and this is the working assumption. Nevertheless, it is not in practice required in so far as the statutory remedies

---

[50] ERA 1996, s. 95(1)(b). This seems illogical, but is brought about for a purely pragmatic reason in that, if it were not to be the case that expiry of limited term contracts amounted to dismissal, employers would employ only on this basis. Indeed, the 'yearly hiring' was historically a common method of retaining a worker.

[51] See for example *McAlwane v Boughton Estates Ltd* [1973] ICR 470; [1973] 2 All ER 299; *Asamoah-Boakye v Walter Rodney Housing Association Ltd* (2000) (unreported – Appeal No: EAT/44/00).

[52] *McAlwane v Boughton Estates* [1973] ICR 470; [1973] 2 All ER 299. See too *Lees v Arthur Greaves Ltd* [1974] ICR 501.

are concerned in that an employee is in a position to give counter-notice, of whatever length, without that affecting the position that the termination is nevertheless by dismissal.[53]

This can be contrasted with the situation, which occurred in a later case,[54] where it was held that the termination was by agreement where employees took early retirement while under notice in order to take a lump sum payment under a pension scheme rather than a redundancy payment. To hold that there would be a dismissal here would, in effect, be entitling the employee not only to the benefit of pension rights on retiring early, but to a redundancy payment on top, for which any contracting out would be considered void. This would constitute an unfair double benefit. The basis for holding that there is an agreement here is thus clearly driven by policy.

Another example which has caused some difficulty is where there is an agreement that the employee is to resign. Several obvious ideas seem to be in conflict here. One consequence would appear to be that there is no dismissal, nor indeed any agreement to terminate, where the employee then resigns as that is an employee termination. This is because the agreement would merely be that the employee terminates the contract, rather than that the termination itself is *by* agreement. Nevertheless, the courts in any event strain to avoid both of these analyses (which do not help the employee) and hold that in such circumstances there is termination by dismissal,[55] unless there is some intervening cause such as an offer by the employer which the employee genuinely finds attractive.[56]

It might be thought that where employees make a request to their employer that they should be allowed to retire early, and the employer agrees to that, even going so far as to say that it requests the employees to do so, the employer's giving of the necessary approval would amount to a dismissal leading to a redundancy payment. However, in the leading case[57] it was held that this was a mere agreement to terminate. It is hard to think that this is not the sort of case which was intended to be covered by the redundancy legislation.

Another type of case that has caused difficulty is where employees have been given leave of absence but have failed to return by an agreed date, with termination as the prior stated outcome in that event. I considered this in a different context in the previous Debate. It is worth reminding ourselves that there are again several possible analyses of these types of cases. One is that

---

[53] ERA 1996, ss. 95(2), 136(3).
[54] *Scott v Coalite Fuels and Chemicals Ltd,* n 48.
[55] *Scott v Formica Ltd* [1975] IRLR 104.
[56] *Sheffield v Oxford Controls Co. Ltd* [1979] IRLR 133; [1979] ICR 396.
[57] *Birch and Humber v University of Liverpool* [1985] IRLR 165; [1985] ICR 470.

the employee has decided not to return by the agreed date and therefore there is a deemed resignation or employee breach. A second is that the event determined by the employer has come about and that this amounts to a dismissal. A third is that the agreement has brought an end to the contract. A fourth is that (where the employee has failed to return through no fault of his own, for example because of bad weather) the contract is terminated by the doctrine of frustration. The courts have fluctuated in their approach on this[58] and have taken refuge in the form of words that have been employed by the parties. However, this can quite often be fortuitous without the parties realizing the distinction that may be drawn between, for example, the words: 'Your contract will be terminated' and 'your contract will be deemed to be terminated'. Therefore, in what is now the leading authority,[59] the Court of Appeal has held that such agreements fall foul of section 203 of the Employment Rights Act 1996. This makes void any agreement which limits the protection of the employment protection legislation. Although this decision is welcomed in principle in that it prevents employers from effectively exerting pressure on employees to sign away their rights, the reasoning seems somewhat flawed. There would seem to be a difference between the situation where an employee signs away rights that they have if they are dismissed, and entering into an agreement which means that there is never a dismissal. In this latter event there is no dismissal in relation to which there are any employment protection rights. The Court of Appeal made it clear, however, that it was more concerned with pragmatic rather than logical issues. If it had not come to this conclusion, one judge said, 'the whole object of the Act can easily be defeated by the inclusion of a term … that if the employee is late for work on the first Monday in any month, or indeed on any day, no matter for what reason, the contract shall automatically terminate'.[60]

CONCLUSION

The position described above can be seen to be typical of the approach of English law to such issues. First, there is the dissimilarity in, and differences in the treatment of, similarly-named concepts when they appear at common law and under statute. Then there is the mixture of the application of analytical logic, policy considerations and pragmatism. Coupled with this is the absence of a rationalized approach to the problem. This is partly because it is true to say that, although the issues surrounding termination by agreement are understood in the sense that they are recognized to exist, they are not considered to be

---

[58] See *British Leyland v Ashraf* [1978] ICR 979; *Midland Electric Manufacturing Co. Ltd v Kanji* [1980] IRLR 185; *Tracey v Zest Equipment Co. Ltd* [1982] ICR 481.
[59] *Igbo v Johnson Matthey Chemicals Ltd* [1986] IRLR 215.
[60] Ibid, at 217.

particularly problematic. In consequence of this, there are no special legislative rules dealing with termination of employment contracts by agreement. Each aspect is dealt with by the courts as and when they arise before them, but there has been no call for, and no sign of, any form of legislative intervention in this area. It would appear to be very likely to remain that way.

Debate 4

Does the law provide employment protection for employees on termination?

The remedies that an employee has on the termination of their contracts of employment, or employment, are often referred to as the employment protection remedies. Indeed, I have frequently done so myself in this book. However, it is doubtful if they are accurately described as such. I have already, in Chapter 3, examined the ways by which the contract of employment and the contract remedies might be used to provide a degree of employment protection, but on the whole this goes no further than the provision of a money payment by way of compensation for employees who lose their jobs. But it is not normally of an amount that is sufficient to be described as a mechanism to protect employees from being sacked. To do that it would have to be a deterrent to the employer. In that the common law has no interest in the fairness of a dismissal but only whether the parties have abided by the terms of their agreement, damages are awarded normally only for the breach of the term to provide adequate notice. That might be a very small amount for employees who have been in employment for a few years only. Neither does it prevent them from being lawfully dismissed, with proper notice, immediately afterwards or at any later time.

Likewise, the law of redundancy does not provide a remedy that can be said to amount to protection for the employee. Many redundancies take place when an employer's business is folding and there are no jobs in the future to be protected. However, that is not necessarily the case. It is quite possible to be made redundant for the opposite reason – because the employer's business is thriving. This is because redundancy is defined in the Employment Rights Act 1996[61] as occurring where the dismissal is attributable wholly or mainly to:

(a) the fact that his employer has ceased, or intends to cease, to carry on the business for the purposes of which the employee was employed by him, or has ceased, or intends to cease, to carry on that business in the place where the employee was so employed; or

---

[61] Section 139(1).

(b) the fact that the requirements of that business for employees to carry out work of a particular kind, or for employees to carry out work of a particular kind in the place where he was so employed, have ceased or diminished or are expected to cease or diminish.

Limb (b), it will be noticed, is not concerned solely with the situation where a business is winding down or closing down. It also covers, for example, where the employer's business is expanding and it becomes worth its while to mechanize tasks previously undertaken by employees. The requirements for employees therefore cease or diminish. The law does not provide real employment protection in those circumstances, for that would amount to a requirement for the employer, whose business is continuing, to retain its workforce. The law does not do that, but provides the employee with money compensation only in the form of a redundancy payment. But, as with the common law claim, this does not in many instances operate as a sufficient deterrent to make it not worthwhile for the employer to dismiss, which would be a secondary way that true employment protection could be given to employees. Statutory redundancy payments are not generous. They are calculated by multiplying the employee's weekly pay by a multiplier depending on age, being one and a half for every year of employment during the whole of which the employee was 41 or over, one for every year during the whole of which the employee was between 22 and 40, and one half for every year between the ages of 18 and 21. The maximum payable is thus equivalent to thirty weeks pay, and this would be appropriate where an employee has been working for twenty years' continuous employment over the age of 41. The amount payable as a redundancy payment, as for an unfair dismissal basic award, is subject to a maximum limit, and the Secretary of State must alter this sum annually in line with the retail price index. The maximum at the time of writing at the end of 2010 stands at £400 per week and the maximum payment is thus now £12,000. This clearly significantly reduces the compensation which would otherwise have been awarded to a large section of the workforce.

It is in the law of unfair dismissal that we come closest to anything that could be identified as true employment protection. As originally envisaged it was intended to provide genuine employment protection. The primary remedies were intended to be reinstatement to the employee's job from which they were dismissed,[62] or re-engagement to another position.[63] These are the

---

[62] Reinstatement is an order that 'the employer shall treat the complainant in all respects as if he had not been dismissed' and must include benefits payable in respect of the period since dismissal and rights and privileges, including seniority and pensions (ERA 1996, ss. 114(1) and (2)). It should not be ordered if it is not practicable for the employer to comply with it or it would be unjust to do so because the employee contributed to the dismissal.

[63] The job must be comparable and suitable and, so far as is reasonably practicable, as favourable as the previous position (ERA 1996, s. 115). It may, however, be with an associated or successor

only remedies that could be properly described as employment protection. However, in reality compensation is awarded in the vast majority of cases. One reason for this is that applicants do not generally want re-employment for the obvious reasons that by the time of the hearing they will have found another job, or because, very understandably, they have no wish to return to work for an employer who has already dismissed them and against whom they have successfully pursued a claim for unfair dismissal in an employment tribunal. Furthermore, the number of employees who ostensibly indicate a wish to claim reinstatement or re-engagement do not in fact wish to. It is a common tactic to increase the employee's bargaining power in the process of negotiations for compensation.[64] It is thus in what I have previously described as the 'secondary' method that employment protection in unfair dismissal law can be provided, that is to say by setting compensation levels that are sufficiently high so as to amount as a deterrent to employers who are thinking of dismissing employees. However, it is arguable that the compensation limits are not sufficient to do this. When New Labour came to power in 1997 it did so with a pledge to remove the compensation ceiling for unfair dismissal. However, although it more than quadrupled the maximum compensatory award to £50,000 – the figure presently stands at £68,400[65] – it did not remove it altogether, with the effect that employees who have not built up a large number of years of continuous employment, or who are high-paid employees, are not entitled to compensation in many instances that would deter their employer from dismissing them.

Compensation consists of two components, the basic and compensatory awards[66] and both may be reduced owing to failure to mitigate the loss or contributory fault. The basic award is calculated as for a redundancy payment, discussed above, and is awarded irrespective of whether the unfair dismissal has caused any loss to the employee. Thus, this part of the claim has a number of caps. There is the maximum number of years of continuous employment that can be taken into account; there is the restriction to continuous employment calculated backwards, not accumulated service; there is also the halving of some of the sum due by the imposition of the multiplier of one half for service before the employee reaches 22 years of age.

---

employer that the tribunal decides what terms should apply and the date by which compliance must be made.

[64] See S. Evans, J. Goodman, and L. Hargreaves, 'Unfair Dismissal Law and Changes in the Role of Trade Unions and Employers' Associations' (1985) 14 *Industrial Law Journal* 91.

[65] The figure is revised annually. There is no maximum award in some cases, where whistleblowers or health and safety representatives are dismissed. There is also an additional award payable, of between 26 and 52 weeks' pay when the employer has failed to comply with a re-employment order. This is capped at present at £20,800.

[66] ERA 1996, s. 118.

The compensatory award is that part of the remedy that could provide the biggest deterrent to the employer. The employment tribunal will assess it to reflect what is just and equitable as compensation having regard to the loss suffered as a result of the dismissal.[67] In *W. Devis & Sons Ltd v Atkins*[68] Viscount Dilhorne thought that the compensatory award had two elements. The first was that regard should be had only to the loss resulting from the dismissal being unfair. The second, however, was that in addition the award must be just and equitable in all the circumstances, and it cannot be just and equitable that a sum should be awarded in compensation when in fact the employee has suffered no injustice in being dismissed. This means that if the employee has suffered no loss because, for example, they have immediately gained a better paid job and would nevertheless have been dismissed if all the necessary procedural protections had been provided to them, they can claim nothing under this head.

The tribunal will make an award under several headings. There will be an award for immediate loss of earnings – this being the net earnings from the date of dismissal to the hearing. Receipt of benefits is ignored because the Government can recoup an equivalent sum from the employer. There will also be a calculation of future loss of earnings, which will depend on how long the dismissed worker is likely to be unemployed, and whether they will have to take a job at a lower rate. If the employee might have been fairly dismissed in the near future, the period of future loss will be reduced to last only until the date of fair dismissal. Loss of fringe benefits will be taken into account, including any expenses reasonably incurred in consequence of the dismissal, and loss of any benefit which the employee might reasonably be expected to have had but for the dismissal. This might cover commission, free housing, food, special travel allowance, and benefits under a share participation scheme. There will also be a sum to cover expenses incurred in looking for new work. Legal expenses in fighting a claim are not, however, recoverable, although they may, in certain restricted circumstances, be included in a costs order. Loss of pension entitlement can in some cases be a very large sum, and its calculation often proves difficult. It is a form of deferred pay. There are two basic forms of pension loss which may be suffered. There is the loss of pension position earned thus far, and also loss of future pension opportunity. Usually it is most appropriate to base the sum lost on the amount of the employee's and employer's contributions made to a future pension. It will take a sacked employee a further year in a new job to obtain statutory employment protection. A fairly nominal sum, usually about £300, is awarded

---

67 ERA 1996, s. 123(1).
68 *W. Devis & Sons Ltd v Atkins* [1977] AC 931; [1977] IRLR 314; [1977] ICR 662.

because of loss in respect of unfair dismissal while the basic award is intended to serve this purpose for loss of redundancy payment. However, the total of these sums may be subject to several deductions, such as for contributory fault by the employee or, a failure to mitigate loss, for example by being slow in obtaining further available employment.

The question arises, then, as to how far the unfair dismissal remedies, in particular compensation, provide an adequate deterrent on the employer to provide the employee with 'secondary' employment protection. This is very difficult to assess. Certainly the legislation was found to have had a significant impact in the early years in a way that could have led to greater employment protection for employees. For example, the argument that always accompanies greater legal rights for employees is that serious financial and economic consequences will be the consequence, particularly in the form of employers being less willing to take on employees. However, there is little evidence for this[69] and was reflected in the introduction of the minimum wage[70]. The growth in the numbers of employees taking cases to employment tribunals could reflect a growing problem with dismissals that are unfair, but it might also be argued that it indicates that employment protection is being provided to an increasing number of employees. On the other hand, some have argued that the very existence of the unfair dismissal legislation has strengthened managerial legitimacy and control, which in turn has meant that employers have not clamoured for it to be overturned.[71]

An inevitable consequence, perhaps, of the employment protection legislation not covering all employees is that there has been an increased use by employers of employees without protection, precisely for that reason. Most obviously this can be said of the growth of temporary and casual employees who have not acquired sufficient continuity of employment. Nevertheless, as Deakin and Morris point out,[72] atypical working is just that, and the majority of employees continue to work on contracts of indefinite duration and acquire job protection.

Unfair dismissal protection is now provided by a statute with the title of the Employment Rights Act 1996, whereas before it was contained in the Employment Protection (Consolidation) Act 1978. It would not be correct to view this change as an indication of an acceptance that legislation does not provide true employment protection, but it is perhaps appropriate.

---

[69] See e.g. W.W. Daniel and E. Stilgoe, *The Impact of Employment Protection Laws* (Policy Studies Institute, 1978).

[70] National Minimum Wage Regulations 1999 (SI 1999 No. 584).

[71] See further B. Hepple, *European Social Dialogue – Alibi or Opportunity?* (Institute of Employment Rights, 1993) p. 95.

[72] Deakin and Morris, *Labour Law,* n 26, p. 514.

Debate 5

How far is the law on unfair dismissal concerned with fairness?

It might seem axiomatic that the provisions in the Employment Rights Act 1996 on unfair dismissal are concerned with fairness, or at any rate, unfairness. To an extent this is obviously true. But it is also true that it ignores, or at least does not pursue, some unfairness in dismissals. It might not seem clear why this should be so. I am not referring here to particular provisions or decisions of the courts in relation to them. That is a type of argument that could be made about any aspect of the fairness of any legislation. I am instead considering an argument that could be made about whole areas of unfairness that it might seem strange for legislation set up precisely to address unfairness to ignore.

Perhaps the most obvious way in which the legislation does not address some unfairness in dismissals lies in the name of the claim itself. It is about the fairness of a dismissal or, in other words, if the employer has acted reasonably in dismissing its employee. It is not concerned about whether the employee has suffered an injustice. So, in cases where the reason for a dismissal was the employee's alleged misconduct, the employment tribunal applies a test that focuses entirely on the reasonableness of the employer's actions. It asks, first, if the employer honestly believed that the employee had committed the offence in question; secondly that there were reasonable grounds for that belief; and finally if the dismissal was within the band of reasonable responses that the employer had open to it.[73] Thus, even if the employment tribunal were to conclude that the employee had not misconducted themselves as alleged, so long as the test is satisfied in relation to the employer the dismissal must be held to be fair. It is difficult to see how ignoring the injustice to the employee whilst concentrating on the employer results in a just solution. If the object of the unfair dismissal legislation were to punish unjust employers that would seem to be a reasonable approach. But if, as I examined in the previous Debate, the purpose of the legislation is to provide employment protection to employees, then this approach would not appear to be one fit for purpose.

This point is also illustrated by the fairness on the occasion of group dismissals. If injustice to the employee were the main focus the law would reach a different result, but as it presently stands, if an employer is aware that one person amongst a group of employees committed an offence but is

---

[73] *British Home Stores v Burchell* [1978] IRLR 379, as qualified by the Court of Appeal's decision in *Sainsbury's Supermarkets v Hitt* [2003] IRLR 23.

reasonably unable to identify which one, it is possible to dismiss the whole group without this being found to be unfair. This is so even though, by definition, the number of innocent employees outnumbers, and perhaps far outnumbers, the guilty party.[74]

A second way by which the law of unfair dismissal ignores injustice is in the idea that reasons why an employee might have been fairly dismissed, but were not a factor in the decision to dismiss because they were discovered only after the dismissal on other grounds had occurred, which will not convert an unfair dismissal into a fair one. This is for similar reasons to the argument considered above in that it is because the fairness of the dismissal is tested in the context of the employer's position. However, justice may be served here by reducing the employee's compensation by 100 per cent, as indeed occurred in the leading case in this area, the House of Lords decision in W. Devis v Atkins.[75]

A final reason why the law of unfair dismissal seems structurally designed to ignore some injustices is that some reasons for dismissal cannot be tested for reasonableness at all. Most dismissals are tested for fairness in unfair dismissal cases, as one might expect, and are termed 'potentially fair' in the process. In other words, once the reason for the dismissal has been established it is then examined to see if the employer acted reasonably in dismissing the employee for that reason. The employer will need to show that it comes under certain categories of dismissal to establish this, such as capability, misconduct or redundancy. In addition there is a 'catch-all' category of 'some other substantial reason' if the specific categories do not seem appropriate.[76] Some dismissals, however, are automatically unfair so that, once the reason for the dismissal is established, it is not tested for fairness and the employer is not able to mount a defence to show that the dismissal was fair.[77]

The following are the reasons which will result in the dismissal being deemed unfair:

---

[74] See *Monie v Coral Racing* [1980] IRLR 464; [1981] ICR 109; *Parr v Whitbread plc t/a Threshers Wine Merchants* [1990] IRLR 39. Furthermore, a dismissal may be fair even though a criminal court decides that the offence was not in fact committed by the applicant – see *Harris (Ipswich) Ltd v Harrison* [1978] IRLR 382; [1978] ICR 1256. However, depending on the facts of the case, this might depend upon differing standards of proof. A criminal court must be convinced of guilt beyond reasonable doubt, whereas the employment tribunal works on the less exacting standard of the balance of probabilities – see *Lees v The Orchard* [1978] IRLR 20.

[75] *W. Devis & Sons Ltd v Atkins*, n 68, 1.

[76] See ERA 1996, s. 98. 'Some other substantial reason' is not *ejusdem generis* with the other categories of dismissal according to R.S. *Components Ltd v Irwin* [1973] IRLR 239; [1973] ICR 535.

[77] There are no automatically fair dismissals. Cases dismissed on grounds of national security appear to be such, but in fact are outside the jurisdiction of employment tribunals. Those cases are simply not heard.

1. Dismissal for reasons connected with pregnancy and childbirth.[78]
2. Dismissal because the employee has a 'spent conviction' or the failure to disclose a spent conviction, by virtue of the Rehabilitation of Offenders Act 1974.
3. Dismissal on a transfer of an undertaking if it, or a reason connected with it, is the reason or principal reason for dismissal.[79]
4. Dismissal because of trade union membership or activities.[80]
5. Dismissal because the employee has asserted a statutory right such as the rights to written particulars of employment; rights to time off for public duties and to look for work or to make arrangements for training; and time off for ante-natal care.
6. Dismissal for taking part in 'protected industrial action' as defined in s. 238A of the Trade Union and Labour Relations (Consolidation) Act 1992.
7. Dismissal for 'whistleblowing' under the Public Interest Disclosure Act 1998.

It may seem unfair on employers that they are always deemed to have dismissed unfairly if any of the above are found to be the reason for the dismissal, but it is not quite as it appears. Clearly public policy plays a significant part in the membership of any of these reasons in the list and so there are wider moral considerations at work here. But it is also the case that, in circumstances where the dismissals looked at objectively might not be considered to be unfair, there is in effect a defence written into the relevant provisions. In other words, what in effect is happening here is that the law in these circumstances provides the employer with a cast-iron reply which is not subjected to counter-argument. For example, it might be thought that it would be unjust on an employer who dismisses an employee for reasons related to pregnancy or childbirth if it were not practicable for her to return to a suitable and appropriate job, and an associated employer offers her a job of the same kind which she unreasonably refuses. Likewise, it might be thought reasonable for a solicitors' firm to dismiss an employee solicitor who has not disclosed a previous criminal conviction. In these, and in other cases, the law provides a 'defence' for the employer in the way of exceptions to the general position.[81] This might be seen to be to put the employer in such cases in an improved position compared to one whereby it needs to make out a specific defence to an employment tribunal based on reasonableness.

---

[78] Maternity and Parental Leave Regulations (SI 1999 No. 3312).
[79] Transfer of Undertakings (Protection of Employment) Regulations 2006 (SI 2006 No. 246).
[80] Trade Union and Labour Relations (Consolidation) Act 1992, s. 152(1).
[81] See, respectively, Maternity and Parental Leave Regulations (SI 1999 No. 3312) Reg. 20(7) and the Rehabilitation of Offenders Act 1974 (Exceptions) Order 1975 (SI 1975 No. 1032).

Further Reading

H. Collins, *Justice in Dismissal* (Clarendon Press, 1993).

W.W. Daniel and E. Stilgoe, *The Impact of Employment Protection Laws* (Policy Studies Institute, 1978).

A.C.L. Davies, 'Judicial Self-Restraint in Labour Law' (2009) 38 *Industrial Law Journal* 278.

A.C.L. Davies, *Perspectives on Labour Law* (Cambridge University Press, 2nd edn, 2009).

P. Elias, 'Unravelling the Concept of Dismissal – I' [1978] *Industrial Law Journal* 16.

S. Evans, J. Goodman, and L. Hargreaves, 'Unfair Dismissal Law and Changes in the Role of Trade Unions and Employers' Associations' (1985) 14 *Industrial Law Journal* 91.

M. Freedland, *The Personal Employment Contract* (Oxford University Press, 2003) ch.6.

B.A. Hepple, *European Social Dialogue – Alibi or Opportunity?* (Institute of Employment Rights, 1993).

J. McMullen (ed.), *Redundancy: The Law and Practice* (Sweet and Maxwell, 3rd. edn, 2010).

6

COLLECTIVE ASPECTS OF EMPLOYMENT

INTRODUCTION

In this chapter I will consider various Debates about the collective aspects of employment. I have already considered one of these in Chapter 2 when I examined the very difficult issues raised by a contractual analysis of collective bargains between trade unions and employees and the effect upon the contracts of employment between employers and employees. In this chapter I will consider two further areas, namely Debates to do with industrial action and the law on trade unions.

Before I embark on these Debates, however, I will step back for a moment and make a brief comment about the law in collective aspects of employment in general in the context of the role of the courts in this area. There has been a long tradition of distrust of the courts by the labour movement, particularly in the nineteenth century when the judges were viewed as highly reactionary in their dealings with working people. They often were, but it is worth remembering that there was widespread fear of the uprisings by the working man that were taking place on the Continent. It was not a reactionary approach rooted in unjustified fears. When the anti-union Combination Acts of 1799 and 1800 were repealed by the Combination Laws Repeal Act in 1824, there was such widespread rioting and disorder that the government felt it necessary to introduce another Combination Act, reversing progress, in the following year. But it cannot be doubted that the innate conservatism of the nineteenth century judiciary also led to some reactionary decisions. There were a number of decisions that are still sources of contempt in the trade union movement today, such as *Hornby v Close*[1] in 1867 when the courts found trade unions to be illegal as they were in restraint of trade. Despite some liberal legislation that followed, notably the Trade Union Act of 1871 which allowed trade unions certain legal powers and status and the

---

[1] *Hornby v Close* (1867) 10 Cox CC 393.

Criminal Law Amendment Act 1871 which de-criminalized many offences relevant to trade union activities. Much of the other legislation eased the lot of trade unions, but the courts continued to reach some notorious decisions, such as *Quinn v Leathem*[2] in 1901 when the House of Lords held that there was a tortious conspiracy where two or more persons combined without justification in industrial action, and *Taff Vale Railway Co. v Amalgamated Society of Railway Servants*[3] in the same year when the House of Lords held that trade unions could be sued despite having unincorporated status imposed upon them by the Trade Union Act of 1871. The decade ended with another highly conservative decision of the House of Lords when it held that a union could not spend its funds on political purposes (at a time when the Labour Party was beginning to emerge out of the trade union movement) because to do so was *ultra vires*, a doctrine applied to corporate bodies.

It is fair to say that the labour movement has never fully recovered from this series of cases, and it displays a level of distrust of the judiciary today, particularly in industrial action disputes. It might therefore be thought that the area of employment law where an alternative to the ordinary courts would be most required would be on the collective side, but this is not the case. Employment tribunals consider individual employment matters. The courts remain the arbiters in collective employment matters, and still do not have the degree of confidence from the labour movement that they would no doubt like.

Debate 1

Does the law give sufficient protection to the parties during industrial action?

OFFICIAL AND UNOFFICIAL INDUSTRIAL ACTION

It is natural that there will be some degree of tension in relationships between employers and employees. The working environment is notorious in this respect, but it reflects the importance of the relationship to both parties. In fact, the term 'both parties' here is too simplistic because, of course, there is often a third agent involved, namely the trade union. Although trade unions are unincorporated bodies (and cannot in law be, or treated as if they were, corporate bodies[4]) consisting of a group of individual worker-members, in

---

[2] *Quinn v Leathem* [1901] AC 495.
[3] *Taff Vale Railway Co. v Amalgamated Society of Railway Servants* [1901] AC 426.
[4] See Trade Union and Labour Relations (Consolidation) Act 1992, s. 10(2). This is subject to some exceptions, as set out in ss. 10(1) and 12.

reality they are of course third parties in the employment environment. Their daily roles are mainly to do with the welfare of their members, financially and in other ways, but occasionally they come to the fore because of industrial conflict. It is for this reason that trade unions might have a public persona that is far more associated with industrial conflict than reflects the reality. In fact the amount of time taken by trade unions in taking industrial action is very small. Nevertheless, the definition of a trade union in law is one that reflects this particular aspect of the functions of trade unions. Section 1 of the Trade Union and Labour Relations (Consolidation) Act 1992 defines a trade union as an organization (whether temporary or permanent) which consists wholly or mainly of workers of one or more descriptions and whose principal purposes include the regulation of relations between workers of that description or those descriptions and employers or employers' associations. It also includes constituent or affiliated organizations, and therefore covers bodies such as the Trades Union Congress. This clearly places an emphasis on just one aspect of the work of trade unions and downplays other important aspects. I will consider the legal status of trade unions in a later Debate.

It is, of course, quite possible for industrial conflict, and industrial action, to occur where no trade union is involved. Industrial action is normally thought of as occurring where there is concerted action by workers of some kind.[5] Action by individual employees is not seen as industrial action but a personal dispute with an employer.[6] There are important consequences, however, if the industrial action involves a trade union, not just for the union but also for the individual members of the trade union taking part in the action. If an employee is dismissed because they were taking part in a strike or other industrial action when everyone else taking part is also dismissed, and none of the employees are re-engaged within three months of the dismissal, the tribunal cannot determine whether the dismissal was fair or unfair.[7] The effect is as if the employer were found to have dismissed the employee for an automatically fair reason because the employee cannot challenge it. In effect, the employer has an immunity. It is not clear why this should be the case, because the employer does not even have to prove that the industrial dispute was the reason for the dismissal. It need only show that the dismissals coincided with the industrial action. The employer might even deliberately provoke the stoppage to remove its workforce and the dismissals could not be challenged in an employment

---

[5] See *Tramp Shipping Corporation v Greenwich Marine Inc.* [1975] ICR 261; [1975] 2 All ER 989.

[6] Action by an individual worker did not qualify as industrial action in *Bowater Containers Ltd v Blake* EAT 522/81 (unreported) but the EAT came to the opposite conclusion in *Lewis and Britton v E. Mason & Sons* [1994] IRLR 4 in which even a mere threat of industrial action by an individual was considered enough to amount to industrial action. I am not aware of any other decisions reaching the same conclusion.

[7] Trade Union and Labour Relations (Consolidation) Act 1992, s. 238(1).

tribunal.[8] However, this general position is subject to an important exception. If only some of those taking part in official industrial action[9] have been dismissed or have not been offered re-engagement within the three-month period, an unfair dismissal claim may be brought[10] and further they will be deemed to have been unfairly dismissed.[11] In other words, the dismissals will be automatically unfair without being tested for reasonableness, in keeping with the notion of preventing (or protecting) employment tribunals from making a decision on the merits of an industrial dispute. However, if the action is unofficial, there is no right to complain of unfair dismissal.[12]

The law on the whole has traditionally been very cautious when it comes to the treatment of trade unions in industrial action. It has been mindful of the strength of opinion that industrial action is arguably a moral right, and one that has been given constitutional protection in other jurisdictions. In so far as trade unions represent employees in taking such action they have a role to play in protecting employees' moral rights and governments have been unwilling to encroach into the idea with the zeal that some of them might have liked to. It has also been aware that the collectivization of labour in the form of trade unions is merely the corollary to the collectivization of capital in the form of the employer and is therefore difficult to challenge. In addition, however, the courts have been aware that their role is not to get into the merits of industrial action, as just mentioned, and to apply, on the whole, standard common law principles in so far as they can without making industrial action to be a special case. Their difficulty in doing this, however, has been that the application of these common law principles has tended to result in the conclusion that industrial action is unlawful. It therefore has been for governments, on the whole, to intervene and correct the consequences flowing from the application of these common law principles.

---

[8] The courts are reluctant for employment tribunals to become involved in the reasons for dismissals in industrial action cases because it would be very difficult to distinguish between doing that and becoming involved in assessing the industrial merits of the dispute. See further *Faust v Power Packing Casemakers Ltd* [1983] IRLR 117.

[9] This is industrial action that has been endorsed or authorized by a trade union. This is defined in the Trade Union and Labour Relations (Consolidation) Act 1992, s. 20 as action that was authorized or endorsed –
(a) by any person empowered by the rules to do, authorize or endorse acts of the kind in question, or
(b) by the principal executive committee or the president or general secretary, or
(c) by any other committee or any other official of the union (whether employed by it or not).
Authorization relates to action yet to be taken, and endorsement to action already begun.

[10] Trade Union and Labour Relations (Consolidation) Act 1992, s. 238(2).

[11] Ibid, s. 238(A).

[12] Ibid, s. 237. There are exceptions for dismissals in the context of jury service, family, health and safety, working time, worker representatives, protected disclosures under the whistleblowing legislation, flexible working, pensions scheme membership, study and training cases and time off for dependants – s. 237(1A).

THE EFFECTIVENESS OF COMMON LAW REMEDIES

There have been three main areas of the common law, supplemented by statute, that have been relevant in industrial action cases, namely the law of contract, the law of torts and criminal law. In each of these areas there has been a great deal of debate as to how far the application of mainstream common law ideas has been, and necessarily or unnecessarily has been, applied so as to deny legal protection to workers engaging in industrial action.

Does the law of contract provide adequate protection?

To apply standard contractual principles to industrial action is fairly easy to do as a simple matter of the application of doctrine. The consideration on a contract of employment moving from the employer is, usually, the payment of wages or a salary. The consideration moving from the employee is the willingness to work. It is not the work itself, if only because the employer is generally under no duty to provide the employee with work.[13] So, if the employee is no longer willing to work, there is a failure of consideration, and where that is total (as with a strike) there is a repudiatory breach of contract. The fact that the unwillingness to work is a breach of contract is enough for the common law to declare industrial action unlawful. It is convenient for the courts that this is so in that it does not involve them in determining the merits of the dispute. Why the workers are on strike is irrelevant, and therefore the merits of those reasons are matters with which the courts are not concerned.

On this analysis, it might be thought that the courts have not displayed any anti-worker sentiment in declaring industrial action unlawful. It seems almost, if not entirely, inevitable in contract theory that this should be the case. The counter-argument to this, however, is that in areas of contract law that might seem to suggest an analysis in the striking[14] workers' favour, the courts do not seem to have been so zealous in applying classical analysis. For example, it might be thought that, in order to avoid being in breach of contract, employees

---

[13] This is, of course, not the case if the contract contains a term, express or implied, to the contrary. Sometimes employees expect more than pay for working, as with an actor taken on for a part in a play who works for the public exposure it will give them. Other employees need to work because part of their pay is determined by the amount of work they do, such as those on commission or doing piece-work. See *Collier v Sunday Referee Publishing Co. Ltd* [1940] 2 KB 647; [1940] 4 All ER 234.

[14] I will refer to strikes and striking here as a shorthand term for industrial action and taking part in industrial action. In the most part there is no significant distinction to be drawn in law between striking and other forms of industrial action. However, where there is I shall make the distinction clear. Forms of industrial action apart from striking include overtime bans (both voluntary and contractual), blacking (whereby particular goods may not be handled as they are connected with the employer who is party to the dispute or in some other way connected with the industrial action), a go-slow, picketing, a work to rule and a go-slow.

could simply give notice to their employer to terminate their contracts of employment. In other words, there could be a concerted resignation by the employees, and not a strike at all, although in reality it would amount to the same thing. This analysis would seem as easy to adopt as that of establishing that there is a breach where no notice has been given. There is, after all, no need to be willing to work for an employer after the employee's notice, validly given, has expired. Of course, industrial action like this would be very difficult for a trade union to organize, not least for two reasons. One is that it is often important for a trade union calling industrial action (let me call it that for that is what in reality it would be) to strike while the iron is hot, if the reader will forgive the pun. Where employees may have to give several months' notice to lawfully terminate their contracts, this would clearly tend against effective action. Secondly, it may be that different employees may have different notice periods. The industrial action would begin in a very staggered way and lose its effectiveness to a significant extent, or the union could identify the longest period of notice an employee might have to give and request all its members to give that period of notice. This would, to say the least, be obviously quite impracticable, and would also mean that there would be no unfair dismissal protection rights. It may be, however, that the threat of such a form of action – industrial action by mass resignation, if you like – of itself would be a powerful tool, but a threat without any realistic prospect of being able to be carried out clearly loses its potency.

In any event, the courts have not applied such an analysis, despite the ease with which they could have done so. They see the reality as being that the workers in giving notice have no intention to terminate their contracts. They intend to return to work once the action is over.[15] This is true in most instances, of course, but it makes a fundamental error of contractual analysis in employment. When an employee resigns they do so by terminating their contracts of employment. That does not connote that they intend to terminate their employment as such. As I have discussed before, an employee's employment may consist in a number of successive contracts of employment, particularly where the employee has been promoted several times. The termination of a contract of employment does not mean in that instance, of course, that employment has terminated. Therefore, it could be argued, the fact that an employee has given notice to terminate their contact of employment does not entail the idea that they are giving notice to terminate their employment. Indeed, the termination of the contract of employment is precisely what the employee intends in many instances when taking industrial action, for the reason that they take the view that it no longer suits

---

[15] See e.g. *Rookes v Barnard* [1964] 2 AC 1129.

them. They want their present contract to be replaced by another, more favourable, contract.

One way the courts have underscored this is by saying that taking industrial action is not only a breach of contract because the workers do not give notice to terminate, but even if they did it would nevertheless amount to a repudiatory breach because it evinces an intention to harm the employer's business.[16] This is quite an extraordinary idea for classical contract theorists in that it takes the courts into the area of determining not just that there has been a breach of contract but that it has come about because of the hostile intention of the party in breach. The courts have traditionally been concerned to keep away from the reasons why a breach of contract has occurred and have merely concerned themselves with the fact of whether one has occurred or not. To concern themselves with motive, particularly in the context of industrial action which can be highly politically charged, is out of line with the classical approach.[17]

Some sympathetic contractual analysis has been displayed by the courts from time to time, and some of it has been quite inventive. So, in *Morgan v Fry*[18] Lord Denning MR, in seeking to bypass the idea that striking involved a breach of contract, suggested that industrial action merely suspends contracts of employment. He reached this conclusion through the argument that there is an implied term that each party to the contract agrees to such a suspension. This is a very difficult idea, particularly because it is not clear on what theoretical basis such a term might be implied. It would hardly be one that is so obvious that the parties must be taken to have agreed to it, and neither could it hardly be said that it is one necessary to give business efficacy to the contract. Nor is it a term 'notorious and certain' – indeed, it would probably come as something of a surprise to both employers and employees. It is also unclear what the position would be if the strike were never settled, or if the employer sought to dismiss the employees during the period of suspension, even unfairly. For these reasons the idea did not gain currency. However, it is striking because of the extent to which at least Lord Denning was prepared to go in applying novel ideas to avoid the conclusion that industrial action necessarily involves a breach of contract. Interestingly, however, although the idea never gained a hold in the courts, something similar can be found in the

---

16 See the decision of the House of Lords in *Miles v Wakefield Metropolitan District Council* [1987] AC 539; [1987] IRLR 193; [1987] AC 368. See too *Secretary of State for Employment v ASLEF (No.2)* [1972] 2 QB 455. Lord Denning MR stated (at 492): 'an act which would otherwise be lawful is rendered unlawful by the motive or object with which it is done'.

17 See the decision of the House of Lords, stating the classical idea, in *Allen v Flood* [1898] AC 1; cf its decision in *Quinn v Leathem* [1901] AC 495. See too E. Ferran, 'Further Deductions From Wages' [1987] 46 *Cambridge Law Journal* 412 and G. Morris, 'Industrial Conflict' (1987) 16 *Industrial Law Journal* 185.

18 *Morgan v Fry* [1968] 2 QB 710; [1968] 3 All ER 452.

law of continuous employment for the purposes of bringing employment protection claims. Whereas some events break continuity some do not, even though they lead to a period where there is no contract of employment. So, where the employee is absent from work due to sickness or injury, a temporary cessation of work, or because of some arrangement or custom to this effect, continuity may be preserved. However, where the absence is due to industrial action, it does not break continuity but neither is it preserved. In other words continuity is not broken but, unlike in the other instances I have mentioned, the period does not count as a period of employment but constitutes a void and those weeks do not count.[19] Looked at another way, there is a suspension of employment during this period for the purposes of calculating continuity much on the lines of Lord Denning's idea in *Morgan v Fry*.

A further example of where the courts have been reluctant to apply traditional contractual analysis where it would be of assistance to workers taking industrial action is where there is a ban on voluntary overtime. This is overtime that is not required under the contract of employment in addition to normal core hours, but which the employee is free to take up at their option.[20] The natural analysis here, it might be thought, is that a ban on overtime which is not contractually required is, by definition, not a breach of contract and therefore lawful. However, this has to be read in the light of the decisions I mentioned above to the effect that a bad motive in carrying out contractual obligations may result in a repudiatory breach. One of the ways in which this can be done is by invoking the idea that contracts of employment contain an implied term of co-operation. This is more of a negative duty not to be obstructive rather than a positive duty to co-operate.[21] It is very general and can be used as a way of placing obligations on workers that are not explicit in the contract. However, to imply this term in the context of industrial action the courts have had to take an approach that might not seem to be in line with contract doctrine, and that is that implied terms are not to be interpreted as 'trumping' express terms. If there is no express term requiring the employee to be available to work overtime, to imply a contractual term to the same effect is to contradict the position of the contract regarding express terms. However, this would be a weak argument. The obvious reply to it is that the implied term is not contradicting an express term but taking advantage of the fact that there is a gap on the point in the express terms, and implied terms only can ever do that. For this reason it would be a good idea, as far as employees are concerned, for their contracts of employment to contain an express term that

---

[19] Employment Rights Act 1996, s. 216(1).
[20] The idea should therefore not be confused with overtime which is unpaid.
[21] See *Secretary of State for Employment v ASLEF (No.2)*, n 16.

there is no requirement to work overtime. But if there were express terms in contracts stating what it does *not* contain that would be a very onerous task.

It might be thought that there is no great importance in the idea that industrial action amounts to a breach of employment contracts. The social reality is that employers are very likely not to sue employees for breach of contract. It would have to be their employees that they would sue on that ground because there is no contractual relationship between employers and the trade union calling the action. This is because collective agreements are very rarely legally enforceable, and contain TINA LEA clauses – 'this is not a legally enforceable agreement'. But even if they were, unless there were a no-strike clause in the collective agreement there would very likely be no breach of that agreement by the union. The breaches of contract in industrial action cases are those of the employment contract by the employee. But even if the employer were minded to sue its employees, in many instances there would be no point in doing so. It is not possible to make employees work as specific performance is not available against the employee, nor to obtain an injunction restraining a breach of a contract of employment if the effect is to compel the employee to work.[22] The employer's remedy would thus lie only in damages. The courts have rejected the idea of making an award to reflect the expenses incurred because of the industrial action[23] and instead will assess loss only as the cost of hiring a substitute.[24] If the employer were running at a loss only nominal damages could be secured, and sometimes strikes may even enhance a company's chance of profitability by reducing wage costs at a time of slack demand.

The position is the same where there is less than full performance of the contract by employees, such as a work to rule or a go-slow. A deliberate refusal in advance of performance to work under the contract as normal, short of an out-and-out strike, completely defeats the employee's contractual claim to wages or salary, and this continues for as long as the refusal to perform goes on. The employer may resist any claim to part-payment on the basis that he makes it clear that he refuses to waive his right to receive full performance.[25] The employer's actual loss recoverable in damages will in most cases be relatively small. It is for these reasons that the law of torts becomes very important in providing the employer with an effective remedy.

22 Trade Union and Labour Relations (Consolidation) Act 1992, s. 236.
23 *Ebbw Vale Steel, Iron and Coal Co. v Tew* (1935) 79 SJ 593.
24 *National Coal Board v Galley* [1958] 1 WLR 16; [1958] 1 All ER 91.
25 *Wiluszynski v Tower Hamlets London Borough Council* [1989] IRLR 259; [1989] ICR 493.

Does the law of torts provide adequate protection?

The real importance for an employer in having a claim in contract is not that it enables the employer to obtain an effective contractual remedy, because it normally would not as I have just discussed. However, it does open up the door to tortious remedies which are much more powerful.

The tort that has proved most effective to employers in industrial action cases has been the tort of inducing a breach of contract. Under this tort the injured party seeks a remedy, not from the party in breach of contract, but with the party who induced the breach in some way. The tort originated, however, in a case that was not concerned with industrial action but an opera impresario seeking to poach a singer with obligations under an existing contract to work for another. Indeed, the tort is now occasionally referred to by its name as the tort of *Lumley v Gye*.[26] Herein, in some ways, lies an initial problem. In that it was not designed as a tort to deal with industrial action it thus perhaps requires special justification as to why it should be applied in such situations. However, the common law, as I have mentioned several times, professes to be uninterested in context but simply whether the forms of action have been complied with. In industrial action cases there certainly seem to be scenarios that square with that in *Lumley v Gye* itself. The tort is committed where a person directly or indirectly induces a party to a contract to break it without legal justification. It will almost always be committed where a union calls industrial action which results in breaches not only of the contracts of employment of the strikers, but also commercial contracts entered into by the employer against whom the action is taken. The great attraction for employers in suing under this head is that the action is taken against the trade union. There is but one defendant and it is the agency that is in control of the industrial action.

The justification for the existence of the tort would seem to be that the party at fault in such cases, be they industrial action cases or others, is the party bringing about the breach. The party in breach of contract to some extent is a tool of the guilty party in causing harm to the innocent party. Not to provide a remedy against an agent who causes an unlawful act to be committed might seem a lacuna in the common law, and one it is justified and natural for it to fill. This is particularly so because the innocent party may not be confined to that party against whom the breach is committed. Sometimes the party in breach can be seen to be an innocent party too. This would be so, for instance, where that party is put into breach, quite involuntarily. So, in industrial action cases, if as a result of its employees' industrial action an employer were unable to fulfil its commercial contracts with other businesses

---

[26] *Lumley v Gye* (1853) 2 E & B 216.

that it supplies with goods or services, it may well be that the employee itself is in breach. As far as those contracts are concerned the employer would appear to be an innocent party, at least in the sense of being put into breach of its commercial contracts against its wishes. In cases like this it would seem that the existence of the tort of inducing a breach of contract is even more justifiable. The business customer of the employer should be able to pursue a remedy, the argument goes, against the agency who is causing the trouble. That is not its contractual partner, who is innocently put in breach, but the trade union who is indirectly inducing the breach of employment contracts of its members, which in turn has caused the breach of the commercial contract between that employer and the customer. However, on further inspection, it would appear that this is not necessarily so, for the following reason.

The likelihood, or at least the possibility, is that in such circumstances there will be a clause in the contract absolving the employer from the breach, which gives rise to particular issues to which I will return later. Such terms are known as *force majeure* clauses, and the issue arises as to whether they excuse a party in breach from that breach, or merely limit the ambit of obligation so that non-performance will not amount to a breach. This is a crucial issue here. If the employer, in breach to its customers against its will, is excused the consequences of, and liability for, the breach by virtue of the *force majeure* clause, the best analysis would seem to be that it remains a breach, but the employer does not pay the normal consequences of it. On the other hand, if the clause is read as limiting the area of the employer's obligations – the employer is under obligations to deliver goods to its customers, but only in circumstances where it is not prevented from doing so for reasons outside its control – there would appear to be no breach of contract where those conditions pertain. There is simply no obligation to perform where reasons outside the employer's control exist such as to prevent it from doing so, and there is consequently no breach.

What is the correct analysis? This is very difficult to say, as both are analytically quite feasible. Of course, the natural answer is to look at the precise terms of the clause and to see which way it tends. The difficulty with that is that the wording might be quite fortuitous and not be intended to have a particular consequence in this regard. In terms of policy the position could be taken that the liability of the guilty party should not exist, or not do so, by an accident of wording of a term of a contract to which it has no access. Whatever one's views on what the liability should be in principle for trade unions who put an employer into a particular legal position as regards their customers, it does not seem rational that it should be dependent upon a term of a commercial contract which they have not seen, or have no right to see. A partial response to this might be that there is a general knowledge of the types of clauses these contracts may contain, and so there is some constructive knowledge which justifies liability should it turn out that the contract in question does contain such a term. But that takes the position only so far. It would still mean that the trade union would escape liability if the contract did not contain a clause that retained liability for the employer, and that would seem unsatisfactory (whatever one's views on whether there should be liability) because, again, it is dependent upon happenstance.

Not surprisingly, then, this has caused some difficulties in the courts. In the leading case of *Torquay Hotel v Cousins*[27] Lord Denning in the Court of Appeal took the view that there was liability even if there were no breach. However, in so doing, he seemed to undermine the whole basis of the tort of inducing a breach of contract in principle. This principle would seem to be that there has been an unlawful act (the breach of contract) but that in addition to the party actually in breach being liable, the party bringing about that breach should itself be liable. It cannot be liable in contract, and so it is liable in tort. But if the view is taken that there is liability even where there is no unlawful act by way of breach, it is difficult to see what the justification for the tort is, for several reasons. First, it would not seem to be grounded in the tort as envisaged in *Lumley v Gye*, not for the reason I previously gave that that case was not one involving industrial action, but because it was a case where there was a breach of contract. A second reason is that it is difficult to see why somebody should be liable at law for bringing about an act by another party which is not itself unlawful – not in the sense that that party is excused the consequences of their unlawful act, but their act is not unlawful in the first place.

For this reason many saw the decision in *Torquay Hotel* as creating a separate, additional, tort rather than being merely an extension of the original tort. While it could be seen that liability for inducing a breach of contract where there was no breach could be another way of interpreting the tort, it is not surprising that the illogicality of that quickly becomes clear. The other alternative available, if there is to be liability, is for this to be founded in a new tort. This came to be known as the tort of interference with contract. Of course, judges on the whole do not like to be seen to be inventing torts and so the pretence that it did not exist other than as a second limb of *Lumley v Gye* persisted in some quarters. But it now has widespread recognition at the highest level, not least because Lord Denning himself repeatedly returned to the theme.[28] By 1983 the existence of the separate tort had been affirmed by the House of Lords in *Hadmor Productions Ltd v Hamilton*.[29]

---

[27] *Torquay Hotel v Cousins* [1969] 2 Ch 106.

[28] See *British Broadcasting Corporation v Hearn* [1977] IRLR 273; [1977] ICR 685; [1977] 1 WLR 1004; *Beaverbrook Newspapers Ltd v Keys* [1978] IRLR 34; [1978] ICR 582; *Associated Newspapers Group v Wade* [1979] IRLR 279; [1979] ICR 664; [1979] 1 WLR 697.

[29] *Hadmor Productions Ltd v Hamilton* [1983] AC 191; [1982] IRLR 102; [1982] ICR 114. See too *Merkur Island Shipping Corporation v Laughton* [1983] 2 AC 570; [1983] IRLR 218. One argument for the existence of

So, the history of trade union tortious liability for calling industrial action has been one of, at common law, increasing liability, decreasing protection for employees who are called to take part in the action by their union and increasing protection for employers. This is shown further by the fact that, the bit between their teeth, the courts have found little reason to restrict the tort to those occasions where there has been a breach of contract. So, other instances of legal liability have sufficed too. For example, a breach of an equitable duty is included so that in *Prudential Assurance Co. v Lorenz*[30] trade union members who refused to submit insurance premiums they had collected to their head office were enjoined from this course of action since it was inducing breach of their equitable duty to account, which they owed as agents to their principal, the claimant. Indeed, in so far as in principal liability is attached to the union because of the unlawful act of another it has caused, it would seem logical perhaps for the tort to cover other forms of unlawfulness too. Likewise, simple inducement is no longer required either. In addition ideas such as procurement, where the party in breach is not induced at all but forced into breach, is also covered, as we have seen. Likewise, the tort has been extended to cover not just direct breaches but indirect breaches too whereby a breach occurs through the agency of another party, as we have seen in the examples above. The courts have sometimes tempered these extensions somewhat by, for example, requiring a separate unlawful act for an indirect breach, but these are not hard to find. In the example I gave above, an employer who is put into breach with their customers is almost always put into breach by virtue of the union's inducement of its members to break their employment contracts. As such, the stringency of the extra requirement is something of an illusion.

The tort of inducing a breach of contract, without further statutory protection for trade unions calling industrial action, is thus a powerful tool in the hands of employers. However, even outside these cases, there have been several calls for many years that there is no justification for the tort of inducement, or at least that there are reasons why it should not be a tort. One objection is that it allows the parties to a contract to create obligations for strangers. This may be true, at least of negative obligations not to interfere with the performance of a contract but, as Roderick Bagshaw has pointed out, this is true also of many other situations, such as on the registration of a patent or the issue of a share certificate.[31] A stronger objection might be that, if the law gave

---

the tort was that there was statutory recognition for it in terms of the statutory immunity that had been given in respect of it. In that this was a prophylactic provision in the event of the tort being seen to be separate from the tort of inducement, the argument that it supported the existence of the tort was somewhat inventive, to put it no higher than that!

30 *Prudential Assurance Co. v Lorenz* (1971) 11 KIR 78.
31 R. Bagshaw, 'Inducing Breach of Contract' in J. Horder (ed.), *Oxford Essays in Jurisprudence* (4th Series) (Oxford University Press, 2000) pp. 131, 133.

no protection against a third party interfering with a contract, particularly a trade union, this would make it harder for employees to leave unsatisfactory employment contracts. But, as Bagshaw also points out,[32] the employee is only bound contractually to those contracts that they have voluntarily entered into. Perhaps the best justification for the tort, and one which cannot be prayed in aid in respect of any possible variation that would not require an actual breach, or the tort of interference with contract that did not involve unlawful acts, is that a party who is the *de facto* procurer of an *unlawful* act should pay some sort of penalty for so doing, or at least should be liable to a party who has suffered because of the unlawful act that the guilty party has brought about.

THE EFFECTIVENESS OF LEGISLATION

Tortious immunity

I began the last paragraph by stating that, without the statutory protection the law provides for trade unions calling industrial action, the law of torts is a powerful tool in the hands of employers. The assumption there, which I would now like to explore further, was that statutory protection takes away the power that tool has. On the face of it, this would certainly seem to be the case. If an act is done in contemplation or furtherance of a trade dispute it is not actionable in tort on the ground only that it induces a breach of contract, interferes with contract, induces any other person to interfere with its performance, constitutes a threat of breach, inducement or interference, or that it constitutes a conspiracy to do any of these things.[33] This is the so-called 'golden formula'. At first blush it would seem to give trade unions an almost blanket immunity to call industrial action. But does it? There are several limitations on this protection for trade unions.

First, it covers only tortious liability. There is no immunity granted for breaches of contract or crime, nor for torts other than those specified which may well occur during industrial action such as trespass, harassment, breach of statutory duty and libel. The consequence, of course, is that the 'discovery' of new torts by the courts means further areas of tortious liability arise that are not covered by the 'immunity'. An example of this is the tort of harassment that emerged in *Thomas v National Union of Mineworkers (South Wales Area)*[34] in 1985. Secondly, the protection extends only to make the torts committed 'not actionable' and they are not made lawful. So torts covered could nevertheless remain unlawful means for the indirect torts.

A third, and major, limitation on the statutory protection is that it is

---

[32] Ibid, p. 134. This article contains a number of convincing arguments for the defence of the tort of inducing a breach of contract which I cannot consider here.
[33] Trade Union and Labour Relations (Consolidation) Act 1992, s. 219.
[34] *Thomas v National Union of Mineworkers (South Wales Area)* [1985] IRLR 136; [1985] 2 WLR 1081.

confined to the rather narrow definition of a 'trade dispute' in the legislation.[35] It must be a dispute between workers and their employer, not with other workers or with other employers. This means that trade unions in the public sector, whose members' pay and conditions are to a large extent influenced by the government but whose employer is another legal entity, are not protected. This is so even if the subject-matter of the dispute is in the normal run of trade disputes in the private sector, such as terms and conditions of employment. In practice this perhaps does not diminish the unions' immunity because all it needs to do is to engineer a further dispute with the employer. This is often not a difficult thing to do, and perhaps consists in an argument with the employer that it is not supporting their employees' case against the government sufficiently. Nevertheless, this would seem to be a highly unsatisfactory state of affairs, because it is not conducive to good industrial relations that additional disputes need to be created in order for trade unions to enjoy legal protection in the event of calling industrial action in the legitimate exercise of protecting their members' terms and conditions of employment. There are exceptions[36] if the dispute has been referred to a joint body where the government is represented and also where it has a statutory duty in relation to the dispute, for example to approve a pay settlement. But these do not cover all situations where the dispute is with the government.

Furthermore, the corporate veil (whereby companies are to be treated as legal persons separate from their real owners) is not lifted as between long-established separate companies in respect of secondary action. So this means that where employer A and employer B are in reality companies owned by the same person, a dispute between employees of employer A cannot be joined by employees of employer B, because they would not be acting in contemplation or furtherance of a dispute with their own employer. It is true that the employer cannot create a new company during the dispute in order to take advantage of this,[37] but a far-sighted employer can take prophylactic measures in order to do so.

The dispute must also relate wholly or mainly to certain matters identified in the legislation. These are:

(a) terms and conditions of employment, or the physical conditions in which any workers are required to work;

(b) engagement or non-engagement, or termination or suspension of employment or the duties of employment, of one or more workers;

---

[35] Trade Union and Labour Relations (Consolidation) Act 1992, s. 244(1).
[36] Ibid, s. 244(2).
[37] *Dimbleby & Sons Ltd v National Union of Journalists* [1984] IRLR 161; [1984] ICR 386; [1984] 1 WLR 427.

(c) allocation of work or the duties of employment as between workers or groups of workers;

(d) matters of discipline;

(e) the membership or non-membership of a trade union on the part of a worker;

(f) facilities for officials of trade unions; and

(g) machinery for negotiation or consultation, and other procedures, relating to any of the foregoing matters, including the recognition by employers or employers' associations of the right of a trade union to represent workers in any such negotiation or consultation or in the carrying out of such procedures.

Therefore, a strike simply against government policy will not of itself be in contemplation or furtherance of a trade dispute, unless it can be related to one of the above matters.

The immunity has also been narrowed in that it must relate wholly or mainly to one or more of these matters. Until 1982 a dispute need only have been 'connected with' them. However, that of course leaves open the possibility that the action may also relate to a matter not in the list.

There is yet a further hurdle which has to be jumped for the trade union to enjoy the immunity. There must be a ballot taken of all those workers likely to be called to take part in the action.[38] However, it is arguable how far this can be said to limit the protection given to trade unions in that they generally place requirements to be satisfied that are quite capable of being satisfied. These relate to, for example, entitlement to vote, notice, balloting methods and so on. Nevertheless they do restrict the ability of a union to call for industrial action in one regard in that the requirement for a ballot in effect rules out wildcat action whereby industrial action is taken on the spur of the moment in immediate response to an act of the employer. It might be thought that it is sometimes legitimate for unions to call on workers to take precipitate action in some circumstances, for example where an employer places a hazardous obligation on its employees. Of course, the employees in those circumstances have no duty to obey such orders, but it is quite a different matter as to the liability of trade unions in calling for action in immediate protest about it.

IS THERE A RIGHT TO PICKET?

Picketing is not a concept, or at least a word, that is known to the law of industrial action. It generally refers simply to the idea that workers place themselves at the entrances and exits of their own workplace, or other workplaces. A century ago the main purpose was to prevent colleagues from

---

[38] Trade Union and Labour Relations (Consolidation) Act 1992, ss. 226–34.

working when there was a strike, or to prevent replacement workers (blackleg labour) from doing the work normally done by striking workers. In the latter part of the century it became, at least in high profile cases such as the miners' strike in 1984–85, more a form of protest involving massed workers (sometimes infiltrated by political militants unconnected with the dispute) which often turned violent.

The main justification of peaceful picketing lies in the right to freedom of speech and of peaceful protest. It is often seen as fundamental and in many countries the right to picket is protected by the constitution. This is, of course, not so in this country, and not only because we do not have a written constitution. The closest we get to the idea is that there may be some protection in the idea that picketing may be a human right, and this has received judicial recognition.[39] Much depends on the practice of the police on the spot in controlling pickets, with relatively little guidance from case-law which has typically proceeded in a very pragmatic way, little determined by principle. This has attracted some criticism.[40] There is, however, an ACAS Code of Practice on Picketing which supplements the law.

It is usually said that, given certain statutory conditions being satisfied, there is a right to picket during industrial disputes.[41] This is an understandable idea, but I would argue it is one that is debatable, at least in literal terms. The 'right' to picket is based upon the idea that picketing is capable of transgressing certain common law and statutory restrictions in the general law (not aimed at picketing *per se*) which are removed by statute in industrial action cases. The possible common law liabilities are several. For example, a breach of the peace might be committed. In *Kavanagh v Hiscock*[42] a policeman claimed he had reason to believe there would be a breach of the peace if an exit from a hospital was not completely clear of pickets, and he thus proceeded to remove those who were waiting to harangue 'blacklegs' being transported to work by bus. The court held that the offence of breach of the peace had been committed and the pickets had no legal right to stop a vehicle without the consent of the driver. What this shows is that it is immaterial whether the breach of the peace is likely to be caused by the pickets themselves, the picketed, or bystanders. It is also an offence at common law to obstruct the public in the exercise or enjoyment of rights common to all, including free passage along the highway. Picketing often falls foul of this prohibition, but

---

[39] See *Gate Gourmet London Ltd v Transport and General Workers Union* [2005] IRLR 881.

[40] See e.g. S. Auerbach, 'Legal Restraint of Picketing: New Trends; New Tensions' (1987) 16 *Industrial Law Journal* 227.

[41] See, for example, S. Deakin and G. Morris, *Labour Law* (Hart Publishing, 5th ed, 2009) at p. 9 where they state that the Trade Dispute Act 1906 'conferred a right to take part in peaceful picketing' for peaceful purposes, which is the ancestor in similar terms of the current legislation.

[42] *Kavanagh v Hiscock* [1984] ICR 282; [1974] QB 600; [1974] 2 All ER 177.

picketing in itself probably does not constitute a common law nuisance.[43] In *J. Lyons & Sons v Wilkins*[44] Lindley LJ thought it did as it constituted an attempt to persuade. But Lord Denning MR in *Hubbard v Pitt*[45] (not an industrial action case) considered that this view had not stood the test of time. He was concerned not to restrict free speech and assembly by restricting picketing, stating that a group of protesters standing on the pavement outside an estate agency, in reasonable numbers and orderly manner, was quite lawful and not a nuisance. However, in *Thomas v NUM (South Wales Area)*[46] Scott J decided that regular picketing of a person's home would in itself be a common law nuisance. In addition it is also possible during picketing to commit a private nuisance, which is an unlawful interference with an individual's enjoyment or use of his land. To sue for the tort, the claimant must have some proprietary interest in land and this action is thus most likely to arise where pickets block an access route. Picketing accompanied by violence, or even merely noise, may be a private nuisance. It may also involve a trespass to the highway. This occurs when the highway is used other than for passing and re-passing. The claimant is the owner of the soil beneath the relevant highway, usually abutting landowners or the local authority. The liability is more apparent than real since few such landowners would be able to show special damage from the picketing.

In addition there are numerous criminal liabilities that might be incurred during picketing. I will give just some examples. By s. 137 of the Highways Act 1980, if a person without lawful authority or excuse, in any way wilfully obstructs the free passage along a highway, an offence is committed. This is a charge frequently brought against pickets. The offence is one of strict liability committed by anyone freely causing an obstruction.[47] In addition, there is statutory control of processions and assemblies under ss. 11 to 16 of the Public Order Act 1986. Section 89 of the Police Act 1996 makes it a criminal offence to obstruct a police constable in the execution of his duty and that duty is to prevent trouble where he reasonably apprehends a breach of the peace as a 'real possibility'. By s. 4A of the Public Order Act 1986 a person is guilty of an offence if they, with intent, cause another person harassment, alarm or distress by using threatening, abusive or insulting words or behaviour or disorderly conduct, or by displaying any writing, sign or other visible

---

[43] Public nuisance is a tort as well as a crime but civil proceedings may be brought only with the consent of the Attorney-General on a relator action.

[44] *J. Lyons & Sons v Wilkins* [1899] 1 Ch 255.

[45] *Hubbard v Pitt* [1975] ICR 308; [1976] QB 142. Lord Denning's comments were in his dissenting judgement, but the majority did not consider the general principle contenting themselves to refrain from interfering in the discretion exercised by the judge in the court below.

[46] *Thomas v National Union of Mineworkers,* n 36.

[47] *Arrowsmith v Jenkins* [1963] 2 QB 561.

representation which is threatening, abusive or insulting. Affray, violent disorder and riot are other possible charges for violent pickets. The former at common law meant unlawful fighting by one or more persons in a public place in such manner that reasonable people might be frightened or intimidated. Section 3 of the Public Order Act 1986 codifies this offence, defining it as the use or threat of unlawful violence to another such as would cause a person of reasonable firmness present to fear for their personal safety. A riot can be charged under s. 1 of the 1986 Act where twelve or more persons use or threaten such violence, and violent disorder under s. 2 where there are three or more persons involved.

There are also several offences specifically aimed at pickets. Section 241 of TULR(C)A 1992 makes it a criminal offence if a person wrongfully and without legal authority:

(a) uses violence or intimidates another;
(b) persistently follows another from place to place;
(c) hides any tools, clothes or other property owned or used by such other person, or deprives him of or hinders him in the use thereof;
(d) watches or besets the house or other place where such other person resides, or works, or carries on business or happens to be, or the approach to such house or place;
(e) follows such other person with two or more other persons in a disorderly manner in or through any street or road.

These are probably enough examples to indicate the degree of possible liability that pickets might incur, both civil and criminal. It may be no surprise, therefore, that statute intervenes to give a degree of protection against some of these liabilities. However, I consider it debatable just how extensive this protection is, for several reasons.

The statutory protection is provided by the Trade Union and Labour Relations (Consolidation) Act 1992, s. 220. This states that it is lawful for a person in contemplation or furtherance of a trade dispute to attend at or near their own place of work or, if they are an official of a trade union, at or near the place of work of a member of the union for the purpose only of obtaining or communicating information, or peacefully persuading any person to work or abstain from working. Notice that the immunity gives protection in relation to liabilities arising from the *attendance* of pickets for peaceful communication and not their criminal or tortious activities while so attending. This might be thought, at the least, to cover trespass, but it does not.[48] There are also restrictions on the numbers of pickets. Although s. 220 contains no specific restriction in this regard, the Code of Practice describes mass picketing as

---

48 *British Airports Authority v Ashton* [1983] IRLR 287; [1983] 1 WLR 1079.

'obstruction if not intimidation' and recommends ensuring that 'in general the number of pickets does not exceed six at any entrance to a workplace, frequently a smaller number will be appropriate'.[49] The courts may take notice of this.

So, the so-called 'right to picket' is very severely restricted, covering liabilities that arise out of mere attendance, by a small number of pickets, and does not cover even trespass. It is also restricted to liabilities that are incurred through being at or near one's place of work. There is no right to be in or on it. And, of course, it covers only the peaceful obtaining or communicating of information, or peacefully persuading workers to work or abstain from working. But, more than this, notice that the right is merely to attend *for the purpose* of doing these things. I would argue that it does not in fact give anyone the right to do those things. Let me give an analogy. If I live in a built-up area I certainly have the right, in the middle of the night, to open my study windows leading onto the street and to seat myself at my 90-stop, four-manual pipe organ, complete with a 32 foot Ophicleide stop, which produces a very loud, reedy, sound – some would say noise. I have the right to do this for the purpose of playing the organ, and I may certainly do so without my neighbours having any legal redress against me. But what I do not have is the legal right actually to play it. It is thus very debatable that there is a legal right to picket in any meaningful sense.

If this was the intention behind the 1992 Act, that would seem to be its effect, although it has to be said that it has not been interpreted in this restrictive, if literal, way. Indeed, the evidence would seem to suggest that the legislation was intended to be particularly helpful to pickets. This can be shown by the special treatment given to secondary picketing. Secondary picketing is picketing which affects an employer who is not the employer party to the trade dispute. It used to be the case that secondary picketing was treated, in the main, no differently from primary picketing. However, during Margaret Thatcher's time as Prime Minister there was a move towards making secondary industrial action of various types unlawful. But some exceptions were retained. One was where the 'secondary employer' was a customer or supplier of the employer in the trade dispute. Another exception was where the secondary employer was an 'associated employer' of the employer party to the trade dispute being, for example, a parent company. Those two exceptions were later repealed, but the secondary picketing exception remains. However, this exception is very narrow. It simply entitles an employee of the employer who is party to the trade dispute to be free of liability in relation to another employer and its employees, such as someone

---

[49] Ibid, para. 31.

making deliveries at the picketing employee's place of work. Nevertheless, it is an exception to the general blanket legal position on secondary action and is significant for that.

HOW EFFECTIVE ARE INJUNCTIONS?

Industrial action is an unusual legal phenomenon in that the opposing parties are both aware that, at some stage in the future, although their relationship has presently broken down, they will need to work together once more. If their intentions were not to do so the workers would simply resign and walk away or the employer would close down its business. What the workers want is the freedom to withdraw their labour and the employers want the workforce to continue working. The employer is not particularly interested in the main in obtaining damages as a remedy as I have mentioned before, not least because an employer who is making a loss might even be in profit during a strike. However, a difficulty for the employer would seem to be the principle that the law will not force employees to work. There is no specific performance available on a contract of employment or injunction to restrain a breach of contract that compels employees to work.[50] It would seem, then, that the employer during strike action is not able to request a court for an injunction to get its workforce back to work.

However, this is not the case. Injunctions seem to be a highly effective remedy for employers in industrial action. This is because there is nothing to prevent the courts from making injunctions to prevent torts. This may seem curious, because the purpose of the unavailability of specific performance and injunctions is partly technical, in that the executory nature of employment contracts makes them difficult to supervise, but it is also because of the principle that no-one should be forced to work. Even if it is a little strong to refer to this as slavery[51] it is something clearly distasteful in a modern industrial democracy. In that case, it might be asked, if the practical effect of awarding an injunction to prevent torts being committed during industrial action is to force the workforce back to work, should there not be the same objection? However, the courts have found no difficulty here.

The use of injunctions to prevent torts can be a very effective weapon in the hands of employers because of the general principles considered by the courts in the decision whether to award them. It used to be the case that the claimant had to establish a *prima facie* case to be entitled to an injunction so that the merits of the case were at least partially aired at an early stage. However, this changed with the decision of the House of Lords in 1975 in the patent law case,

---

[50] Trade Union and Labour Relations (Consolidation) Act 1992, s. 236.
[51] See *De Francesco v Barnum* (1890) 43 ChD 165; 59 LJ Ch 151.

American Cyanamid Co. Ltd v Ethicon Ltd.[52] The House of Lords held that it is necessary only for the claimant to have an arguable case, and that there is a serious issue to be tried. In deciding whether to award an injunction the judge should apply a balance of convenience test. This has the effect of assisting an employer because the balance of convenience more often than not lies with it – the status quo is that there is no industrial action. It is balanced to some degree only by the claimant having to give an undertaking to compensate the defendant in damages if they have suffered loss as a result of its issue and the court hearing the case at full trial determines, on reviewing all the evidence, that the injunction should not in fact have been granted. This is, however, of little use in dispute cases to a union enjoined because, first, full trials are very few and far between and, secondly, because the loss which the union could prove it has suffered by not being able to strike is likely to be nominal. The difficulty for the union is that once the impetus for the industrial action has been lost because of the issuing of an injunction it may be very difficult to revive. Further, the employer can make arrangements to defeat a subsequent strike, such as organizing supplies or subcontracting its work to other firms. Therefore, to redress this imbalance somewhat, the Trade Union and Labour Relations (Consolidation) Act 1992, s. 221(1) states that if there might be a 'trade dispute' defence to an injunction, the court must not grant relief without notice unless all reasonable steps have been taken to notify the other side of the application and to give them an opportunity of putting their side of the story. Further, s. 221(2) states that on an application for an interim injunction the court must 'have regard' to the likelihood that the defendant would succeed at trial with a trade dispute defence. However, section 221(2) applies only in relation to the torts specified in s. 219(1). These are inducing breaches of contract, conspiracy and intimidation. If other torts are committed, the ordinary test will apply.

One important factor in the decision is that the courts may take the public interest into account, particularly if there would be immediate threats to health and safety in the event of a strike.[53] This again works heavily in the employer's favour, as do several other considerations. First, all the employer needs to do is to obtain an interim injunction. This is, in theory, an injunction that is awarded pending a full trial when all the issues can be properly aired. This is why the tests for granting it are 'holding' ideas, to preserve the status quo, to consider the balance of convenience and so on. But the practical reality is that cases very rarely go to a full trial for the simple reason that an interim injunction normally provides the employer with all it needs. It has the effect

---

[52] *American Cyanamid Co. Ltd v Ethicon Ltd* [1975] AC 396; [1975] 2 WLR 316.
[53] *Beaverbrook Newspapers Ltd v Keys* [1978] IRLR 34; [1978] ICR 582.

of killing off the industrial action and forcing the employees back to work. Secondly an interim injunction can be granted very quickly. An application may be made by an application notice and the claimant must in most circumstances give three days' notice. However, this may be dispensed with in cases of urgency and an application may even pre-date the issue of a claim form in the action. If an interim injunction without notice to the opposing party is granted the absent defendants will usually be given leave to apply to discharge it on short notice.

Another factor which seems to weigh very heavily in the employer's favour is that the consequences of failing to abide by the injunction are extremely serious. The employer may apply for committal of the trade union or one or more of its officers for contempt of court leading to a fine or imprisonment. Not surprisingly, courts insist that all procedural aspects of a committal for contempt are fully complied with, and therefore the injunction must be served personally on the defendant except in the most exceptional circumstances such as when it has been given wide coverage in the media. The union may be in contempt of court if it does not prevent its officials from acting in contempt of court. The court may imprison the guilty party for up to two years,[54] fine or issue an order to give security for good behaviour. The largest fine so far levied was £250,000 on the National Union of Mineworkers in 1984.

However, the very powerful remedy of sequestration is available as a last resort. This works by sequestrating all the real and personal property of the union or other person subject to the order. In recent strike cases chartered accountants have usually been appointed to be the sequestrators. The writ binds all the property of the person sequestered from the date of its issue, and the sequestrators enter at once to take possession of both real and personal estate. The sequestrators act as officers of the court, and may from time to time be given directions by the judge. Any resistance or interference by any person with the sequestrators carrying out their proper duties is in itself a contempt of court.

It can be seen, therefore, that far from being impotent in the face of industrial action, there is an argument that the employer has a very significant arsenal of measures available to it. It undercuts in a major way any idea that there exists a legal right to strike in any meaningful sense.

---

54 Contempt of Court Act 1981, s. 14.

Debate 2

How justified is it for the law to intervene in trade union affairs?

One of the main arguments that could be made in favour of the idea that trade unions should be free from legal intervention is that they are, in essence, private bodies, rather like a club. The courts have tried to ascribe corporate status to them, or quasi-corporate status,[55] but cannot now do so. Their status is now determined by the Trade Union and Labour Relations (Consolidation) Act 1992 which states that it is not possible for trade unions to have corporate status giving them a legal identity separate from their members, nor can they be treated as if they had corporate status, as quasi-corporate bodies.[56] It is possible for them, however, to make contracts, to sue and be sued in their own names, be prosecuted, have their property held for them on trust and have court judgements, orders and awards enforced against them.[57] In other respects they are similar to other unincorporated bodies.

On the other hand, it has long been recognized that trade unions have a public persona and have a great influence in the national economy and in national politics. It is often stated that the Labour Party and the trade unions have a very close connection but it is, of course, much closer than that in that the Labour Party was born of the trade union movement. It is much more of a parent-child relationship than a friendly acquaintance. Such has been the perception of the power of trade unions that they were treated very suspiciously by the courts in the nineteenth century. They were seen as something of a danger to national life, and the possible harbinger of Jacobinism and other seeds of revolution. This manifested itself in the legal idea that trade unions were unlawful bodies in that they were in restraint of trade.[58] This idea is still important enough for the 1992 Act to have a provision in it specifically making it clear that trade unions are not unlawful by reason only that they are in restraint of trade.[59] Notice, however, that the Act does not state that unions are not to be treated as if they were in restraint of trade, but that legal consequences are not to follow by reason only that they are in restraint of trade.

The political aspect of trade unions is something which has been seen to give governments *locus* to intervene in the internal affairs of trade unions. This

---

55 See *Taff Vale Railway Company v Amalgamated Society of Railway Servants* [1901] AC 426; *Bonsor v Musicians' Union* [1956] AC 104.

56 Trade Union and Labour Relations (Consolidation) Act 1992, s. 10.

57 Ibid, ss. 10, 12.

58 *Hornby v Close* (1867) 2 LR QB.

59 Trade Union and Labour Relations (Consolidation) Act 1992, s. 11.

is most directly to be seen in the legal control on their political funds. The courts have been astute to the possibilities of doing this since the emergence of the Labour Party from the trade union movement over a century ago. Most notoriously the House of Lords decided in *Amalgamated Society of Railway Servants v Osborne*[60] in 1910 that the use of union funds for political purposes was illegal, as unions were empowered to pursue only those objects permitted in the Trade Union Act 1871 and this was not one of them. This had a significant impact on the development of the Labour Party but this proved to be but temporary as three years later the Liberal Government secured the passage of the Trade Union Act 1913. This Act permitted unions to pursue any object sanctioned by their constitution, although it placed restrictions on the funds which could be used for political purposes. TULR(C)A 1992, s. 71(1) now states that payments for political purposes can be made only from a separate political fund. Political objects are defined in s. 72(1) and covers contributions to the funds and expenses of a political party, provision of any service or property for a political party, expenditure in connection with the registration of electors, the candidature of any person or the selection of any candidate, the maintenance of any holder of a political office (including an MP, MEP, local councillor, or party office-holder), and holding a party political conference or meeting (including sending observers or other non-participants). In addition every form of political advertising is covered. The oversight of political funds is not carried out primarily by the courts but by an official called the Certification Officer who has sometimes taken a wide view of what amounts to 'political'. For example, in *Richards v NUM*[61] the Certification Officer held that money spent on a march and Parliamentary lobby against Government cuts should have come from the union's political fund.

There would appear to be good justification for treating the political activities of trade unions as something different from the rest of their activities. As we have already seen, the law defines trade unions in terms of their principal purposes including the regulation of relations between workers and their employer.[62] This is a somewhat narrow view of trade unions, but it makes no mention of political activity. And, of course, it is quite possible to belong to a trade union without being a member or even a supporter of the political party (normally but not exclusively the Labour Party of course) supported by the union. For this reason it is possible not to pay into the union's political fund, which means that a member can opt out of that part of their membership dues that would otherwise be paid into the political fund.[63] If they do so they may

---

[60] *Amalgamated Society of Railway Servants v Osborne* [1910] AC 10.
[61] *Richards v National Union of Mineworkers* [1981] IRLR 247.
[62] Trade Union and Labour Relations (Consolidation) Act 1992, s. 1.
[63] Ibid, s. 84(1).

not be excluded from any benefits of the union, nor placed at a disability or disadvantage compared with other members of the union because they have opted out.[64] So much seems unexceptionable apart from one consideration. In this regard trade unions would seem to be parallel to companies, from which much of the funding for the Conservative Party is derived. And yet there is no right for company members (shareholders) as individuals to opt out of political payments. They may do so collectively at a general meeting of the company, but there is no individual right. This puts into even sharper relief the intention of Margaret Thatcher when she was Prime Minister in the early 1980s to change the law so that union members had to opt in to making payments into the political fund rather than simply having the right to opt out. Not surprisingly, in the light of the position regarding companies, she seems to have been persuaded that this was not feasible on political grounds.

The public nature of trade unions has also been the basis for intervention in union rule books. For example, Lord Denning saw the rules of the unions not as agreements whose terms the law allows the members to determine, but instead rather more like local authority by-laws.[65] This led him to the view that the rules, if they were unreasonable, could be declared invalid by the courts as contrary to natural justice. This would not be applied to the constitution of a purely private body. The important difference here, for Lord Denning, was the extent of trade union power, to the point of being able to deprive workers of their livelihoods. This is less so now, of course, since the demise of legal support for the closed shop. In fact between 1974 and 1984 unions had virtually complete freedom over what went into their rule books except regarding the political fund and the right to resign membership. Nevertheless, some union rules may be held to be illegal at common law. In *Drake v Morgan*[66] in 1978 the House of Lords held that a general union policy to pay the fines of members who were convicted of unlawful picketing would be unlawful.[67] In *Thomas v National Union of Mineworkers (South Wales Area)*[68] in 1985, one of the cases arising out of the 1984–85 miners' strike, Scott J decided that it would be *ultra vires* the rules of the union for its officials to embark upon and finance a form of picketing as that would be bound to involve criminal acts.

In many respects the argument that there is too much interference in the rule books of trade unions would seem to be unfounded in that the courts are very often simply applying the approach that they do with regards to other private documents. For example, the courts imply terms into the rule book

---

[64] Ibid, s. 82(1).
[65] *Edwards v Halliwell* [1950] 2 All ER 1064.
[66] *Drake v Morgan* [1978] ICR 56.
[67] It is now, however, unlawful under statute to make such payments by virtue of Trade Union and Labour Relations (Consolidation) Act 1992, s. 15.
[68] *Thomas v National Union of Mineworkers*, n 36.

much in the same way that they would do for any contract. So, applying the officious bystander test, the courts have required reasonable notice to be given to members of important meetings[69] and a power to discipline members was implied in *McVitae v Unison*.[70] However, the courts have refused to imply that members be entitled to vote by proxy,[71] or that a member should abide by all reasonable directions of the union.[72]

On the other hand, sometimes the courts apply ideas to rule books that are arguably inappropriate. For example, rule books are rather like the articles of association of a company, providing for the institutions which govern the union. The courts must sometimes restrain a union organ which acts *ultra vires* (beyond its legal capacity). Similarly, the rule in *Foss v Harbottle*[73] (that the proper plaintiff where there are procedural irregularities should be the body itself and not a member) is sometimes applied. However, both the *ultra vires* concept and the rule in *Foss v Harbottle* are relevant to corporate bodies. There is therefore a strong argument that, being unincorporated associations, trade unions should not be subject to these ideas.[74]

Debate 3

Should there be a right not to be a trade union member?

The right not to be a member of a trade union is primarily about the extent to which the law should not underpin closed shops.

Before the law first turned its attention to the institution of the closed shop in the form of the Industrial Relations Act 1971, most were informal and flexible arrangements which had grown up over time often supported only by custom and practice in the work place or industry concerned. With the introduction of protection against unfair dismissal in the same Act, it was provided that an employer who dismissed a non-unionist in accordance with a valid closed shop agreement (and few were valid) had dismissed fairly. Nevertheless, the arguments against legal support for the closed shop eventually won the day during Margaret Thatcher's tenure as Prime Minister, and the law on this is now contained in the Trade Union and Labour Relations (Consolidation) Act 1992.[75] It is not true to say that the Employment Act 1988 made closed shops unlawful, as is sometimes claimed, but they have become very difficult in law to maintain.

---

[69] *MacLelland v National Union of Journalists* [1975] ICR 116.
[70] *McVitae v Unison* [1996] IRLR 33.
[71] *Goring v British Actors' Equity Association* [1987] IRLR 122.
[72] *Radford v NATSOPA* [1972] ICR 484.
[73] *Foss v Harbottle* (1843) 2 Hare 461.
[74] See Lord Wedderburn, 'Trade Union Law' (1985) 14 *Industrial Law Journal* 127.
[75] Trade Union and Labour Relations (Consolidation) Act 1992, ss. 137, 138, 152, 174–177, and 222.

There are several strong arguments both for and against providing legal support for the closed shop. It has been a matter of great, sometimes fierce, debate whether the law should support closed shops, remove all support or indeed make them unlawful. To some people, closed shops are abhorrent in that they see compulsory union membership in order to obtain a particular job as an attack on fundamental freedoms. They have argued that the closed shop abuses human rights, and that individual liberty must come before any potential industrial relations gains. They contend that, consistent with a right to belong to a trade union, a symbol of a free society is the right to dissociate. The European Court of Human Rights has indeed held[76] in 1981 that the closed shop breaches Article 11 of the European Convention on Human Rights, which provides that everyone has the right to freedom of peaceful assembly and to freedom of association with others, including the right to form and join trade unions for the protection of their interests.

On the other hand the idea has been supported by others as an important tool to strengthen the unions' hands in collective bargaining. It is also seen as a justified method by which the collectivization of capital and management in a business in the form of the employer can be counter-balanced by the collectivization of labour in the form of the trade union. But occasionally it has been seen as an important tool for employers too. When there is a closed shop the employer embarking on collective bargaining is aware that the union officials in front of it represent the entire workforce. It also removes multi-unionism and the possibilities that this entails for inter-union rivalries and discord.

Another argument is that some groups of workers are so fragmented that they are impossible to organize without compulsory unionism, and consequently collective bargaining could not be carried on in those areas without the institution of the closed shop. This was considered to be an argument strong enough to lead to the exemption in the Industrial Relations Act 1971 for certain workers, such as seamen and actors, to be in 'approved closed shops'. However, these did not survive the reforms of the Thatcher Government's legislation. It is also argued that, as all employees, whether union members or not, reap the benefit of the union's efforts in collective bargaining, they should pay for that by being required to be members of it. Alternatively it was argued that the non-member should pay a sum equivalent to the union subscription to charity so that they do not end up in pocket by virtue of non-membership. This was recognized in the Industrial Relations Act which contained just such a provision.

---

[76] See *Young, James and Webster v United Kingdom* [1981] IRLR 408; (1982) 4 EHRR 38.

Debate 4

What is the basis of union membership rights and duties?

If trade unions were simply like clubs, and purely private bodies as their unincorporated legal status might suggest, there would be little justification for a great deal of regulation by statute or interference from the courts. Naturally, they would be subject to the general law in the same way that other bodies are, and there would appear to be good reasons why they would be subject to the law on, for example, discrimination, health and safety, and general employment law. That would appear to be incontrovertible. What would be less clear are any special measures or ideas to be applied to trade unions, over and above the general law.

However, as I have discussed earlier in this chapter, trade unions are not simply like private clubs, and there would appear to be good reasons to support arguments as to why there should be law dedicated to their legal status and activities. Not least is the public side of trade unions and their major economic power, at least in the sense of their ability to provide a co-operation between the workforce and business that is fundamental to a thriving economy, and the flipside to that, which is their potential to cause enormous economic disruption. There is also the power that has existed in trade unions, particularly when the closed shop was given extensive legal support, in relation to individuals and their jobs. When the refusal of trade union membership takes place in a context where membership is required in order to comply with a closed shop agreement, that clearly can be devastating to individual job prospects and security.

To a government, like that of Margaret Thatcher's between 1979 and 1990 that sought to curb trade union power, it was a useful technique to delay removing legal support for the closed shop. Some in the Conservative Party would no doubt have liked to have made closed shop agreements illegal from the outset of the Thatcher administration. However, this did not happen – and indeed never happened. It is not illegal even now to enter into a 'union membership agreement', as closed shop agreements were known in law. What is unlawful is to refuse employment to someone because they do, or do not, belong to a trade union.[77] The Conservative government took its time in reaching this situation, first of all introducing measures against the post-entry closed shop whereby employees were required to join a trade union within a period after taking up employment. These became almost unworkable, due to

---

[77] Trade Union and Labour Relations (Consolidation) Act 1992, s. 137. This also covers the situation where the claimant is unwilling to accept a requirement: (a) to take steps to be, or to remain or not to become, a member of a trade union, or (b) to make payments or suffer deductions in the event of not being a member of a trade union.

the requirement for high ballot majorities, followed as late as 1988 with the Employment Act of that year making refusal of a job due to trade union membership or non-membership subject to a right of employees to bring claims in an industrial tribunal. Then the pre-entry closed shop was given similar treatment in the Employment Act of 1990. It might seem surprising now that this was the course of events, given the well-known attitude of the government at that time to trade unions. However, the rationale for providing extensive protection to employees made most sense when it was still possible to operate a closed shop, for it was then that they were most vulnerable. By delaying the most extensive measures against the closed shop it was politically easier to introduce protection for individuals. Of course, once the closed shop was removed from the industrial scene the rationale for these measures became weaker but by that time the political hurdles had been overcome. The Labour Party no longer had the stomach to fight this, even if it any longer had the ideological desire to do so given its overriding objective of distancing itself from its militant past in order to make it more attractive to the electorate. So, it should come as no surprise that the thirteen years of Labour government between 1997 and 2010 saw no back-pedalling in relation to these rights.

IS THE BASIS OF A RIGHT TO JOIN A TRADE UNION ADEQUATE?

One limb of the legal foundation of trade union membership rights is clearly the right to join the union. Another is the right not to be expelled from it. There is also the right to resign membership. These may appear to be separate aspects of the right to belong to a trade union, and indeed throw up very similar issues. However, there are important differences, and I will therefore consider the first two independently.[78]

An employee has the right to join a trade union as against their employer by virtue of the Trade Union and Labour Relations (Consolidation) Act, s. 152. This states that a dismissal is automatically unfair, without the need to test it against the requirements of reasonableness, if it occurs at least mainly because the employee proposes to become a member of a trade union. It is otherwise treated in the same way as other cases of unfair dismissal, except that there is a minimum basic award payable. This provides, as I have described it elsewhere, 'secondary employment protection' for the employee. It is also unlawful if the employer, for the same reasons, takes action short of

---

[78] I take it as self-evident that, in the absence of a closed shop, there are no arguments that could be put forward for preventing a trade union member from resigning membership. For example, arguments from the position of members not being entitled to take the benefits of non-membership that have been accrued by the efforts and money of those in membership ultimately are reduced, in the context of the right to resign membership, to compulsory membership.

dismissal, such as refusing to promote the employee or withholding benefits of some description.[79] This may take a number of forms.

The legal right to join a trade union, as against the union, is now to be found in s. 174 of the 1992 Act. The exclusion of an individual from membership is permitted only in certain circumstances. The first is when that member does not satisfy an enforceable membership requirement. A requirement is enforceable for these purposes only if it restricts membership solely by reference to one or more of the following criteria: employment in a specified trade, industry or profession; occupational description (including grade level or category of appointment) and possession of specified trade, industrial or professional qualifications or work experience. Suspension from the benefits of union membership, however, is not covered.[80] The second is where the person does not qualify for membership because the union operates only in a particular part of Great Britain. Others are where, in the case of a trade union whose purpose is confined to a particular employer or group of employers, the member is not employed by that employer or the exclusion or expulsion is entirely attributable to that person's conduct. This excludes the possibility of exclusion or expulsion in reliance on agreement between trade unions for regulation of their relationships with each other which were enshrined in the Bridlington Principles. These were an agreement between unions, under the auspices of the Trades Union Congress, to prevent inter-union rivalry and the poaching of the members of other unions.

Now that the closed shop is no longer a feature of industrial life, the arguments for the right to join seem to be weaker than they once were. Certainly, the idea that it is rooted in the right to work, even if that ever had any firm foundation,[81] is no longer relevant. The only significant argument, other than in the exceptions just mentioned, would appear to be that, under the European Convention on Human Rights, there is a right of freedom of assembly and association in Article 11. This provides that:

1. Everyone has the right to freedom of peaceful assembly and to freedom of association with others, including the right to form and to join trade unions for the protection of his interests.

2. No restrictions shall be placed on the exercise of these rights other than such as are prescribed by law and are necessary in a democratic society in the interests of national security or public safety, for the prevention of

---

[79] Trade Union and Labour Relations (Consolidation) Act 1992, s. 146.

[80] NACODS v Gluchowski [1996] IRLR 252.

[81] Lord Denning MR attempted in Nagle v Feilden [1966] 2 QB 633; [1966] 1 All ER 689 to introduce the novel concept in English law of a right to work, in order to enable a woman to be admitted to the Jockey Club, so that she could work as a trainer. However, despite one or two cases which are sometimes taken to support the idea, it has not developed. See e.g. Edwards v SOGAT [1971] Ch 354; [1970] 3 All ER 689.

disorder or crime, for the protection of health or morals or for the protection of the rights or freedom of others ...

There is nothing in Article 11 that relates to this freedom being necessary as a gateway into employment, and it is thus not restricted to closed shop cases.[82] As such, it would seem to cover the right to join a trade union even where a closed shop does not exist. A major difficulty, however, with any right to join an organization rooted in the right of association is that the right not to associate with those with whom one wishes not to associate would seem to be implied. Thus, trade unions, as representative of the collection of individual members, would seem to have the right to refuse membership to another. So, in *ASLEF v United Kingdom*[83] in 2007 the European Court of Human Rights held that it was a matter for trade unions themselves to draw up conditions of membership, subject to a reasonable exercise of their decision-making powers. This would seem to provide a lesser degree of protection than TULR(C)A, s. 174 itself. The right, therefore, appears not to be very extensive.

IS THE BASIS OF A RIGHT TO REMAIN A TRADE UNION MEMBER ADEQUATE?

Much of the law on the right to remain a member of a trade union, or not to be expelled, is the same as that for the right to join. So s. 174 of the Trade Union and Labour Relations (Consolidation) Act 1992 giving the right not to be excluded from membership applies to expulsion too. Also, if an employer dismisses an employee because they remain a union member during employment, that is an automatically unfair dismissal under s. 152 of the same Act. However, there would appear to be a difference in principle between the right to join a union and the right to remain in it. The right to join is, clearly, the right not to be denied a benefit, namely that of membership. The basis of the claim therefore is rooted in the idea that the would-be member is denied something they do not have. It would seem in circumstances such as that, (absent discrimination, caprice or arbitrariness) an employee has less of a foundation for a claim than one based on existing membership. This is because in that case to have membership taken away is a form of theft. It is to have something that in a sense one owns removed for reasons, it would need to be claimed, that had no justification. So, there would seem to be two important distinctions here, I would suggest. One is that the basis of the claim itself differs between exclusion and expulsion. The second is the burden of proof for the claim. In other words, it would appear to be arguable, at least as a starting point of principle, that there is a greater burden on a body that seeks

---

[82] However, see the important case of *Young, James and Webster v United Kingdom*, n 76 on the application of Article 11 to the closed shop.
[83] *ASLEF v United Kingdom* [2007] IRLR 361.

to take away from somebody something that they already have compared with a denial of something that they presently do not have. If for no other reason this would seem to be sustainable from the vantage of preservation of the *status quo*.

Further Reading

S. Auerbach, 'Legal Restraint of Picketing: New Trends; New Tensions' (1987) 16 *Industrial Law Journal* 227.

R. Bagshaw, 'Inducing Breach of Contract' in J. Horder (ed.), *Oxford Essays in Jurisprudence* (4th Series) (Oxford University Press, 2000).

A. Bogg, *The Democratic Aspects of Trade Union Recognition* (Oxford University Press, 2009).

H. Carty, *An Analysis of the European Torts* (Oxford University Press, 2001).

H. Carty, 'The Economic Torts in the 21st Century' (2008) 124 *Law Quarterly Review* 641.

K.D. Ewing, 'The Function of Trade Unions' (2005) 34 *Industrial Law Journal* 1.

E. Ferran, 'Further Deductions From Wages' [1987] 46 *Cambridge Law Journal* 412.

D. Howarth, 'Against *Lumley v. Gye*' (2005) 68 *Modern Law Review* 195.

G. Morris, 'Industrial Conflict' (1987) 16 *Industrial Law Journal* 185.

T. Novitz, *International and European Protection of the Right to Strike* (Oxford University Press, 2003).

H. Simester, and W. Chan, 'Inducing Breach of Contract: One Tort or Two' (2004) 63 *Cambridge Law Journal* 132.

Lord Wedderburn, 'Trade Union Law' (1985) 14 *Industrial Law Journal* 127.

7

HUMAN RIGHTS AND EMPLOYMENT

INTRODUCTION

It is highly probable that anyone who had not given a great deal of thought to the concept of human rights and how they differ from other rights will nevertheless be aware that the idea has relevance in law as well as morality. They most probably would also be aware that the United Nations Declaration of Human Rights exists, created in the aftermath of the Second World War. They will almost certainly know that the Human Rights Act 1998 gave effect to the European Convention on Human Rights (or the European Convention for the Protection of Human Rights and Fundamental Freedoms) which was adopted by the Council of Europe in 1950, and came into force in 1953. Its role was to protect individuals' rights against infringement by states.[1] They might know that the Equality Act 2006 created the Commission on Equality and Human Rights to underpin its work in the United Kingdom. But what the idea of human rights is, and what its relationship with domestic employment law amounts to, will probably be issues that are much less clear in the mind of the interested observer. It is to this, therefore, that I first turn.

Debate 1

Is the idea of human rights in employment clear?

Anyone unacquainted with the idea of human rights, on being asked what they thought the term might refer to, would probably be rather perplexed. No doubt they would presume that the term 'human' was used in contradistinction to rights that were not held by humans. That would mean

---

[1] See generally, S. Palmer, 'Human Rights: Implications for Labour Law' (2000) 59 *Cambridge Law Journal* 168.

either inanimate objects or animals. The possibility that the former could have rights would no doubt seem peculiar and counter-intuitive. It would also probably be something that they had never heard of. To a lawyer, this might be tempered by the knowledge that corporate bodies have rights, but they would probably be aware that some theorists argue that this is just a useful fiction.[2] The alternative is that human rights are to be contrasted with animal rights. There are certainly some people who believe that animals have rights, and not simply that there are rights held by humans that concern animals. However, Peter Singer, who is often attributed as being the major proponent of the idea, in fact does not base his argument for the ethical treatment of animals on the notion that animals have rights.[3] In any event, it is clear that the concept of human rights goes much further than something that is to be contrasted with non-human rights, of whatever form, inanimate or animal. They are to be contrasted with other types of human rights in the sense of rights, other than 'human rights', held by human beings.

This would probably take our perplexed observer to the notion that human rights are in a sense more fundamental than other rights. This can be in two forms. The first is the Kantian idea that human rights are entrenched rights in the sense that they cannot be traded against anything else. They have, to use John Rawls' term, 'lexical priority' over other rights.[4] They are incommensurable. It is this aspect of those rights that makes them distinguishable from other 'ordinary' rights, legal or otherwise, because the latter can always be 'trumped'

---

[2] The fiction theory of corporate personality is not universally held. There are other common explanations. One is that a corporate body's legal personality is simply an amalgam of the legal features of its individual members. Another is that corporate personality is not a fiction in that it does exist in a real sense, but only in some metaphysical way. All three ideas have their difficulties. The term 'fiction' usually denotes the idea that something is held out as true but which is known by the person creating it, and others aware of it, not to be true. But corporate personality does exist in the real legal world in the sense that, for example, it is possible to go to court and enforce a company's legal rights in a way that Harry Potter or Homer Simpson could not. Neither is it true that a company's tax liabilities are merely a collection of the tax liabilities of its shareholders *qua* shareholders. None of them are liable to corporation tax. Then the idea that a company has 'real' existence, but only in some metaphysical sense, is an idea that seems to have little credence in the physical world of law. Perhaps it is best seen as a concept the meaning of which is simply determined by the occasions on which we choose to use the word. So, a trick in a game of cards as a concept is clearly not a fiction, nor a simple amalgam of four cards, nor does it have a metaphysical existence. It is a word and an idea that we use when given conditions have been met (see H.L.A. Hart, 'Definition and Theory in Jurisprudence' [1954] *Law Quarterly Review* 70). I explain this idea here in some detail not to explain alternatives to the idea that corporate personality is explicable as a fiction but because, of course, this approach would also seem to be relevant to the idea of why humans might have human rights and, indeed, rights in any form.

[3] See P. Singer, 'The Fable of the Fox and the Unliberated Animals' [1978] *Ethics* 119.

[4] J. Rawls, *A Theory of Justice* (Harvard University Press, 1971). The term 'lexical' is short for 'lexicographical' which is the basis for the ordering of words in a dictionary. All words beginning with A appear before any beginning with B, regardless of the position in the alphabet of the second and subsequent letters of the words. In other words, lexical priority entails the idea that one principle must be completely satisfied before embarking on the satisfaction of any other principle.

in some way by some other right or consideration. The idea obviously is widely discussed in the context of natural law. It could be reduced to the idea that human rights are those rights that, regardless of whom one is or what one has done, cannot be taken away. So, the right to life would entail the notion that even Adolf Hitler or Osama bin Laden had the right not to be killed for their terrible crimes. It would also entail the idea that, if the right to vote in general elections is a human right, even prisoners cannot be denied it. And, if the right to a family life is a human right, perhaps people should not be imprisoned at all.

If the concept of a human right is to be seen in such terms this would lead to this chapter being even shorter than it is. It would be very difficult to argue without eccentricity that whatever one has done there are rights in relation to one's job that can never be taken away. It may be that there are such overriding rights and that these are best described as 'human rights'. However, this is not the place to enter into that debate, interesting though it is. The point here is that, if there are such rights and that is what is meant by 'human rights', there would not appear to be any employment rights in that category. There are clearly rights of that type, if the argument is taken, that would relate to employment, such as the notion that employers, even if they may fire employees, may not fire shots at them. We can leave such pedantry behind.

So, we are left with the second approach to human rights I identified, which is the idea that there are rights that are more fundamental in some ways than others. In other words, that they may not be rights that cannot be trumped by any other right or idea, but nevertheless are superior in some shape or form to other rights. If we take that on board we can now start to relate the idea of human rights to the context of employment rights. We can ask questions that are relevant to employment because human rights then connotes the notion that rights need to be balanced against each other. Is the employee's right to strike one that counter-balances the employer's right to a loyal and co-operative workforce and does not put it into breaches of legal obligations to others? Is the employer's right to run its business in the most efficient way one that overrides the employee's right not to be dismissed unfairly? Is the employee's right to have personal characteristics (such as age, disability, race, sex) disregarded in the context of employment trumped by an employer's freedom to employ only those people it wishes to? The difficulty with this concept of human rights is that, of course, all rights in this second approach have the characteristic that they can be trumped by another right or consideration. They have this characteristic by definition. If that is the case, and human rights are to be defined in this way, it follows that they do not differ from any other type of right. It takes us nowhere in differentiating human rights from any other type of right.

A further possibility is that human rights are differentiated from any other type of right by content rather than by form. In other words, it is not their 'status' that defines human rights as such, in terms of incommensurability or superiority, but what they are about. They are human rights in the sense that they are about the essence of what it is to be a human being. They are concerned with fundamental ideas of the sanctity or inviolability of human life, human dignity, liberty and freedoms, respect and so on. It is here that we may be coming closer to the role that human rights have in the employment context. Protection of one's capacity to work, the freedom from unfair treatment during employment and protection of one's job itself are all fundamental to achieving life goals at one extreme and the attainment of minimum standards of living at the other.

A particular difficulty that arises here for our purposes is that this conception of a human right is both very vague and rooted in controversial ethical ideas. That it may also connote the notion that these rights are universal does not mean that they are uncontroversial. They can be highly controversial, particularly as they are rarely discussed other than in the context of balancing with other rights or considerations, such as national security and penal theory. And in that they are rooted in ethics – some would argue that they are primarily ethical[5] – human rights raise a great number of fundamental philosophical issues which it is not possible to enter into here in a way that would be likely for us to reach accepted positions to form the basis on which to discuss human rights in employment.

Furthermore, in that I am considering human rights here within the context of law that in our system is seen primarily from a positivist viewpoint, this creates further difficulties. Legal positivism involves the notion that the test or tests of legal validity – what makes something a law – are purely factual and not contentual.[6] For example, a Bill becomes an Act of Parliament and hence law in our system by passing through procedural hoops, namely receiving majorities in the House of Commons and the House of Lords before receiving the Royal Assent. There are similar procedural tests for other types of law, like precedent. These tests are not dependent in positivist theory on the *content* of those laws. They do not, for example, have to pass tests of morality, reasonableness or even comprehensibility in order to be law. Now positivism is seen in contradistinction to natural law theories in particular which are often taken to entail the notion that law has to pass a moral test in order to be law.

---

[5] See e.g. A. Sen, 'Elements of a Theory of Human Rights' (2004) 32 *Philosophy and Public Affairs* 315 and M. Freeman, *Lloyd's Introduction to Jurisprudence* (Sweet and Maxwell, 8th edn, 2008) p. 399f.

[6] See particularly H.L.A. Hart, *The Concept of Law* (Clarendon Press, 2nd edn. 1994). Cf. R Dworkin, *Justice in Robes* (Harvard University Press, 2006).

It is not in fact the case that this is necessarily a claim by natural lawyers[7] but the point here is that this is often taken to be the case and, even if it is not based on natural law ideas as such, the idea that positive law has to comply with some higher ethical and universal standard is clearly claimed by some human rights theorists. I am not making a claim (at least here) that positivism provides the best understanding of legal validity, but merely note that the notion of human rights as just described does not match with what are commonly understood tests in our domestic legal system of what something needs to be in order to be law.

So, it would seem that I can, in examining domestic employment law in the context of human rights, proceed on the basis only of what has been described as human rights in domestic law in general. This means that employment law needs to be examined in the light of the European Convention on Human Rights as incorporated (it is said) into United Kingdom law by the Human Rights Act 1998. This Act came into force for most purposes in 2000 and is designed to achieve three main aims. The first is that legislation should be interpreted in accordance with the Convention. The second is that acts of public bodies that are not in compliance with the Convention are unlawful, and thirdly to give courts the right to make declarations of incompatibility between domestic legislation and the Convention. So, under section 3 of the Act all courts and tribunals, when determining questions which arise in connection with a Convention right, must take into account judgments of the European Court of Human Rights, so far as relevant and possible. This means that the courts are not to be bound by previous interpretations of existing legislation by higher domestic courts if they are incompatible with the Convention. However, if domestic primary legislation is unambiguous and simply cannot be interpreted in accordance with the Convention, the domestic statute must be implemented. A statutory instrument will, however, be struck down if inconsistent with Convention rights unless the primary legislation prevents the removal of the incompatibility.

All public authorities must act in compliance with the Convention, unless prevented by domestic legislation from doing so, and it is unlawful for a public authority to act in a way which is incompatible with a Convention right.[8] Courts and tribunals are public authorities for the purpose of the Act, so courts and employment tribunals themselves act unlawfully if they breach Convention rights.

---

[7] See e.g. J. Finnis, *Natural Law and Natural Rights* (Clarendon Press, 1980).
[8] Human Rights Act 1998, s. 6.

Debate 2

Are any employment rights human rights?

If we take to mean by a human right those rights that are recognized by the European Convention on Human Rights, and which are necessarily recognized in the interpretation of domestic law by virtue of the Human Rights Act 1998, it is arguable that there are many circumstances in the world of work where human rights may be infringed. However, it is debatable how far the Convention has been successful in granting adequate protection against human rights violations. I will not attempt to give a thoroughly balanced consideration of that question here but instead concentrate on the argument that the Convention has not been as successful in this regard as it might have been.

FORCED OR COMPULSORY LABOUR

The most obviously relevant article of the Convention to employment is not one that in modern Britain has a great deal of practical significance. Article 4 states that there is a right not to be required to perform forced or compulsory labour. In any event, the UK already has this idea in its employment law, in that the Employment Rights Act 1996, s. 236 states that 'no court shall issue an order compelling any employee to do any work or attend at any place for the doing of any work'. However, there are those such as Douglas Brodie who have cogently argued that specific performance should be available against employees.[9]

DISCRIMINATION

Another article of the Convention that is reflected particularly in domestic legislation in the employment context, although not exclusively so, is Article 14. This states that the enjoyment of the rights and freedoms in the Convention are to be secured without discrimination on any ground such as sex, race, colour, language, religion, political or other opinion, national or social origin, association with a national minority, property, birth or other status. It goes further than United Kingdom law in the extent of its coverage, including such matters as political opinions and social origin, but on the other hand does not include, for example, disability or marital status. However, the use of the words 'such as' indicates that the categories of prohibited discrimination may include other grounds not mentioned.

---

[9] D. Brodie, 'Specific Performance and Employment Contracts' (1998) 27 *Industrial Law Journal* 37.

PEACEFUL ASSEMBLY AND ASSOCIATION

Article 11 is a much more significant provision on the face of it in the context of employment, although it is debatable how far it reaches in practice. Article 11 states that everyone has the right to freedom of peaceful assembly and to freedom of association with others, including the right to form and to join trade unions. It also states that there should be no restrictions placed on the exercise of these rights other than such as are prescribed by law and are necessary in a democratic society in the interests of national security or public safety, for the prevention of disorder or crime, for the protection of health or morals or for the protection of the rights and freedoms of others. However, Article 11 does not prevent the imposition of lawful restrictions on the exercise of these rights by members of the armed forces, of the police or the State.

The rights in respect of membership of trade unions are very important. However, the context in which the European Court on Human Rights first considered the issue in this context was with regard to the closed shop which, as I have discussed in a previous chapter, is no longer of practical significance in that the law now does not provide support for closed shops, without making them unlawful as such. In the early 1980s, in the case of *Young, James and Webster v United Kingdom*[10] the Court stated that the idea of freedom of association implied some measure of freedom of choice as to its exercise so that the freedom to associate included, to some extent, the freedom not to associate.[11] However, the Court held in *ASLEF v United Kingdom*[12] in 2007 that it would be in contravention of Article 11 to exclude or expel people from membership of trade unions because of their membership in political organizations.

Article 11 has also been used to attempt to require an employer to recognize a union. Membership of a trade union that is not recognized may be of very little value, and so it can be seen as a necessary corollary to the protection of the right to join a union. However, in *Swedish Engine Drivers' Union v Sweden*[13] the Court held that Article 11 did not require a Member State to treat trade unions in any particular way, and collective bargaining was not inherent in the right to form and join a trade union. It did also state, however, that there was a right in trade unions that they should be heard.

In so far as the government is concerned the wide discretion it has over matters of national security has also been instrumental in giving human rights protection in the field of trade unions. The best known example of this is when Margaret Thatcher, in her role as Minister for the Civil Service, banned unions

---

[10] *Young, James and Webster v United Kingdom* [1981] IRLR 408; (1982) 4 EHRR 38.

[11] See too on this point *Cheall v United Kingdom* (1986) 8 EHRR 74.

[12] *ASLEF v United Kingdom* [2007] IRLR 361.

[13] *Swedish Engine Drivers' Union v Sweden* (1979–80) 1 EHRR 617.

recruiting at the Government Communications Headquarters in Cheltenham – GCHQ. The union's complaint was rejected in *CCSU v United Kingdom*[14] on the basis that the workers there were working for the administration of the State.

Further examples of where Article 11 has failed to give protection to workers where it might have been thought that it would do so is in relation to workers on strike. In *NATFHE v United Kingdom*[15] in 1998 it was held that that the obligation on a union to disclose the names of union members taking part in a ballot did not infringe the Convention in that it was not a significant limitation on the right to take strike action. But there is no general right to strike guaranteed by the Convention according to the Court in *Schmidt and Dahlstrom v Sweden*.[16] It stated that the right to strike was not inherent in the right to freedom of association, and accordingly the State was free to restrict the right to strike as it saw fit. However, the Court did hold in *Wilson and the NUJ; Palmer, Wyeth and the RMT; Doolan and others v United Kingdom*[17] that the failure of the United Kingdom to outlaw a practice whereby employers could offer financial inducements to employees not to belong to a union, or members to withdraw their membership, was a breach of Article 11 resulting in amending legislation.[18]

FAIR HEARINGS

It is naturally important that employees have a right to a fair hearing of their grievances in an employment tribunal. Article 6 is relevant in this regard as it provides that, in civil cases as well as in criminal, everyone is entitled to a fair and public hearing within a reasonable time by an independent and impartial tribunal established by law. It might be thought that this again is of little practical importance in employment cases in the United Kingdom. Employment tribunals are held in public, according to fair forensic principles, with independent judges and wing members, with cases normally being held within about three months of their inception by the employee's application, the decision and the reasons for it normally being given immediately at the end of the hearing. However, there have been occasions where this article has been prayed in aid in employment cases. Indeed, to take the latter point, in *Kwamin v Abbey National plc*[19] the Employment Appeal Tribunal held that an excessive delay between a tribunal hearing and the promulgation of its decision will contravene Article 6.

---

14 *Council of Civil Service Unions v United Kingdom* (1988) 10 EHRR 269.
15 *National Association of Teachers in Further and Higher Education v United Kingdom* (1998) 25 EHRR CD 122.
16 *Schmidt and Dahlstrom v Sweden* (1979–80) 1 EHRR 632.
17 *Wilson and the NUJ; Palmer, Wyeth and the RMT; Doolan and others v United Kingdom* [2002] IRLR 568.
18 See further, K.D. Ewing, 'The Implications of *Wilson and Palmer*' [2003] 32 *Industrial Law Journal* 1.
19 *Kwamin v Abbey National plc* [2004] ICR 841.

The area where perhaps there might seem to be the greatest possibility in practice of contravening Article 6 is with regard to public hearings. Employment tribunals sometimes make restricted reporting orders and hold private hearings. However, there are exceptions in the Convention to the general rule that hearings should be held in public such as to protect the private life of the parties and it is likely that most cases fall within the exceptions to the rule.

Another employment case where it was argued that Article 6 had been breached is *Smith v Secretary of State for Trade and Industry*.[20] Because the tribunal lay members are appointed by the Department of Business, Innovation and Skills, the issue arose (in relation to its predecessor) as to whether those members could be truly impartial in a case in which the Department was involved as a party. The Employment Appeal Tribunal came to the view that it could not reach a decision on the matter because, if the employment tribunal were not impartial for this reason, neither would it be so itself. The issue raised in this case was perhaps more cosmetic than real. However, in that an employment case that goes up to the Supreme Court probably will have been through two tribunals and the Court of Appeal before – a longer ladder than in other cases – there is the possibility that the length of period that might pass before the case is finally settled might breach Article 6. But again, this is more apparent than real given the short period that it normally takes to get a case to an employment tribunal hearing. However, a long time can elapse where a case goes on to appeal to the Court of Appeal or Supreme Court and is then remitted and after reconsideration by the employment tribunal again goes back up the judicial hierarchy. But this is no different to cases in other areas of law.

Another feature inherent in the concept of a fair trial at the heart of Article 6 is the idea of 'equality of arms' between the parties. The unavailability of legal assistance in respect of complicated issues has been held to be a breach of the principles of a fair trial, and the unavailability of Legal Aid in employment tribunals may be an issue here. In *Airey v Ireland*[21] in 1979 the Court stated that there may be a breach of Article 6 if the case were of such complexity that the assistance of a lawyer was necessary to present an applicant's case properly and satisfactorily. However, the Court has declined to follow this line of reasoning in other cases.[22]

---

[20] *Smith v Secretary of State for Trade and Industry* [2000] ICR 69.
[21] *Airey v Ireland* (1979) 2 EHRR 305.
[22] See e.g. *Munro v United Kingdom* (1987) 52 DR 158.

PRIVATE AND FAMILY LIFE

Other articles of the Convention may seem less relevant to employment, but that is not necessarily so. Take, for example, Article 8 which states that everyone has a right to have their private and family life, home and correspondence, respected. This is subject to public authorities being legally entitled to interfere in so far as is necessary in a democratic society in the interests of national security, public safety or the economic well-being of the country, for the prevention of disorder or crime, for the protection of health and morals, or for the protection of the rights and freedom of others. The individual's right under Article 8 is not absolute – it amounts to an entitlement to be respected only in this regard. But it does extend into the workplace, and can affect such matters as the employer's medical screening of employees,[23] and security procedures[24] if they impinge, for example, on a person's dignity. It may even cover such issues as the right to have a dress code in the workplace.

Privacy considerations are clearly raised under Article 8 in respect of a number of recent employment practices, such as the use of closed circuit television, eavesdropping on telephone calls and the monitoring of email correspondence. However, the Employment Appeal Tribunal held in *McGowan v Scottish Water*[25] that an employer did not infringe Article 8 in covertly videoing an employee's home in order to see if he was falsifying timesheets. The reasons were not 'external or whimsical'. This, again, shows the extent to which such rights are not by any stretch fundamental or incommensurable. The courts take into account the balance of interests and commercial interests and necessity to an extent perhaps far greater than might be assumed.

FREEDOM OF EXPRESSION

Issues relating to dress codes may be considered to raise human rights issues under Article 10 as well as under Article 8. Article 10 states that everyone has the right to freedom of expression, including the freedom to hold opinions and to receive and impart information and ideas without interference by public authorities and regardless of frontiers. But, again, this right is tempered by the requirement for formalities, conditions, restrictions or penalties as are prescribed by law and are necessary in a democratic society in the interests of national security, territorial integrity or public safety, for the prevention of disorder or crime, for the protection of health or morals, for the protection of

---

23 *MS v Sweden* (1997) 3 BHRC 248.
24 See e.g. *Niemitz v Germany* (1993) 16 EHRR 97.
25 *McGowan v Scottish Water* [2005] IRLR 167.

the reputation or rights of others, for preventing the disclosure of information received in confidence, or for maintaining the authority and impartiality of the judiciary. It would seem to be no coincidence that the exceptions to the operation of the right take rather longer space to explain than the right does itself. The barrier does not seem particularly difficult to hurdle. So, in *Ahmad v United Kingdom*[26] the test was stated to be whether there is a pressing social need. In *Morissens v Belgium*[27] it was said that by entering the civil service as a teacher the applicant had accepted certain restrictions on the exercise of her freedom of expression and in *B v United Kingdom*[28] an atomic weapons worker who criticized atomic weapons in public was found to be justifiably disciplined.

OTHER HUMAN RIGHTS

There are two other articles of the Convention that may be of relevance in employment. The first is Article 3 which concerns subjection to torture, inhuman or degrading treatment or punishment. This would seem to cover only extreme cases of maltreatment, and outside the context where a claimant would be seeking an employment remedy.

The second is Article 9 which opens up greater possibilities. This provides that: everyone has the right to freedom of thought, conscience and religion including the freedom to change religion or belief, and the freedom, either alone or in community with others and in public or private, to manifest religion or belief, in worship, teaching, practice and observance. Limitations on the freedom to manifest one's religion or beliefs should be those only prescribed by law and necessary in a democratic society in the interests of public safety, for the protection of public order, health or morals, or for the protection of the rights and freedoms of others.

This seems to give employees of public authorities a general entitlement to practise their religion and, more importantly, not to be disciplined or dismissed for doing so. It also provides employees of private bodies with some protection if they are dismissed, since a dismissal on grounds which infringe a Convention right will be unlikely to be found to be fair. This is because employment tribunals must interpret the Employment Rights Act 1996 containing the protection against unfair dismissal in a way that is consistent with the Convention.

The right is limited however, and does not, for example, extend to the

---

[26] *Ahmad v United Kingdom* [1997] EHRLR 670.
[27] *Morrisens v Belgium* (1988) 56 DR 127.
[28] *B v United Kingdom* (1990) 46 DR 278.

right to time off for employees practising their religion during working time because they have the opportunity to take employment at times other than when they need, for instance, to pray.[29] Neither does the Convention help those employees who refuse to work on Sundays because of their Christian beliefs.[30] However, domestic legislation in any event goes further in that it gives employees rights to refuse to work on Sundays, at least in the form of making contractual requirements so to work unenforceable.[31]

An important limitation on the application of Article 9 is that the Court has said that a balance must be struck between the religious views and the essential needs of the job, including the ethos of the organization in which the applicant works.[32] However, s. 13 of the Human Rights Act 1998 states that a court or tribunal must have particular regard to the importance of that right.

CONCLUSION

Whilst it is the case that there are clearly a number of circumstances in which the idea of human rights are relevant in the employment context, it would thus seem that there are a number of difficulties associated with it. Some go a long way outside internal matters of employment law. The notion of what a human right amounts to is highly problematic. Whether it is meaningful other than in an ethical context is a matter of debate. And whether, in a civilized society, it provides much more than a background context to employment law is also open to question. Many opportunities available to the courts to open up employment further to human rights have not been taken up. It is hardly to be doubted that in the future human rights will continue to be a feature of employment law as well as to other areas of law, but how much of a role it will have to play has yet to be seen.

Further Reading

R. Allen, A. Beale and R. Crasnow, *Employment Law and Human Rights* (Oxford University Press, 2nd edn, 2007).

P. Alston (ed.), *Labour Law as Human Rights* (Oxford University Press, 2005).

A.C.L. Davies, *Perspectives on Labour Law* (Cambridge University Press, 2nd edn, 2009).

J. Finnis, *Natural Law and Natural Rights* (Clarendon Press, 1980).

S. Fredman, *Human Rights Transformed: Positive Rights and Positive Duties* (Oxford University Press, 2008).

---

[29] See *Ahmad v United Kingdom* (1982) EHRR 126.
[30] See *Stedman v United Kingdom* (1977) 23 EHRR CD 168.
[31] Employment Rights Act 1996, ss. 40–43.
[32] *Kalac v Turkey* (1999) 27 EHRR 522. See also *Eweida v British Airways plc* [2010] IRLR 322; *McFarlane v Relate Avon Ltd* [2010] IRLR 872.

C. Ovey and R. White, *Jacobs and White: The European Convention on Human Rights* (Oxford University Press, 4th edn, 2006).

S. Palmer, 'Human Rights: Implications for Labour Law' (2000) 59 *Cambridge Law Journal* 168.

A. Sen, 'Elements of a Theory of Human Rights' (2004) 32 *Philosophy and Public Affairs* 315.

P. Singer, 'The Fable of the Fox and the Unliberated Animals' [1978] *Ethics* 119.

8

THE EMPLOYMENT LEGAL SYSTEM

INTRODUCTION

It is a striking feature of employment law that cases concerning individuals' work issues will be dealt with by a tribunal rather than a court. And yet disputes about jobs are some of the most serious that can take place in a person's life. It might be one thing for a legal dispute about the merchantable quality of an iron or a television to be dealt with outside the normal court system, but quite another for, together with family, the most important aspect of life and human relationships to be determined in such a way. This idea underpins each of the Debates in the present chapter. First, I pose the question as to whether the employment tribunal system is in need of reform. Then I examine whether the appeals process in employment cases could be improved.

Debate **1**

Are employment tribunals in need of reform?

Employment tribunals plainly are intended as an alternative[1] to the court system in employment cases. Whether it is necessary for them to be so is an altogether different question. When they were created in the mid 1960s,[2] as industrial tribunals, they had very limited jurisdiction, hearing only appeals in industrial training levy cases. Their jurisdiction is now far greater than that and covers not just statutory claims such as unfair dismissal, discrimination and unlawful deductions from wages, but also since the late 1990s breach of contract claims at common law on termination of employment. (Before then,

---

[1] The word 'alternative' here does not indicate that there is, outside breach of contract cases which may be taken to the county court, any element of choice involved. On the whole, where employment tribunals have jurisdiction, it is exclusive.
[2] See Industrial Training Act 1964.

breach of contract claims were heard exclusively in the county court or the High Court). 236,100 claims were accepted by employment tribunals in the year up to March 2009, up 150,100 from the year before. Of course, many of these did not go to a full hearing,[3] but it is nevertheless a substantial workload.

As with many tribunals they were created to achieve a number of laudable aims, namely accessibility, speed, informality, and cheapness.[4] I will look at each of these elements in turn, but it is worth noting what is not in the jurisdiction of employment tribunals. One notable exception is collective labour law cases, as I mentioned in the previous chapter. The area of labour law where, due to the level of distrust of the courts that have historically existed, one might imagine that an alternative to the mainstream courts would have been put in place, this has not occurred. Collective employment matters remain in general to be decided there, with individual employment matters to be dealt with in employment tribunals.

ACCESSIBILITY

The first feature to require a system of employment tribunals, in the Donovan Commission's opinion,[5] is accessibility. There can be little doubt that on this score tribunals are superior to the ordinary courts. A typical case in an employment tribunal would take about three months to come up for hearing, compared to many more months or even years for cases in the ordinary courts. The process by which a case is begun is also straightforward, with the claimant simply filling in a simple form called an ET1 within the time limit, which is often three months.[6] The ET1 asks for details such as the name and address of the claimant, the details of the person against whom relief is sought, and the grounds of the claim, which need not go into more than basic detail identifying it as within the jurisdiction of the employment tribunal.[7] This must be sent to the tribunal office for the area in which the employee worked. The employer will then respond on form ET3, which must be done within 28 days. The response will give the employer's details, and whether or not it intends to defend the claim. The employer may also counter-claim.

Although this indicates that employment tribunals are reasonably accessible, the courts' attitude towards the various time limits is quite strict. However, some principles have been established for the more common types

---

[3] Normally around three-quarters of cases do not reach hearing – see ACAS Annual Report and Accounts 2009–10.

[4] See the Donovan Commission Report (the Royal Commission on Trade Unions and Employers' Associations 1965–1968) Cmnd 3623 at para. 578.

[5] Ibid.

[6] Originally there was no requirement for this form to be completed.

[7] See *Grimmer v KLM Cityhopper Ltd* [2005] IRLR 596.

of valid excuse for delay. One frequently encountered is that internal proceedings arising out of the dismissal were pending at the same time, and that it was reasonable to delay the application to the employment tribunal in order not to prejudice them.[8] Naturally, in cases where the parties are physically prevented from submitting their documentation, such as absence abroad or a postal strike or some untoward or unexpected event, the courts have been more lenient.[9] If a party has been discouraged, impeded, misled or deceived,[10] or was unaware of an important fact,[11] these too may lead to an extension. However, these approaches may well soon be solely of historical interest if the system becomes fully electronic, as is quite possible. In *Initial Electronic Security Systems Ltd v Avdic* (2005)[12] the Employment Appeal Tribunal held that a claim submitted by e-mail eight hours ahead of the deadline but not received in time was acceptable when the sender was given no indication by that time that it had not been received.

Employment tribunals are also reasonably accessible in terms of location. There are twenty-six centres in Britain[13] with further tribunals sitting in Northern Ireland. They are also available for sitting on most days of the working week.

SPEED

I have already described how most cases come to hearing, if they do at all, within about three months after the ET1 has been submitted. This is therefore a significant entry on the credit side in so far as speediness is concerned. However, it should also be understood that dealing with a case speedily does not necessarily mean that the consequences of a particular employment event are most expeditiously dealt with. For example, it may be that for an employee who is well paid, but not greatly so, it is not worth their while bringing claims in a tribunal, for example for unfair dismissal. But they may be well paid enough for a breach of contract claim to be outside the employment tribunal's

---

[8] See *Crown Agents for Overseas Governments and Administration v Lawal* [1978] IRLR 542; [1979] ICR 103 but compare *Bodha v Hampshire Area Health Authority* [1982] ICR 200 and *Croydon Health Authority v Jaufurally* [1986] ICR 4.

[9] See e.g. *Walls Meat Co. Ltd v Khan* [1978] IRLR 499; [1979] ICR 52.

[10] *Porter v Brandridge* [1978] IRLR 271.

[11] *Machine Tool Industry Research Association v Simpson* [1988] IRLR 212; [1988] ICR 588 cf. *Belling & Lee v Burford* [1982] ICR 454.

[12] *Initial Electronic Security Systems Ltd v Avdic* [2005] IRLR 671.

[13] Namely in Aberdeen, Ashford, Bedford, Birmingham, Brighton, Bristol, Bury St Edmunds, Cardiff, Dundee, Edinburgh, Exeter, Glasgow, Leeds, Leicester, Liverpool, London Central, London East, London South, Manchester, Newcastle, Nottingham, Reading, Sheffield, Shrewsbury, Southampton and Watford. The Tribunals Service website in fact lists 27 venues, but those for East London and London East are the same.

limit for hearing such claims.[14] In that event, their case would need to be taken to a county court or the High Court. If there is some issue about whether the employee was dismissed or resigned, thus becoming intentionally unemployed, there might be an issue here relating to benefits (such as jobseeker's allowance or income support) to be considered by another tribunal, the Social Security and Child Support Tribunal. Furthermore, as the employment tribunal is not a court, this means that it does not have the power to enforce its orders. Even where, for example in an unfair dismissal case, the employment tribunal makes an order that the employee be re-employed by the employer in one way or another, if the employer fails to do so there is no contempt of court. The order is merely commuted to a money payment, although this may be enhanced. As with any court to some extent, but more so with tribunals, it is one matter to win a case and have an order made in your favour, but it is another matter actually receiving what is owed to you. In the final resort recourse has to be made to the county court or High Court to enforce the order made by the tribunal, but that can be the start of a lengthy, expensive and possibly fruitless exercise. Thus, although the time it might take for individual cases to reach a hearing may be quick, the accumulated time, as well as effort, might be quite considerable.

There are other features that lend to cases being treated speedily. For example, the Employment Rights Act 1996, s. 111(3) and (4) permits a premature claim, so that where a dismissal takes place with notice the employee may make a claim during that notice period. Once an ET1 has been submitted by the employee and the response by the employer has been made by way of the ET3, ACAS[15] is informed, and a representative will attempt to get the parties to reach a settlement. The focus of this is not to achieve a fair result, or to work for either of the parties in the preparation of their claim. Rather it is on reaching a settlement, whatever that may be, so that the case does not go to a hearing. This has the effect of expediting the resolution of individual cases, but it has the secondary effect of freeing the tribunals of cases so that those that will go to a hearing can be heard more quickly.

The hearing can be dealt with most efficiently if the parties have prepared their cases well, and have cleared the ground of any contentious issues that can be resolved before the hearing. So, the gathering of evidence is often an important part of the pre-hearing process, and the employment tribunal has the power to order the discovery of documents which are relevant and necessary to the proceedings. The parties will then receive a 'directions letter' informing them what has to be revealed. This will not cover documents that

---

14 Currently £25,000.
15 The Advisory, Conciliation and Arbitration Service.

are privileged, such as legal advice to one of the parties from a solicitor. A party might be ordered to produce a written witness statement, stating what the evidence will be to be given by a party they intend to call at the hearing. It is possible for the tribunal of itself, or on application of one of the parties, to hold a case management discussion or a pre-hearing review, which is often heard by the employment judge sitting alone. If the result of this is that the tribunal is of the view that a party's case has no reasonable prospect of success it may make an order for a deposit of up to £500 to be paid and warn that, should they lose at the hearing, they may have an order of costs made against them as well as losing their deposit. In addition, the tribunal may strike out an originating application or the notice of appearance if it considers that it, or the manner in which the case is presented, is scandalous, misconceived, or vexatious. All of this may appear to delay the case reaching a hearing, but in that it may prevent cases from going to a hearing pointlessly, it has a weeding-out effect and may increase the speed with which the caseload of tribunals in the round can be handled.

In the majority of cases, which involve little or no legal argument and turn on the interpretation of the evidence, they are heard in half a day, or perhaps a full day, which compares very favourably to cases heard in the ordinary courts. The employment judge will, in most cases, give both the decision of the tribunal immediately as well as outline reasons for the decision which might later be reduced to writing. Some employment judges tape this part of the proceedings in order to have a full record of what the parties were told at the hearing. Although in the ordinary courts there will often be an immediate decision in the same way, the incidence of reserved judgements when the decision of the court is given later, perhaps in several months time, is significantly greater.

INFORMALITY

The speed of employment tribunal hearings is associated with the informality with which the tribunal conducts proceedings. To some extent, tribunals have become more formal as time has progressed, and perhaps inevitably. The increasingly technical aspects of employment law means that tribunals often need to deal with matters with which self-represented parties have little or no knowledge or understanding. The informality of proceedings in this regard would be aided by the absence of lawyers, which was originally intended to be the norm. However, lawyers are often present. This is not, however, simply because of the growing technicality of the law. If informality is thought to be a virtue because it helps the parties feel at ease, that is mistaken if the consequence is that the parties have to present their own cases. Many parties prefer to have lawyers doing their work for them in a formal way rather than representing themselves in what, for all its claims to informality, can nevertheless be a very intimidating atmosphere for the ordinary person.[16] Even as early as 1988 research suggested that the majority of employers preferred to be represented by lawyers, with just below half of employees taking the same view.[17] This is despite the fact that parties pay their own costs in most circumstances, win or lose and, although there is a high number of lawyers who are prepared to take cases on a no-win-no-fee basis, or even *pro bono*, this is perhaps surprising. It is not surprising that many lawyers in employment tribunals are not at the expensive end of the range, and it has long been thought that it is a good forum for pupil barristers in particular to cut their advocacy teeth. Even if true, this is most unfortunate. Cases in employment tribunals are not concerned with damaged bicycles or faulty microwaves, but about livelihoods, and most often about whether an employee has been unfairly deprived of their entire source of income and career prospects.

The tribunal is free to conduct proceedings as it considers most appropriate. The regulations state that: 'so far as it appears appropriate to do so, the chairman or tribunal shall seek to avoid formality in his or its proceedings and shall not be bound by any enactment or rule of law relating to the admissibility of evidence in proceedings before the courts'.[18] Also the tribunal: 'shall make such enquiries of persons appearing before him or it and of witnesses as he or it considers appropriate and shall otherwise conduct the hearing in such manner as he or it considers most appropriate for the clarification of the issues and generally for the just handling of the proceedings'.[19] There are not normally opening addresses. But, usually, normal court practice applies whereby the party with the burden of proof puts their case first and calls, in the order determined by the tribunal, witnesses who are then cross-examined, with the process repeated for the other side. At the end of the evidence there are closing addresses. Although the tribunal is addressed formally, the case is heard throughout with everyone seated.

It is perhaps detrimental in the pursuit of informality that chairmen of employment tribunals are now styled 'employment judges'. It does give a gravitas to the proceedings and perhaps the respect with which chairmen are held, but this may in turn lead to greater formality, the notion that employment tribunals are courts of law rather than alternatives to them and, perhaps in a few cases, the instilling of a sense of self-importance detrimental to an informal atmosphere.

---

[16] See P. Latreille, J. Latreille, and K.G. Knight, 'Making a Difference? Legal Representation in Employment Tribunal Cases: Evidence from a Survey of Representatives' (2005) 34 *Industrial Law Journal* 308.

[17] J. Smallcome, *Lay Representation in Industrial Tribunals* (unpublished Ph.D thesis, University of Exeter, 1988).

[18] Employment Tribunals (Constitution and Rules of Procedure) Regulations 2004 (SI 2004 No. 1861) r. 14(2).

[19] Ibid, r. 14(3).

EXPENSE

Employment tribunals are unlike courts in that costs on the whole do not follow the action, with each party paying their own, whether they win or lose.[20] But even this does not deter a growing number of parties, particularly employers, from hiring lawyers, as I have already mentioned. But claimants often engage some other form of representation rather than representing themselves, perhaps from their trade union, the local Citizens' Advice Bureau or a lawyers' *pro bono* organization, such as the Free Representation Unit.

However, it is possible for costs to be awarded and they are in a small minority of cases. These may be against the parties themselves or their representatives, called 'wasted costs'. The sums can be substantial, with the tribunal having the power to make an order up to £10,000, but this might be greater if they are referred for determination to the county court. In 2009–10 there were 412 orders made in total, excluding wasted costs and preparation orders in favour of in-house representatives and litigants in person. The highest award was against two respondents for £13,942 (the only award above £10,000). The average award was for £2,288, but there were 31 above £8,000 and below £10,000, of which 2 were awarded to claimants and 29 to employers. Overall, claimants had costs awarded in their favour in 88 cases, but in favour of respondents in 324 cases.[21]

Awards might be made in various circumstances such as where a party has been vexatious, abusive, disruptive or otherwise unreasonable or where there has been a failure to comply with an order or Practice Direction. Costs may also be awarded where the bringing or conduct of the proceedings is misconceived, for example where the party has no real prospect of success. Costs must be awarded against a respondent in circumstances where the claimant in an unfair dismissal case wishes to be reinstated into their old job or re-engaged by the same employer in another job, the employer knows about this at least seven days before the hearing and has obtained an adjournment based on its inability to adduce evidence relating to the availability of these jobs. Costs must also be awarded where a party has been ordered to pay a deposit and the decision has gone against them.

Particularly because ACAS will become involved in cases which might lead to a hearing in an employment tribunal, the attempt to get a settlement is a major feature of the process. In the ordinary civil courts, if the winning party obtains judgement on less favourable terms than had previously been offered to them by the losing party, costs from the date of the offer will normally be awarded against them. The offer is known as a '*Calderbank* letter', and is revealed to the court after the trial and before an order as to remedies is made. These are not

---

[20] See generally, J. Bowers et al, *Blackstone's Employment Law Practice* (Oxford University Press, 2008).
[21] *Employment Tribunal and EAT Statistics 2009–10* (Ministry of Justice, 2010).

normally treated in the same way in employment tribunals, unless the losing party was so unreasonable in their attempt to get a better offer that the tribunal believes it to be justifiable to make a costs order against them.[22]

Because costs are not awarded in the vast majority of cases it might be worthwhile for a party to consider the use of contingency fees whereby the lawyer taking the case does not accept a fee unless the party wins the case. It may be that this is of more benefit to employees than to employers.[23]

It is thus not always the case that taking a case to an employment tribunal is financially risk-free, although it is normally much cheaper than taking a case through the ordinary courts. At least, this is so as far as the parties themselves are concerned. But there is also another context in which the cost aspect of employment tribunals needs to be examined, and that is the costs of running the system itself.

All tribunals come within the Tribunals Service. Although employment tribunals come under the Tribunals Service's jurisdiction, they are treated differently from other tribunals because of the differences between the needs of employment tribunals and administrative tribunals. The former deal with disputes between parties and the latter deal with disputes between parties and the State. Therefore the description of other tribunals as First Tier Tribunals or Upper Tribunals does not apply in the employment context. Responsibility for administering employment tribunals and the Employment Appeal Tribunal rests with the Ministry of Justice, by virtue of the Tribunals, Courts and Enforcement Act 2007. However, the Department of Business, Innovation and Skills (BIS) has responsibility for, among other things, the Rules of Procedure of employment tribunals.

The cost of running the employment tribunal system is thus not an easy figure to determine, for several reasons. One is that in the calculation the running costs need to be offset against the cost of the alternative, in the main the cost of the county court system. A large number of variables would apply to that calculation, not least that the number of cases taken to county courts if employment tribunals did not exist might be considerably lower, particularly if costs did follow the action and cases were longer. Another reason why the figure is difficult to determine is that the tribunals under the aegis of the Tribunals Service are in the main different to employment tribunals, which operate somewhat out of the main in that regard. However, it is possible to

---

22 See *Kopel v Safeway Stores plc* [2003] IRLR 753. In this case the successful claimant pursuing claims for discrimination had turned down a settlement in order pursue claims under the European Convention on Human Rights which the tribunal felt to be ludicrous and awarded £5,000 costs against her.
23 See J.A. Johnson and G. Hammersley, 'Access to Justice: No Win No Fee, What Chance of Justice?' (2005) 14 *Nottingham Law Journal* 19.

assess the importance of employment tribunals to some extent, at least, within the context of the cost of the Tribunals Service as a whole. The Tribunals Service is made up of 36 separate jurisdictions, but employment cases received by them comprise about 30 per cent of the total. The Tribunals Service as a whole had gross expenditure on operating costs for 2009–10 of £355.4 million. There was a significant increase in expenditure overall from the previous year which the Tribunals Service attributed to an increase of six per cent in judicial activity.[24]

CONCLUSION

It can be seen from the above discussion that, in terms of the advantageous features of tribunals identified by the Donovan Commission in 1968 of accessibility, speed, informality and cheapness, it remains in many regards that a good case can be made out today for employment tribunals. Nevertheless, in each regard there are some improvements that could be made, and some ground that, over the years, has been lost. This has been recognized within government, and in 2002 the Department of Trade and Industry set up an Employment Tribunals System Taskforce precisely to consider the most efficient operation of the system in the light of increasing numbers of cases being heard by tribunals and rising costs.

There are many reforms that perhaps could be made in addition to those I have considered already under the Donovan criteria. For example, as in many areas of law, there has been a growing awareness recently of the possibilities of arbitration, or mediation, in employment cases. ACAS has an important role here, as I have mentioned before, but it could perhaps be developed. According to its Annual Report for 2009–10, ACAS received 87,421 net cases for conciliation from employment tribunals[25] compared to 77,478 in 2008–09, representing an increase of 13 per cent year on year. The Department of Business, Innovation and Skills assesses the performance of ACAS in conciliation in terms of potential tribunal hearing days saved as a result of its intervention. In 2009–10 it achieved 52 per cent in short period cases, 74 per cent in standard period cases and 84 per cent in open period cases. Across all cases 78 per cent of potential hearing days were saved. This, it might be thought, represents something of a success story for the organization.

Further thought could also be given to the constitution of employment tribunals. However, I will give here an example of a possible reform that is debatably misconceived. It comes as a surprise to many to find that a tribunal

---

[24] See Tribunals Service, Annual Report and Accounts, 2009–10 at pp. 12 and 58.
[25] This figure excludes actual and potential equal pay cases in local government and the National Health Service which constitute a special case which would distort the figures.

which consists of a lawyer chair and two further members representing employers and trade unions could, in the vast majority of cases, reach a unanimous decision. This might indicate the strength of such a constitution, but the opposite could be argued. Could not the two wing members be abandoned for the very reason that the employment judge would reach the same result without them? This is similar to an argument that could be made out for the abolition of juries in criminal trials. Judges are often heard to comment in favour of juries that they should be retained because they reach the right answer in the overwhelming number of cases. That, on the contrary, I would argue, suggests that they should be abolished. In those small number of cases where juries disagree with the judges and get it wrong (as the judges' comments imply) that is an argument for them not being involved with those cases. In the others, where they agree with the judge, they are superfluous. The difference with employment tribunals, however, is that there are no juries and judges who deliberate separately. In employment tribunals the fact that the members discuss the case amongst themselves might lead to a different result than if they had not done so. It is not that tribunal members reach a compromise, which would offend notions of justice. It is that they, through a process of discussion, may reach a conclusion together that they might not have done separately.

Debate 2

Should the appeal process be reformed in employment cases?

Appeals from employment tribunals are heard in the Employment Appeal Tribunal. The Donovan Committee's criteria for tribunals relating to accessibility, speed, informality and cheapness also apply equally well to the EAT. So, in so far as they are similar, the points for reform just considered for employment tribunals apply equally as well to the EAT.

One of these similarities, however, is curious. Like employment tribunals, the EAT usually has three members who are of different status. The chairman is a High Court judge or circuit judge and the wing members are likewise taken from the ranks of employers and workers and can be very senior figures. But, unlike employment tribunals which mainly deal with issues of fact, albeit within the context of the application of the facts to the law, appeals in the EAT are generally on points of law only.[26] Furthermore, the lay members may

---

[26] These rare exceptions in regard of some trade matters and where it is argued that an employment tribunal clearly has reached a perverse decision on the facts – see *Yeboah v Crofton* [2002] IRLR 634.

outvote the judge, and have done so. It is difficult to see what role lay members might have in this process as a matter of fact, and also difficult to see what justification there is for their membership.

Although constituted on the same lines as employment tribunals, the EAT is a different creature in a number of respects, most obviously of course in the number of cases with which it has to deal.[27] But because these cases are appeals on points of law, the incidence of lawyer representation is also greater. Given that, the question arises as to the necessity for a dedicated tribunal, particularly as the chair is a member of the judiciary in the ordinary courts. Furthermore, with two tribunals in the process before the case returns to the ordinary courts – appeals from the EAT go to the Court of Appeal – this can add an extra tier to case histories. A case reaching the Supreme Court will normally have already been heard in two tribunals and a court below, whereas other cases will have been heard in just two courts below. This, of course, would seem to cut across the claim that tribunals are a speedy method of achieving resolution of disputes, although it has to be remembered that a case will take only about three months from inception to become a hearing in an employment tribunal. This is a fraction of the time that cases sometimes take to reach the Supreme Court.

However, it would seem, somewhat surprisingly perhaps, that few employment cases reaching the highest court follow what might be thought to be this paradigm course. A few years ago I undertook a study of employment cases that reached the House of Lords between 1998 and 2003.[28] A particularly striking feature of my survey was that, of the 35 employment cases heard by the House of Lords during that period, only nineteen came up through the paradigm route. The other cases originated in the High Court and the county court in the main, but one began with a decision by a district judge in a magistrates' court which went to the Lords via the divisional court.

Some other very interesting results emerged from this research. The first was the number of cases considered by the Lords as a proportion of its overall caseload. In those years, there were 307 civil cases determined by the House of Lords, primarily on appeal from the Court of Appeal, in England and Wales. Of these, on my categorization – what counts as an employment case is not absolutely clear – thirty were employment cases, amounting to around ten per

---

[27] The EAT hears appeals from employment tribunals. In the year 2009–10 1,963 appeals were received. Of these 244 were rejected as they were out of time, 843 were rejected because they had no reasonable prospect of success, 169 were withdrawn prior to registration, and 115 afterwards. There were 22 appeals struck out and 56 dismissed at preliminary hearings. Just 403 were disposed of at a full hearing (see The Tribunals Service, Employment Tribunal and EAT Statistics 2009–10). The figures do not deal with Northern Ireland.

[28] S. Honeyball, 'Employment law and the Appellate Committee of the House of Lords' [2005] *Civil Justice Quarterly* 364.

cent of the House of Lords' caseload. This was a high percentage of the overall number of cases heard by the Lords given that the official figures were broken down into twenty different areas of law. It compares with a total of eight employment cases heard in the Lords in the far longer period between 1952 and 1968, these being six trade union and restrictive practices cases and two master and servant cases. One reason for this would seem to be the far greater amount of employment legislation in the period of the survey than there was before 1968. Having said that, a substantial portion of cases – fourteen – concerned common law claims, at least in part.

Given that unfair dismissal is by far the most common claim in employment law, as we have seen, it is surprising that just four cases in the period covered by my research concerned this claim. Most common were contract, tort and discrimination cases. Contract issues appeared ten times, tort seven times and discrimination issues seventeen times. European Union law appeared to be a significant issue in only three cases. It is also interesting that there was only one case involving an issue of collective labour law. This was almost certainly a consequence of the declining role and influence generally of trade unions.

I also found that the chances of success in the House of Lords were heavily weighted in favour of employers. Employees succeeded in just eleven cases whereas employers succeeded in 21. Employee-appellants were successful eight times and employer-appellants eleven times.[29] However, when employees were respondents they were successful in just four cases whereas employer-respondents were successful in thirteen cases. It is not at all clear why there should have been this disparity. The Government, however, was very successful. It was involved in six cases, and won them all.

This Debate is about reform of the appeal process in employment cases. My findings considered above raise obvious prompts for considering reform. Each of them raises particular issues that can be considered separately. They also raise the general issue as to why the appeal process at the highest level seems to be out of kilter with issues on the ground. However, it is easy to identify what is problematic. It is far more difficult to identify possible solutions. This is so particularly with the following issue.

It is clearly important for the parties in a case to have faith in the legal system. It is more difficult where the further a case travels up the appeal ladder the more likely it is that the wrong result will be reached. Of the nineteen cases in my survey which originated in industrial/employment tribunals, their decisions were upheld in seven cases in the Lords but were not in eight. However, the EAT did not fare well by comparison, with its decisions

---

[29] Not all cases in the sample involved both employers and employees.

being upheld by the Lords on only six occasions, while eight were not. But the Court of Appeal fared even worse.[30] It was reversed by the House of Lords in eight cases out of fourteen and was upheld in just six. In fact, in only two cases out of fifteen was a stand-alone decision of the Court of Appeal upheld by the Lords on the same grounds without some element of reversal. So, it seems, the further up the appeal ladder that an employment case progresses, the more likely it is to be wrongly decided. Of course, this argument is predicated on the idea that the highest court reaches the right result when not agreeing with the various courts and tribunals below. However, if this is not the case it entails the even more disturbing idea that the trail of mistakes includes even the highest court itself.[31]

Further Reading

J. Bowers et al, *Blackstone's Employment Law Practice* (Oxford University Press, 2008).

M. Burton, 'The Employment Appeal Tribunal: October 2002 – July 2005' (2005) 34 *Industrial Law Journal* 273.

Donovan Commission Report (the Royal Commission on Trade Unions and Employers' Associations 1965–1968) Cmnd 3623.

S. Honeyball, 'Employment Law and the Appellate Committee of the House of Lords' [2005] *Civil Justice Quarterly* 364.

J.A. Johnson and G. Hammersley, 'Access to Justice: No Win No Fee, What Chance of Justice?' (2005) 14 *Nottingham Law Journal* 19.

P. Latreille, J. Latreille, and K.G. Knight, 'Making a Difference? Legal Representation in Employment Tribunal Cases: Evidence from a Survey of Representatives' (2005) 34 *Industrial Law Journal* 308.

---

[30] This does not include those cases where a reference was made to the European Court of Justice, nor, two partial reversals in consolidated appeals as instances of cases where the Court of Appeal was reversed.

[31] Of course, the situation may have changed since my survey was undertaken, and it has to be kept in mind that the Appellate Committee of the House of Lords has since then been replaced by the Supreme Court, but there is no evidence available as yet to this effect.

INDEX

Agency workers 35, 50–52
Alston, Peter 198
Aristotle 101–102
Atiyah, Patrick 25, 27
Auerbach, Simon 170

Bagshaw, Roderick 166
Bargaining power 14, 37, 76
Barnard, Catherine 81, 96
Blair, Tony 57
Bogg, Alan 186
Bowers, John 48, 121, 206
Brodie, Douglas 2, 70, 192

Carty, Hazel 186
Castle, Barbara 98
Collective labour law
    Blacking 158
    Closed shop 180–181
    Force majeure 164
    Go-slow 158
    Golden formula 167
    Inducing breach of contract 166
    Industrial action 41, 67–68, 132,
        138–139, 152, 154–163,
        165–176
    Injunctions 174–176
    Official and unofficial industrial action
        155–163
    Overtime bans 158–162
    Picketing 158, 169–174
    Striking 158, 176
    Tort 163–167, 211
    Tortious immunity 167–169
    Trade dispute 168

Trade union membership 182–185
    Work to rule 158
Collins, Hugh 11–12, 32, 37, 79, 92, 153
Common law 61, 91, 95, 97, 158
Constructive dismissal 62–63
Contouris, Nicola 52, 71
Cross, Rupert 27

Dahrendorf, Ralf 103
Daniel, William Wentworth 149
Davies, Anne 153, 198
Deakin, Simon 3, 7, 20, 25, 27, 29,
        31–32, 62, 71, 132–133, 138–139,
        149
Devlin, Lord 108
Discrimination 97, 99–100, 103, 107–108,
        111–112, 116–117, 119, 125, 192,
        211
    Associative discrimination 109–110,
        112–113, 117
    But-for test 119
    Causation 100, 116
    Direct discrimination 114, 116–122
    Equality 99, 102–103, 105–107
    Indirect discrimination 100, 116–118,
        120–122
    Pregnancy 5, 42, 102, 104, 107,
        116–119, 124–125, 152
    Reasonableness 97
    Rights 108–109
    Unified approach 99–100
Dworkin, Ronald 10, 12

Economy 75, 107, 177, 182
Elias, Patrick 130, 153, 175

Employment contract
  Atypical workers 50–53
  Collective agreements 53–56
  Collective bargains *see* Collective
    agreements
  Effective date of termination 58
  Fixed term contracts 52
  Frustration 56–58
  History 35
  Illegal contracts 59–60
  Implied terms 68–70, 75, 80, 91–92, 97
  Limited term contracts 52
  Post-employment contract 44
  Pre-employment contract 38–43
  Restrictive covenants 44–47
  Transfer of undertakings 47–49
  Work rules 67
  Written statement of terms 65, 84–85
    Consideration 74, 86
    Contractual restrictions 76
    Creation 83–86
    Variation of terms 86–88
Employment
  Common usage test 6
  Control test 5, 21, 25
  Definition 1–33
  Economic reality test 5
  Integration test 5
  Multiple test 5
  Policy 10–12
  Self-employment 2
  Tests 5–7
  Unified analysis 20–29
Employment tribunal 200–212
  Accessibility 201–202
  Appeal process 200, 209
  Expense 206–208
  Informality 204–205
  Speed 202–204
Equal pay 105–108
European Union 71, 74, 128, 140, 211
Evans, Stephen 79, 147
Ewing, Keith 76, 80, 186, 194

Feminist legal theory 103
Ferran, Eilis 186
Finnis, John 191
Fredman, Sandra 87, 105, 198

Freedland, Mark 31–32, 43, 75, 78, 92,
  94–95, 129, 153
Freeman, Michael 190

Gladstone, William 103
Goodman, J 79, 147

Hammersley, Geraldine 207
Hargreaves, Leslie 147
Hart, Herbert 9, 27, 58, 108, 188
Health and safety 70–71, 74, 115, 175
Hepple, Bob 49, 93
Hitler, Adolf 183
Human rights 187–198
  Fair hearings 194–195
  Freedom of expression 196–197
  Peaceful assembly and association
    193–194
  Private and family life 196
  Trade unions 193
Hume, David 101

Johnson, Jane 207
Jurisprudence 13, 110

Labour party 183
Laden, Osama Bin 189
Latreille, Paul 205
Legal positivism 190–191
Liability in tort 6

Maine, Henry 65, 71
McKendrick, Ewan 21
McLean, Hazel 54
McMullen, John 48, 153
Merritt, Adrian 62
Mogridge, Christine 59
Morality 12, 56, 60, 103, 113, 187, 190

Napier, Brian 32
Natural law 189–191
Novitz, Tonia 186

Palmer, Stephanie 187, 199
Part-time work 107
Pitt, Gwyneth 18
Plato 5

Rawls, John 188
Reform 98, 181, 200, 208–211
Rogers, Horton 19, 43

Sen, Amartya 190
Simpson, Brian 10
Singer, Peter 188
Smallcome, Jeffrey 205
Stilgoe, Elizabeth 149

Termination
    Compensation 127, 146–147
    Constructive dismissal 134–136
    Continuous employment 44, 66, 84,
        123, 125, 127–128, 146–147, 161
    Dismissal 128–30, 133–135, 138–140,
        143–144, 150–152
    Employer termination 130–133
    Employment statutes 121, 123–124
    Fairness 150–152
    Non-renewal of a limited term contract
        133–134
    Redundancy 6, 19–20, 24, 33, 40,
        49–50, 55, 57–58, 66, 70–71, 74,
        78, 87, 124–127, 129–130, 141,
        143, 145–147, 149, 151

Re-engagement 146
Reinstatement 146
Remedies 10, 28–29, 52, 59–60, 63,
        75–81, 103, 125–129, 131–132,
        135, 138, 142, 145, 148,
        162–164, 174, 176, 197
Self-dismissal 138
Termination by agreement 139–142,
        142–144
Thatcher, Margaret 173, 179, 180, 182,
        193
Tiley, John 19

Unfair dismissal 66, 74–75, 78–79, 82, 89,
        124–125, 127, 137, 146, 149–152,
        200, 203, 211

Vicarious liability 4, 6

Walter, James 13
Wedderburn, Lord 8, 11, 186
Westen, Peter 101
Williams, Glanville 6, 33
Wilson, Harold 98
Wittgenstein, Ludwig 5
Wynn-Evans, Charles 50